Famous Stable Celebrates 400 Years

From Associated Press Reports

LIPICE, Yugoslavia — The Lippizaner stable, which supplied its famous white thoroughbreds to Vienna's royal court and the Spanish Riding School there for more than three cent...

THE HAPSBURG MONARCHY

THE HAPSBURG MONARCHY

BY

HENRY WICKHAM STEED

NEW YORK

Howard Fertig

1969

First published in 1913; 2nd edition 1914 [here reprinted]

<small>HOWARD FERTIG, INC. EDITION</small> 1969
Published by permission of Constable and Co. Ltd.

All rights reserved.

This book is copyright under the Berne Convention.
Apart from any fair dealing for the purposes of private
study, research, criticism or review, no portion may be
reproduced by any process without written permission.
Enquiries should be addressed to the publishers.

Library of Congress Catalog Card Number: 68-9601

PRINTED IN THE UNITED STATES OF AMERICA
BY NOBLE OFFSET PRINTERS, INC.

DEDICATION

A Roman road, tall elms, an ancient fane,
Woodland and mead studded with Tudor towers,
God's acre, gladdened by unbidden flowers
That bloom and yearly die to live again ;
Peace, luminous as sunset after rain,—
An old-world peace, careless of days and hours,
Sure of the blue beyond the sky that lowers,
Certain that neither Love nor Faith is vain.

Oh ! ye that rest beneath yon hallowed sod
Yet urge with memory's strength our feet to move
In childlike steps along the path ye trod :
Know that we hope and strive e'en as ye strove,
Know that we seek as ye our way to God,
Know that we live as ye by faith and love.

PREFACE TO THE SECOND EDITION

FEW changes have been made in preparing a Second Edition of this book. No important event has occurred to render necessary the employment of the past tense where in the First Edition the present tense was used. The illness of the Emperor Francis Joseph has, it is true, suggested that the time may presently come when his personality and his reign will be matters of historical but no longer of contemporary interest. Fortunately, his robust constitution seems once more to be getting the better of the only serious physical weakness that has ever afflicted him, and questions as to what will happen when he shall no longer rule over the Hapsburg lands are again losing their point. To such questions this book supplies a tentative answer. If Francis Joseph's successor be granted health and the mental stability that goes with health, it is probable that the transition from the old reign to the new will take place without hitch or shock. Later on grave problems are likely to arise ; but this book will have been written in vain should it fail to persuade open-minded readers that every act of an Austro-Hungarian monarch needs to be judged without prejudice, and, above all, without the intellectual conservatism that applies to a new ruler the standards applied to the old, and distrusts change because change involves uncertainty.

One minor event affecting this book nevertheless requires brief notice. At the end of April a subordinate Austrian police official discovered, either spontaneously or under advice from interested quarters, a passage in the First Edition which, torn from its context, could be interpreted as constituting " the crime of insult to Majesty." He denounced *The Hapsburg Monarchy* to the Public Prosecutor, who, as is usual in such cases, ordered the confiscation of the two, or perhaps three, copies that remained unsold in Vienna, and forbade the circulation of the book in Austria. The incriminated passage, which will be found on page 30, has been left unchanged in the Second Edition. Had it contained any " insult to Majesty " or any historical or psychological inaccuracy, I should not have hesitated to revise it. Proof enough of its truth is to be found not only in this book but in any fair account of Francis Joseph's reign.

But I take this opportunity to correct a misapprehension that seems to be implied in a question asked by the most competent Austrian reviewer of the First Edition, Professor Ottokar Weber of Prague, who, writing in the *Frankfurter Zeitung*, the leading German Liberal organ, on April 5, said, " Steed has observed keenly, has studied also the previous history of Austria, and, as the result of his studies, observation and research, he gives us this book which can be described as one of the most sagacious ever written on Austria. Without party or race prejudice, he judges clearly the complicated conditions of our fatherland. Expert facility of expression, the power to cast his observations in aphoristic form, make the perusal of his four chapters extremely fascinating. . . . He conceives the medley of peoples in Austria-Hungary as a product of dynastic attachment to the House of Hapsburg, as being held together by loyalty to the hoary monarch whose unselfishness, generosity and justice the author emphasizes, though he cannot avoid remarking that Francis Joseph can be constitutional—to the point of injustice. In the mouth of an Englishman is this praise or is it blame? One hardly knows."

It is neither praise nor blame. It is the historical truth. The arrangements tacitly or explicitly made by Francis Joseph with the Austrian-German party under Auersperg between 1871 and 1879, and with the Magyar Liberal Party under the elder Tisza, 1875-1890, gave each of those parties and races a free hand in the administrative oppression of their opponents, and were maintained as long as the Germans and the Magyars furnished without flinching money and recruits for the army. Further instances might be cited, particularly in regard to the ill-treatment of Croatia-Slavonia and of the Rumanes and other non-Magyar races of Hungary by various Magyar governments. But all these instances go to substantiate the main thesis of this book—that, to the head of the Hapsburg dynasty, races and peoples, governments and systems of government, statesmen, officials and politicians, appear as simple factors in the problem of preserving the dynastic inheritance which, in his own firm belief, the Monarch has been divinely appointed to administer for its own good and for that of the Imperial and Royal House.

LONDON, *May* 1914.

PREFACE TO THE FIRST EDITION

THE purpose of this book is to record, before they fade or
become over-simplified by memory, the impressions received
and the conclusions reached during ten years' work in Austria-
Hungary. Many foreign writers have already dealt with
Austrian, Hungarian, and Austro-Hungarian questions. Some
have written hastily, some have studied profoundly and some
have reproduced material obtained from official sources ; but,
unless I am mistaken, none have enjoyed the advantage—
or laboured under the disadvantage—of having lived for a
decade the daily life of the country and of having been
obliged to preserve in regard to it a critical if not a judicial
attitude. Such writers have, as a rule and necessarily, dealt
chiefly with externals, gathering and working on documents
or reproducing impressions received and information collected
during visits and journeys. Much of their work has been
based on precise knowledge of recorded facts, statistics, race
idiosyncrasies and historical developments, and is, therefore,
of permanent value even though it sometimes lack discern-
ment of the peculiar realities that lie behind the complicated
phenomena of public and social life in the Hapsburg
dominions. My object is not to tread again the ground they
have trodden, but rather to offer the fruits of individual
experience and reflection as a modest contribution to the
difficult task of rendering Austro-Hungarian tendencies and

problems less incomprehensible to the outside world. Though in dealing with those problems some degree of juridical differentiation and terminological distinction is inevitable, I have tried to dwell less upon points of difference than upon the features and interests that are common to the peoples ruled by the House of Hapsburg. The Hapsburg Monarchy requires synthetic treatment. In the case of a country so diversified, analysis is fruitful of confusion. The ablest disquisition upon the constitutional history and State rights of Hungary or Bohemia, the most exact statistical treatise upon races and languages, is apt to leave the foreign reader bewildered and disheartened. Even at the risk of scandalizing believers in the Dual System as the last word of Austro-Hungarian political development, it is needful to insist upon the essential unity of the Hapsburg Lands, although that unity is, and may increasingly become, a unity in diversity. For this unity no better name can be found than " The Hapsburg Monarchy." The constitutionally correct names " Austria-Hungary " and " Austro-Hungarian Monarchy " are poor substitutes for the old comprehensive designations " Austria " and " The Austrian Monarchy," which expressed more adequately than the present compound terms the political individuality of the Hapsburg peoples. This individuality is only hidden, not dead ; and despite recent blunders and shortcomings, there may yet be good ground for the belief that, whenever the head of the dynasty shall call for a common effort, or in the hour of common need, the spirit of Grillparzer's famous lines will again be vindicated as it was during the annexation crisis of 1908–9 :

> Die Gott als Slav' und Magyaren schuf,
> Sie streiten um Worte nicht hämisch,
> Sie folgen, ob deutsch auch der Feldherrnruf:
> Denn "Vorwärts !" ist ungrisch und böhmisch.

Gemeinsame Hilf' in gemeinsamer Not
Hat Reiche und Staaten gegründet ;
Der Mensch ist ein Einsamer nur im Tod,
Doch Leben und Streben verbündet.

Errors, weakness, or prejudice on the part of the Monarch,
of statesmen, or of races may, it is true, bring the Monarchy
again to the verge of ruin ; disaster may seem to portend
the fulfilment of prophecies of disintegration ; but I have
been unable to perceive during ten years of constant observation and experience—years, moreover, filled with struggle
and crisis—any sufficient reason why, with moderate foresight on the part of the Dynasty, the Hapsburg Monarchy
should not retain its rightful place in the European community.   Its internal crises are often crises of growth rather
than of decay.   The intense belief in a better future that
animates the best " Hapsburgians " is in itself an earnest
that their faith is not, or need not be, vain.   Whatever
censure, whatever criticisms may be found in the following
pages are to be taken as subject to this main principle, and
as evidence of the writer's desire, when pointing out blemishes,
to indicate the expediency and the possibility of remedy.

CONTENTS

INTRODUCTION

THE Hapsburg Monarchy has ever been a butt for epigram. Napoleon and Talleyrand, Metternich and Bismarck, Gladstone and countless other statesmen, writers and diplomatists have whetted their wit or vented their indignation upon the semi-anonymous polity which, surviving the dissolution of the "Holy Roman" Empire, continues to own the sway of the House of Austria. From the Napoleonic gibe at the eternal tardiness of Austria down to Metternich's sarcastic confession that "Asia begins on the Landstrasse"—the eastern suburb of Vienna—and to Gladstone's exclamation that nowhere in the world has Austria ever done good, these apophthegms, one and all, had reference to the defective quality of the Austrian "soul." Lagarde, the famous German writer, even denied the existence of an Austrian "soul." "Prussia," he declared, "has not enough body for her soul; Austria no soul for her very ample body." [1] Lagarde wrote in 1853 before Prussia found scope for her energies in the unification of Germany and before Austria was born again in the form of Austria-Hungary; but in some respects his stricture holds good. "Austria" has never yet quite "found herself." The Austrian question is whether she can "find herself,"—a question on which it would be rash to dogmatize, above all negatively. Though the House of Hapsburg is one of the oldest of dynasties, its peoples are one of the youngest of nations and often seem unconscious of their nationhood. The very words "nation" and "nationality" have for them a special and restricted meaning.

[1] *Deutsche Schriften*, p. 35.

Austrian Germans speak of their "nation" and mean primarily the Germans of Bohemia, the Tyrol, Upper and Lower Austria, Moravia, Styria and Carinthia, and secondarily their brethren *draussen im Reich*, that is, in the German Empire. Czechs, Croatians, Serbs, Slovenes, Poles, and Ruthenes or Little Russians, nay, even the Jews of the Zionist persuasion, likewise refer to their several "nations" in an ethnical sense. The idea of an "Austrian" nationhood, with its uniting virtue, is lacking, nor is the want supplied by what is called the "State idea." True, Austrians and Hungarians alike employ the term "Fatherland," but they usually limit its application to their own half of the Monarchy; *Gesamtpatriotismus*, or patriotism embracing the whole Monarchy, is the privilege of a few. Such "soul" as "Austria" possesses is mainly dynastic ; and the principal bond between the Hapsburg peoples is devotion to the person of the Monarch, who, ruling by right Divine in various constitutional guises, is the chief factor in each State separately and in both States jointly. The Dual Monarchy depends upon the Crown more fully and more truly than any other European realm. The dynasty is not only the pivot and centre but the living force of the body-politic. The Army, the Navy, the Bureaucracy and, in a sense, the Church are dynastic projections. "Austria" can only "find herself" when her aspirations run parallel to those of the dynasty, or when dynastic purpose coincides with popular necessity. Here, more than elsewhere, union is, or might be, strength ; here, more than elsewhere, division signifies weakness and waste. "Viribus Unitis," the Emperor Francis Joseph's motto, defines indeed the "Austrian" ideal—but reality would often be more aptly indicated were the rims of the coins that bear the motto to be inscribed with the precept "Divide et impera" and the ruler's effigy to be surrounded by the unchanging though unconfessed Hapsburg maxim, "Voluntas Imperatoris Suprema Lex esto!"

Yet, despite a statecraft frequently "soulless," the Emperor Francis Joseph has cultivated, and succeeded in maintaining throughout the greater part of his reign, such a relationship between the dynasty and most of its peoples that the Crown has come to be regarded as a personal possession of its subjects to an extent hardly to be paralleled in Germany, in Italy, or perhaps even in England. This personal relationship is one of the chief realities that lie behind Austro-Hungarian Constitutional appearances, a reality not without drawbacks corresponding to its vital significance. Personal in its embodiment, it involves the extension of the personal principle to all departments of public life, and produces, through its action upon a popular character predisposed by temperament and tradition to yield to its influence, a vagueness and instability baffling to non-Austrians. "What is incomprehensible to every non-Austrian, nay, the eternally unintelligible about Austria, is the Asiatic in Austria," wrote in 1871 Ferdinand Kürnberger,[1] the ablest Austrian essayist of the second half of the nineteenth century. But, he added, "Austria is not really unintelligible; it must be comprehended as a kind of Asia. 'Europe' and 'Asia' are very precise ideas. Europe means Law; Asia means arbitrary rule. Europe means respect for facts; Asia means the purely personal. Europe is the man; Asia is at once the old man and the child. With this key you may solve all Austrian riddles."

And again :

"Did I say that Asia is both a child and an old man? Austria also. The way our people, lively, light-living, changeable, dance up to all things with verve and grace is like a rosy children's ball. But note well that in all this South German liveliness and Slav changeability, in this whole rapid whirl of *persons*, the thing itself remains Asiatically stiff, inert, conservative, sphinx-dead and spectrally hoary, not having budged an inch since Biblical times. For this reason the most daring innovations come easier to us than to other States—because they are only new names. . . . We might proclaim Atheism as the State religion and the

[1] *Siegelringe*, 1st edition, pp. 220-225.

Cardinal-Archbishop would celebrate an atheistic High Mass in the Cathedral."

Thirty-five years after the publication of this essay Austria astonished Europe by introducing universal suffrage overnight.   Hitherto this "daring innovation" has indeed seemed, or been caused to seem, little more than a "new name"; and it is a typically Austrian paradox that an extension of popular rights should have been dictated to Parliament by the Crown from above and forced on from below by socialist organizations working in harmony with the Crown.   In point of fact the introduction of universal suffrage was the fulfilment of a dynastic plan long formed and tenaciously pursued.   To regard it simply as a "popular victory" would be to overlook the circumstance that, in the Hapsburg Monarchy, most things have another than their surface meaning, fulfil another than their ostensible function. While such a country is not susceptible of definition by epigram, synthetic treatment is required to make it approximately intelligible.   The portrait of " Austria " can best be drawn in bold outline by hands consciously careless of distracting detail.

However the portrait be drawn, the question of method is important.   Neither the purely historical nor the contemporary-photographic method is entirely satisfactory, nor can the ethnographical method quite serve the purpose. Historical continuity assuredly exists, despite abrupt changes and dislocations; statistical returns and reports on local conditions are valuable ; ethnography is likewise of service, provided it be borne in mind that what is essential in Austria is not so much the individual characteristics of the various race groups as the mixing, the blending of those characteristics and groups in and through the common State and in the service of the common dynasty.   Could the Monarchy be divided into race compartments, each carefully segregated and only linked together, like the cells of a battery, by confluent wires, a long step might be taken towards disintegration.   Rigid centralization, on the other hand, might crush some particles to the detriment of internal solidity. Some writers suggest that Switzerland offers an excellent model for Austrian imitation, but forget that Switzerland has never had an Imperial tradition nor been the object of a dynastic policy separate from and stronger than the interests of any one of the Helvetian races. The "Austrian" problem is a problem *sui generis*, not to be solved on principle or in the light of theory. The line of "Austrian" development seems to lie in the direction of continual readjustment of the relations between ethnic groups under the auspices of the dynasty. Such development must naturally involve both weakness and strength— weakness, by reason of inevitable loose-jointedness and of the tendency towards inter-racial jealousy and conflict; and strength, by reason of the subordination of all parts to the common head and of the subtle and often unconscious current that causes individual groups to tingle with unitary senti- ment at moments of effort or exaltation. No eye-witness of the procession of the Austrian peoples that passed before the Emperor on his Diamond Jubilee in June 1908 can have failed to realize the immense reserves of devotion to the Crown and its wearer that lie accumulated even in the farthest districts of the Hapsburg dominions; nor can those who lived through the annexation crisis of the following winter have failed to hear the strong, regular pulsations of " Austrian " hearts, glad of an albeit insignificant pretext to beat in pride and unison. The Hapsburg peoples are not very wise, not over-cultivated, not overburdened with political sense, but they have in them at their best moments, be those moments of defeat or of triumph, a unitary instinct that seems to draw nourishment from their common past. The influence of the Imperial tradition outlasting the sacrifice of the Holy Roman-German Imperial title; the permanent effects of the artificial but pitilessly effective standardization of political and religious sentiment by Jesuit Fathers and fanatical monarchs during and after the Counter-Reforma- tion; the force of a doctrine of Divine Right incomparably rigid and worked out consistently in and through a State conceived as a projection of the Ruler's person ; the rationalization and centralization of the governing apparatus in a spirit of "enlightened despotism" by Joseph II. under French encyclopedist influences ; the brusque reaction after the death of a favourite Austrian Archduchess, Marie Antoinette, on a French revolutionary scaffold ; the rise of Napoleon and the dogged struggle for existence against his armies ; the growth of the idea of Nationality, abhorred by Metternich as "the Revolution," and by him hampered and oppugned ; the short-lived triumph of liberal Constitutionalism in 1848 ; the dynastic struggle with Hungary, and the revolts at Vienna and Prague ; the ensuing years of black reaction under Alexander Bach, culminating in the Concordat of 1855 ; the loss of Lombardy in 1859, of Venice and of German hegemony in 1866 ; the consequent concentration of Imperial and State attention upon internal readjustment, which, starting from the Settlement with Hungary and the Austrian Constitution of 1867, led in 1879 to the breaking of the supremacy of the German element in Austria at the instance of the Crown and to the subsequent rise of Slav influence,—all these factors, events and vicissitudes seem to have left an indelible mark on Austrian minds and to have created an odd sort of fellowship, an unavowed feeling of retrospective comradeship in weal and woe, which no present strife can entirely efface or subdue.   And beneath this feeling lies the consciousness that, throughout the centuries with their struggles and changes, one Imperial House, one Imperial dynasty, has reigned over, if it has not always governed, those whom it regards in a special sense as "its" peoples.

A few years ago it was and, to some extent, it still is the fashion to consider the Hapsburg realms as an ill-assorted congeries of races and lands devoid of internal cohesion, a kind of Stoic polity made up of ethnic atoms in fortuitous concourse and ready to resolve itself into its constituent elements whenever external pressure should be

displaced or the personal prestige of Francis Joseph should
be removed.   Palacký's phrase, " If Austria did not exist it
would be necessary to invent her," suggested, indeed, a
reason—the reason of expediency—for the existence of the
Monarchy, but failed adequately to express its real *raison
d'être*.   It seemed to indicate that the Monarchy is a useful
lumber-room or scrap-heap for broken or detached fragments
of other peoples, and gave no hint of the truth that the main
thing in the Monarchy is the living force of the dynasty.
Some developments in recent years have doubtless tended
to obscure this truth.   The "Los von Rom," *i.e.* "Los von
Habsburg" movement of the later 'nineties and the sedulous
Pan-German propaganda for which it was a cloak and a
pretext; the separatist tendencies of the Magyar gentry
and of their Jewish allies in Hungary; the "Neo-Slav"
agitation; and, latterly, the growing sense of solidarity
between the various branches of the Serbo-Croatian or
Southern Slav race,—these and many minor phenomena
have helped to encourage a belief in the decrepitude of the
Monarchy and to hide the importance of the dynastic influence.   The temptation to ignore fundamental facts is
to-day very strong.   A cheap daily press, eager for sensa-
tions and prone to taboo "philosophic doubt" as likely to
place too heavy a strain upon the intelligence of its readers,
has discouraged reflection and created an appetite for
"knowledge" in portable lozenge form.   Dynasties, moreover, are not positively popular.   Though their potential
utility is freely recognized, though the Italian, British, and
German Imperial thrones appear to stand firmer to-day
than they stood twenty or thirty years ago, the public
apologists of the monarchical principle scarcely form a
majority among political philosophers.   Faith in the Divine
Right of Kings has faded and is not likely to revive.   But
the record of some republics and the advantages of continuity secured by some monarchies have assuredly reinforced the monarchical position and brought into play
utilitarian considerations that would have seemed impious

to legitimists of the old school. Perception that "monarchy" and "democracy" are not antithetical terms and that a crowned democracy may be as efficient a guardian of individual right and social liberty as any republic, is gradually spreading, and the average man seems instinctively to understand that, in the modern world, tyranny is more likely to come from oligarchies than from monarchs—less indeed from aristocratic or feudal than from economic oligarchies, groups of industrial magnates, financiers, banks, and distributive organizations. Against tyranny from such quarters the natural ally of the people is, or might be, the Crown. Parliament is no sufficient safeguard, for parliaments can be bought, influenced, or gerrymandered into conscious or inadvertent alliance with the economic princes of the world. Monarchs and dynasties should have little to fear unless they so identify themselves or allow themselves to be identified with plutocratic undertakings as to seem to stand for anti-popular tendencies. Several examples of the danger of an intimate association of rulers or reigning families with money-making enterprises might be culled from recent European history. One of the reasons for the popularity and prestige of the Austrian Emperor among his subjects is his entire freedom from personal interest in economic concerns. He has never been suspected of having an axe to grind for himself or for his family. Like some of his greatest predecessors, he has ever had an eye for the needs of the people and has played an important, sometimes a decisive, part in every enlargement of popular right and in every work for the promotion of popular welfare. Despite some relapses into absolutist cynicism and into a callousness towards the administrative ill-treatment of races and provinces that is scarcely explicable by the doctrine of respect for constitutional limitations, the Crown in Austria and in Hungary has frequently identified itself with the people, even at the cost, or perhaps with the object, of curtailing the power of dominant parties and castes. The Crown is therefore not merely a dead-weight valuable for

the automatic maintenance of equilibrium, but a living force
consciously exerting itself to counteract or impede undue
accumulations of social and political power.   Like the
Austrian problem itself, the functions of the Crown must be
expressed in terms of dynamics, not of statics ; and as long
as the Crown exercises these functions so long is it likely
to be invincible.

   .   .   .   .   .   .

    Next in importance to the Crown stand the institutions
of State, the Army, the Church, the Police, and the Bureaucracy, which form the bony framework of the body-politic.
Of these institutions the Army is the most important.   Its
influence is, on the whole, educative both in a pedagogical
and in a political sense.   It is, in the case of recruits from
the less advanced races, veritably a primary school, teaching
not only the " three R's," but cleanliness, self-control, and
habits of discipline.   It inculcates, moreover, unitary sentiment and devotion to the dynasty.   In spirit it is far more
democratic than the German army.   The bulk of Austro-
Hungarian officers are drawn not, as in Germany, from the
aristocracy and the nobility, but rather from the middle and
lower middle classes.   Austro-Hungarian officers are, for
the most part, hard-working, hard-living men, unspoiled by
luxury, and striving to subsist on little more than their
meagre pay.   They stand nearer than the German officers to
the common soldier.   Cases of ill-treatment of men by officers
are rare.   The subaltern who should restrict his intercourse
with his men to the shouting of a few words of command
would soon be found wanting.   The bulk of Austro-
Hungarian regiments are racially composite.   Their officers
must speak enough of the languages of the men to be able
to supplement the German words of command with detailed
instructions and explanations in the mother-tongues of the
rank and file.   There results a personal relationship that
renders the Army in Austria-Hungary a more human and
humanizing organization than in Germany.   Race feeling
may be noticeable here and there, but, broadly speaking,

the Army is the greatest asset not only of the Crown but of the Monarchy at large.

Of the Church it is impossible to speak with equal confidence. It has great power, vast wealth, and little living faith. It is an institution, not an evangelizing nor always a purifying agency. "In tutta Vienna non ho trovato una sola anima" was the sad verdict of a profoundly religious foreign friar after considerable experience of the Austrian ecclesiastical world. The religious movement, nicknamed "Modernist," that affected some of the best minds in the French, Italian, German, and English branches of the Roman Church, left Austria-Hungary practically untouched. Austria has not produced a single "Modernist" of note. One solitary priest who pleaded for greater spirituality in a book called *Nostra Maxima Culpa* was speedily silenced and is now forgotten. One Hungarian bishop revealed spiritual tendencies in a series of books and pastoral letters, but found himself condemned and obliged to retract. These are the only signs of loftier aspiration in the Church of Austria and Hungary. The rest is domination, intrigue, enjoyment of fat revenues, and maintenance of control over a people very observant of religious form and very void of religious feeling. In such conditions "Clericalism" flourishes.

Clericalism is one of the cardinal forces in the Monarchy, a force not merely defensive and conservative, but aggressive and sometimes almost revolutionary. The essence of Clericalism is the abuse of religious allegiance and of legitimate ecclesiastical organization for political and economic purposes. Its deleterious effects on public life proceed from its inherent dishonesty—a dishonesty comparable to that of the Jewish financial and political organizations that work under the guise of "Liberalism." Clericalism claims transcendental sanction for worldly manœuvres, and tricks out its dream of theocratical domination in democratic raiment. It encourages lip service to religious forms, puts a premium on clever hypocrisy, confounds consciences by employing immoral means for the attainment of professedly moral ends, and while pretending to lead the people towards well-being in this world and beatitude in the next, corrupts their very fibre. In every Clerical movement and organization there are two categories of individuals who give it force and respectability—the fanatics and the unconscious. The former believe in the sanctity of their cause and, by devotion to its catchwords and to its leaders, impart to the movement momentum and vigour ; the latter form the rank and file of the Clerical army, following the banner wherever it may lead, and awakening only to a sense of their position when defeat or internal scandal rouses them from somnambulism. Since the Counter-Reformation, Clericalism has played an important and usually, though not invariably, a sinister part in Austria. Save during the periods when Imperial displeasure or counter-intrigue curtailed their power, the Jesuits have marshalled and led the "Black" battalions. The history of the Jesuit Counter-Reformation in the Hapsburg dominions forms one of the most terrible chapters in the annals of politico-religious crime—crime that seems to have blunted the moral sense and blighted the religious potentiality of whole classes of Hapsburg subjects. During recent years there has been much futile controversy between ex-Jesuits and Jesuits on the question whether the doctrine that "the end justifies the means" or that "evil may be done in order that good may come" is inculcated by the Company of Jesus. It would probably be vain to search authentic Jesuit records and publications for an enunciation of any such principle. The Jesuits have no need to crystallize their practice into traitorous maxims. Their motto "Ad Majorem Dei Gloriam" covers all requirements. How can any act undertaken for the greater glory of a Deity who is good partake of the nature of evil ? The fundamental ambiguity and intellectual immorality of the Jesuit attitude proceed from its incompatibility with the postulates of simple Christianity. Christian morality is frankly absolute. For it Good is Good, and proceeds from God, the Fountain-head of Goodness ; Evil is Evil, and proceeds from the Devil, the

Father of Lies.   Christian consciences are moulded to distinguish instinctively between good and evil, and are
exhorted to cleave to the one and eschew the other.   Into
this world of moral antithesis comes the Jesuit with his
doctrine of relativity, maintaining, in practice if not in
precept, that all is good provided it redound to the greater
glory of God, of which the Company of Jesus is the special
custodian.   The immorality of the Jesuit position depends
not upon the thesis of the relativity of good and evil which,
as a philosophical proposition, is sounder than the orthodox
Christian thesis, but in the adoption of such a position
within the pale of Christianity, and under the aegis of the
Vicar of Christ.   However deftly subtle theologians may
mask the fundamental contradiction between the Jesuit
position and the simple sense of Christian doctrine, the
contradiction remains and perennially causes " little ones "
to stumble.

Nevertheless it would be unjust to cast the blame for the
demoralization of Austria on to Jesuitism and Clericalism
alone.   A part scarcely less deleterious has been played
during the last generation by anti-Clerical " Liberalism."
Like most things Austrian, " Liberalism " gradually acquired
a significance very different from its ostensible meaning.
Its catchwords " freedom," " progress," " culture," " civilization," originally the rallying-cries of democratic enthusiasts
and reformers, gradually became mere shibboleths by which
a rapacious clique recognized its own partisans.   The
natural and healthy reaction against the State " system "
of Alexander Bach, a system that co-ordinated with mar-
vellous skill the agencies of the Police, the Church, the
Bureaucracy and the Army in the work of stamping the
progressive spirit out of Austria, brought into power during
the later 'sixties and the 'seventies of last century, a party
that strove for a time to correct the worst anachronisms and
to remedy the most flagrant abuses of the obscurantist past.
But " liberty " and " freedom " in Austria then meant, in
most cases, liberty for the clever, quick-witted, indefatigable

Jew to prey upon a public and a political world totally unfit for defence against or competition with him. Fresh from Talmud and synagogue, and consequently trained to conjure with the law and skilled in intrigue, the invading Semite arrived from Galicia or Hungary and carried everything before him. Unknown and therefore unchecked by public opinion, without any "stake in the country" and therefore reckless, he sought only to gratify his insatiable appetite for wealth and power. The Press, which he invaded, corrupted, and dominated, denounced resistance to him as "religious intolerance," and clamour for protection against him as "anti-Liberal." Little by little the "Liberal" Jew established himself, as he thought, in an impregnable position. But the excess of the evil brought, if not remedy, at least a palliative in the ugly form of an anti-Semitic agitation that drew strength from the financial and building crisis of 1873. For that crisis the Jews were not alone responsible, though their unbridled speculative habits and mushroom fortunes undoubtedly started the speculative mania which led to the crash; and while the aristocracy and the middle classes, which had been caught by the mania, lost heavily in the inevitable catastrophe, the Jews extricated themselves more nimbly and were little the worse. Resentment and envy rapidly found vent in an anti-Jewish outcry that made of the Jew a scapegoat for the sins of the community. The Jewish "Liberal" Press hastened to denounce as "religious" intolerance this not unnatural reaction; and the Catholic Church, taking the hint, added a "religious" count to the general indictment. The anti-Semitic movement might have subsided as soon as the Jews had learned the lesson of prudence, had not a demagogue of genius, Dr. Karl Lueger, placed himself at its head and used it to bear him aloft to the Burgomastership of Vienna. Though often a Jew-baiter, Lueger was no Jew-hater. He knew the Jews too well to cherish indiscriminate rancour against them, however wildly he may have talked in his political harangues. Some of his close friends throughout life were Jews, to one of whom he paid, shortly before his death, a public tribute of gratitude and admiration.   Had his political career not been blocked at the outset by the dog-in-the-manger attitude of the Vienna " Liberals," Lueger might perhaps have saved the " Liberal " party from itself and have prolonged its lease of power.   But he was determined to find his opportunity, and found it in leading the " Christian Social anti-Semitic " forces to an assault upon the strong places of Jewish and capitalistic liberalism.   His great political talent, his personal integrity, his ability to put Viennese ideas into Viennese words, his freedom from Jewish Liberal " progressive " cant, gained him an ascendancy over his native city and a prestige in the Empire such as few Austrian politicians had previously enjoyed.   His often ruthless agitation against the Jews, his fiery denunciations of their malpractices, rendered in the long run a service to the Jews themselves by compelling them, under pressure, to observe a circumspection of which they had previously seemed incapable.   The better Jews, indeed, soon recognized that Lueger had been to them a blessing in disguise by tempering the immoderation that is a prominent Jewish failing.   On the other hand, Lueger's agitation was attended by many drawbacks.   While it rendered an immense service to Austria by rousing an " Austrian " consciousness, and by revealing to a public opinion which decades of pseudo-liberal influence had hypnotized, the real character of the Magyar State and of the Austrian position in regard to Hungary, it tended to degrade political controversy to a pothouse level and to raise local interests and cupidities to the rank of political principles.   It set party advantages above social and electoral justice, facilitated a revival of militant Clericalism in a peculiarly dangerous form, and replaced, albeit inadvertently, a system of " Liberal " corruption and Jewish tyranny by a " Christian Social " concatenation of interests and offices scarcely less tyrannical and corrupt. In a word, the employment of impure means to attain ends not in themselves impure entailed consequences almost as deleterious as the evils Lueger had set out to combat.

The importance of Lueger must, however, be measured by the change he wrought in the character of Austrian politics, and especially in the politics of the Austrian Germans. He killed the "Los von Rom" movement and its potential disloyalty to the House of Hapsburg; and he gave to the Austrian bureaucratic machine an impulse stronger than any it had received since the days of Joseph II. The bureaucracy is, in Austria, the material of which the fabric of the State is composed. The English expression "civil service" is not a synonym for "bureaucracy." Despite "officialism" and "red tape," the English civil service has not yet fully acquired a consciousness that it is not a "service" but a government, *the* government. In Austria this consciousness exists and is assiduously cultivated. The idea of a "civil service" conveys to English minds a notion that the Departments of State serve both the Crown and the public. The Austrian bureaucracy, on the contrary, conceives itself theoretically as the executive instrument of the will of the Crown, and practically as invested with a mission to govern the public. A wide gulf still yawns between the Anglo-Saxon standpoint that government is the delegation by the governed of certain administrative and disciplinary functions to organs created for the purpose, and the Roman conception that government is a good in itself, something superior to the governed in its nature and attributes. That the State exists for the service of the public is a conception foreign to the bureaucratic mind, which is moulded on the principle that the community exists for the State and derives its well-being from and through the State. The members of the bureaucracy, with their carefully graduated hierarchy reaching from the copying-clerk to the steps of the throne, form a privileged class whose maintenance absorbs a large proportion of the public revenues. It is true that in Austria there long lingered the tradition inspired by Joseph II. that the privileged position of the bureaucratic class connotes an obligation to fulfil certain duties and to give proof positive of its superiority by promoting the general welfare, checking abuses, and administering national resources faithfully without other sanction or reward than the consciousness of duty well done. The Josephine tradition, despite its Germanizing and centralizing tendencies, produced much of what was best in the Austrian administration. It infused a certain idealism into bureaucratic routine and inculcated the doctrine that the functionaries of the State were *de facto* if not *de jure* the trustees of the community at large. This comparatively liberal tradition survived the " Systems " of Metternich and Bach, the Concordat and the various constitutional experiments of the early 'sixties, and lasted till nearly the end of last century. The rise of the Christian Social movement under Lueger's leadership marked, in a sense, the end of the Josephine tradition and the beginning of a semi-Clerical tendency towards State and municipal socialism that has aggravated the Austrian bureaucratic problem and has to some extent changed its very character.

Great social and political movements usually have their source " beneath the threshold " of public consciousness. They are rarely " created " by any single man or circumstance. Ideas germinate simultaneously, often unconsciously, in many minds, but come to maturity only in minds fertile or spacious enough to permit of their development. The supreme artist, the poet, the convincing writer, the popular leader, the great statesman, rarely " create " in the sense of producing something new in substance. They give a new form, corresponding to the tastes, needs, or instincts of the day, or of the morrow, to substances already awaiting the shaping hand. Too great originality is apt to be sterile. It meets no need and finds no mate for the work of propagation. Judged by the highest " creative " standards Lueger was not a great man ; judged by Austrian and Viennese standards he was greater than any of his contemporaries. He represented the instinctive revolt of the average man against the tyranny of conscienceless liquid wealth, the protest of the small producer or tradesman against the crushing force of agglomerations of capital, the rebellion of all save the "fittest" against the cruelties of ruthless competition. Unhampered by the notions of economic schoolmen, he brought to bear upon political and economic problems the sober sense of a robust intelligence. Whereas Socialism of the Marxist type regards economic development as a natural process tending towards the subjugation of individual initiative by the force of capitalist organization until that organization shall itself be expropriated by the revolutionary force of the organized proletariate, the "Christian" Socialism of Lueger sought immediate solutions for social problems in two different and apparently —but only apparently—contradictory directions. While, on the one hand, he turned resolutely towards the protection of the "small man"—the butcher, the baker, the greengrocer, the chimney sweep, and the tinker,—against the power of the large, mainly Jewish, enterprises which in Germany were crushing the "small man" out of existence, he advocated, on the other hand, a consistent policy of State and municipal Socialism. He gave a powerful impulse to, if he did not actually inspire, the "middle-class policy" of the Government, a policy based on a belief that society may be the poorer for the destruction of small independent existences, and that industrial or commercial "efficiency" is not the last word of social or political well-being. Under the influence of the ideas he represented, legislative checks were placed upon the growth of monopolies ; wages and spheres of competition were regulated ; and a deliberate attempt was made to individualize the workman and to personalize his work. Ten or twenty years hence this part of his policy may be pronounced a "failure," many of the artificial restrictions it imposed may have to be removed, but it will not necessarily follow that they were useless. They may be seen to have served a good purpose in allowing time to be gained for maturer consideration of social questions, in damming back the tide of raw capitalism, and in encouraging a sound belief that the banker and the trust magnate do not rule by right divine.

This part of Lueger's policy was carried out chiefly by the bureaucracy to whose instincts it appealed. It afforded the bureaucracy, in fact, another opportunity to govern and to establish its authority over a further region of public life. But the curse of every bureaucratic system is that, as soon as any department or ministry has been created, it develops a consciousness of its own and becomes an end in itself with interests, ambitions, and instincts of self-preservation quite apart from the purpose it was established to fulfil. Similarly, in the other direction of Lueger's activity — the municipalization and the nationalization of public services,—the object of protecting the public against capitalistic exploitation was, in some though not in all circumstances, attained at the cost of creating fresh armies of bureaucrats to do, less efficiently and more expensively, work previously done by the servants of private companies or individuals. This disadvantage is inherent in all municipalization and nationalization. It is inevitable, and becomes tolerable only when it clearly represents a lesser evil or the avoidance of a greater risk. Nationalization for the sake of nationalization is not only expensive and productive of inefficiency, but tends to become politically dangerous by creating a class of able-bodied dependents upon the public exchequer whose services to the community are rarely commensurate with the power they wield and with the privileges they enjoy. They are apt, moreover, to form, voluntarily or involuntarily, electoral *clientèles* of which the influence may eventually compromise the working of representative institutions. Indeed, Lueger and his lieutenants deliberately used municipalization to reinforce their electoral following. They troubled little about theories and ulterior effects. They saw an advantage to be gained, an abuse to be remedied, a danger to be averted, and took the shortest road to their object.   As the Jews represented capitalist individualism masquerading as "Liberalism," Lueger struck at them—but met his match in the Social Democratic movement which, under Jewish leadership, gathered force as rapidly as "Liberalism" lost it. "Red" Socialism compelled the "Black" Socialists under Lueger to assume the defensive.   He, the genial, irreverent demagogue, gradually became the champion of law and order, the darling of the Church, a pillar of the Throne, a symbol of all that is positively and consciously conservative in the State.   In this posture he died, after having set an indelible stamp on modern Austria.   He left no successor, and his associates have since disgraced and degraded his work.   But he had shown that even a sceptical, artistically emotional, intellectually lazy, and politely conceited folk like the Viennese will respond to the touch of a real leader, and that the non-Viennese Austrians who, in virile quality are superior to those of the capital, rise to the idea of common patriotism and joint effort when it is proclaimed with direct conviction.   When a new Lueger appears he may be neither anti-Semitic, nor Clerical, nor even "Christian Social," but may need to bend his energies towards the liberation of the people from bureaucratic tyranny as Lueger strove to preserve it from the grasp of rampant and immature capitalism.   But it will be long before the Lueger tradition dies—the tradition that Austria, with all her faults, weaknesses, and "Asiatic" characteristics, is a living, growing, cohesive, not a decrepit State ; that the interests of the people are mainly coincident with those of the dynasty ; that the Austrian Germans, though the leading, are not the only State-preserving element, and that their first duty is to their country and their second to their race ; that Slav and Jew are entitled to equality of treatment and consideration in so far as they are loyal to Crown and Fatherland, but that whoever dallies with trans-frontier affinities is unworthy of his "Austrian" birthright.   Lueger at his best represented what is strongest in the Austrian "soul," a soul still inadequate to its body and still seeking for opportunities of expression and growth.   Before its opportunity is found, the body may pass through many a convulsion and even undergo changes of form.   Change and convulsion should, however, herald not the approach of death but rather the entrance into a new and stronger life.

CHAPTER I

So much attention has been paid to single aspects of the Austro-Hungarian problem, and so much stress laid upon its complexity, that the essential character of the Hapsburg Monarchy as a dynastic estate has been lost sight of. "Austria" has been conceived by most modern writers as a multiplicity, whereas it is indispensable that it be regarded in the first place as a monarchical unity. Homage of a sorry sort has, indeed, been paid to the importance of the Emperor Francis Joseph by the dissemination of the view that, upon his death, his realms may fall asunder; but this questionable tribute has been offered rather to the person of a single monarch than to the monarchical office he has filled for more than two generations. The degree in which the occupant is transcended by the office, and the individual ruler by the monarchical function, has not been adequately recognized. Confusion of thought has resulted, and from it an attitude of apprehensive bewilderment in regard to all things Austrian.

A further cause of confusion has been the spread of inaccurate notions of the power of the Hapsburg Crown. Since Austria is to all appearances a Constitutional and Parliamentary Empire, and Hungary a Kingdom proud in the possession of a "thousand-year-old Constitution," the Austro-Hungarian Monarch, that is to say, the Emperor Francis Joseph, has been conceived as a passive element of equilibrium, as a kind of keystone in a tottering arch, a keystone, moreover, of such special weight and shape as to be unique and individually indispensable.   The truth, amply demonstrated by Hapsburg history and instinctively recognized by the majority of Hapsburg subjects, is that the passive functions of the Crown are of minor importance in comparison with its functions as an active, driving, sometimes aggressive force that has frequently proved itself stronger than any other force in its dominions.   If, in regard to the passive functions of the Crown, metaphor be permissible, they may be likened to those of the gyroscope, in resisting automatically the influences that tend to deflect the moving structure of Hapsburg states and peoples from the course marked out by dynastic interest, and, even when exposed for a moment to checks or perturbations too violent to be immediately withstood, spinning on noiselessly in discharge of a self-contained mission to correct the deflection and restore continuity.

Yet it may be contended that while Hapsburg history reveals the potential importance of the monarchical office, it reveals likewise the importance of the " personal equation " and the untoward effects of mental insufficiency or positive wrongheadedness on the part of individual rulers.   Hence, it may be argued, the supreme importance of the Emperor Francis Joseph, whose personal characteristics are known and whose devotion to duty, incomparable experience, and statesmanlike wisdom form an invaluable asset in the political balance-sheet of his dominions and of Europe ; whereas the characteristics of his presumptive successors are unknown, or, in so far as known, hardly promise adequately to replace those of the veteran Emperor.   Though, in point of fact, the personal and political characteristics of the Emperor Francis Joseph are less known than they are commonly supposed to be, while those of his presumptive successors cannot fairly be judged before their heads have borne the weight of the Crown and their shoulders the burden of dynastic responsibility, it is necessary to insist that, in Austria-Hungary, the only misgivings entertained in regard to the future concern not the practical certainty that the Heir Presumptive will succeed smoothly to the Imperial estate, but the possibility that, after succeeding, he may use the immense power inherent in the monarchical function in order to pursue a policy distasteful to some sections of his subjects. If apprehension there be, it is not based on fear lest the demise of the Crown involve the demise or disintegration of the Monarchy, but lest trouble arise during the adjustment of things to the new Monarch's conception of his dynastic " mission."

It is hard to escape the influence of contemporary notions and phenomena. Even the few octogenarians who remember the revolution of 1848, the abdication of Ferdinand and the accession of Francis Joseph, the long series of errors and misfortunes that marked the process of transition from Unitary Absolutism to Constitutional Dualism, find it difficult to recall the conception of the Emperor Francis Joseph's personal and political character that prevailed in Austria and abroad throughout the first half of his reign. Forty-six years of peace, broken only by the Bosnian campaign of 1878–79, have cast a retrospective glamour over the earlier decades, and have dulled the vision even of eyes accustomed to detect permanent features beneath changing forms. Yet it is undeniable that the experiments undertaken and the mistakes committed between 1848 and 1867 throw more light upon the veritable nature of the Hapsburg Monarchy and the power of the Crown than the developments since the Dual System was established. Only those who hold the Dual System to be the final form of the Monarchy, and believe the influence of the Crown to be subordinate to the observance of Dualist principles, can ignore the changes that have been wrought in the Dual System itself, or close their minds to the possibility that the Crown may eventually be compelled by those very considerations of dynastic interest which inspired the settlement of 1867 to recast the constitutional framework of its dominions in another mould. It is no reflection upon the Constitutional loyalty of the Emperor

Francis Joseph to urge that, were he a younger man, he himself might be driven to undo in part the work of his own hands ; nor would it be just to question *a priori* the wisdom of his successors should changed conditions and altered necessities dictate a departure from the later methods of Francis Joseph. Each Hapsburg ruler interprets in his own way the " mission " with which he believes Providence to have entrusted him.

In the Empire of Austria or, as its clumsy constitutional title runs, in the " Kingdoms and Lands represented in the Reichsrath," the idea of popular sovereignty has never been recognized. Under the Fundamental Statute, or Constitution, granted in December 1867, the Emperor is, indeed, bound to exercise his executive power through certain organs of the State, and the constitutional validity of his acts depends, as regards Imperial matters, upon the assent of the Reichsrath or Imperial Parliament, and, in provincial matters, upon the assent of the local Diets. But he remains none the less Emperor by Divine right, and is far from wearing his crown, like the King of Italy, " by the grace of God and the will of the Nation." The peoples of Austria are the peoples of the Emperor almost in a feudal sense ; and though the " Magyar Nation " stands in a different relationship to the Wearer of the Sacred Crown of St. Stephen, the constitutional power of the crowned King of Hungary is far greater than some current Magyar political literature may suggest. The " Magyar nation," in the Constitutional sense, consists practically of those citizens whose political rights the Constitution expressly recognizes. A favourite phrase of Magyar orators when descanting upon the dangers of universal suffrage is that " the bastions of the Constitution " can only be opened to citizens of recognized Magyar sentiment. The conception has not greatly changed since the beginning of the sixteenth century, when, in his Tripartitum Code, Verböczy defined the " people " as the " prelates, barons, and other magnates, also the nobles, but not the commoners." Though many of the Magyar commoners have been enfranchised since 1848, the "nation" in Hungary is still a close corporation standing in a special relationship to the Monarch with whom it makes a fresh bargain at every coronation. Much of the uncertainty in regard to the future of the Hapsburg dominions springs from apprehension lest the future monarch should conceive his "mission" to consist in the reduction of the Magyars to a position in the Monarchy commensurate with their numerical importance and with their status as a minority among the citizens of Hungary; and lest he, drawing his inspiration from the reign of Joseph II. rather than from the later years of Francis Joseph, should seek to substitute for the Dual System some form of centralized unity. Such an effort would be by no means unprecedented in Hapsburg history, and, if deftly and vigorously made, by no means certain to fail.

The Hapsburgs have been defined by a modern Austrian writer[1] as "born artists," in that they lack the sense of reality and create a special world for themselves, each according to his own temperament or "mission." Lands, peoples, and men are their materials. In this respect Ferdinand II. and Joseph II. were the most typical. Ferdinand, drawing his inspiration from the Virgin Mary under Jesuit guidance, accomplished the terrible miracle of transforming Austria in thirty years from a Protestant into a Catholic country. Determined to save the souls of his people, he fulfilled to the letter his saying, "Better a desert than a land of heretics." The thoroughness of his work, and the consistency with which he earned, by fire and sword, confiscation and banishment, torture and execution, his proud title, *Catholicae Fidei Acerrimus Defensor*, are hard to realize in our modern world of tentative policies and halting performance. Ferdinand II. made Austria materially and morally a desert, some parts of which have never since blossomed; but he made it Catholic. Joseph II., the enthroned Jacobin, drawing his inspiration from the Goddess

[1] Hermann Bahr, *Wien*, pp. 19-30.

of Reason, sought to transform his realms and peoples according to a strictly logical, rational plan. "His people is to be what he thinks a people of free citizens ought to be," writes Hermann Bahr in a brilliant historical analysis of the Hapsburg spirit. "This he decrees. His idea determines the life of the nation. He enquires not whether the nation will, or can, whether conditions allow it to conform itself to his idea ; nor understands that the child cannot suddenly deny its father, that to-day can never quite abjure yesterday, that nothing human arises by word of command. ' All this has now ceased, my Lord Chancellor !' he writes to Kolowrat. What existed before him has suddenly to cease. A new world has to begin. And by a stroke of the pen, his bundle of matrimonially-acquired provinces is appointed a modern state. He believes that human life can be ' drafted ' on paper. ' Abolish ' and ' transform ' are his favourite words ; they constantly recur. . . . His ' transformation ' proceeds not from the inner necessities of men and things, but from ' principles,' from Reason. ' An Empire over which I rule must be governed according to my principles. . . . Since I ascended the throne and donned the first diadem of the world, I have made Philosophy the Lawgiver of my Empire. In pursuance of philosophical logic Austria will be given another form.' Here hides the secret of all Hapsburg policy : Austria is always to be given another form in pursuance of some logic or other. To let her grow by herself, according to her nature, does not occur to the Hapsburgs. It is always the mind that is to transform everything, the Ruler's mind alone." [2]

Bahr, however, does less than justice to the inherent soundness of many of Joseph's "principles," and overlooks the fact that but for his untimely death he might himself have corrected the asperities of his "System," instead of withdrawing, in a fit of death-bed despondency, most of the decrees that embodied it. Indeed, modern Hungarian

[1] *Wien*, pp. 26-27.　　　　　　[2] *Wien*, pp. 26-28.

writers like the historian Professor Henrik Marczali admit that, notwithstanding the resistance of the Magyars to the reforming policy of Joseph (whom they nicknamed a *király kalapos*, or " hatted," *i.e.* uncrowned King), his death and failure were a misfortune for Hungary. The mind of Joseph cannot be better studied than in the remarkable Memorandum on the condition of the Austrian Monarchy[1] which he addressed to his mother, the Empress Maria Theresa, in 1765, fifteen years before his accession to the Austrian Throne. Like some of his predecessors, and like Francis Joseph, at least, among his successors, Joseph II. was penetrated by a sense of duty towards his subjects. In regard to the duties and pleasures of the Sovereign he wrote in his quaint French : " Surtout que sa maxime inviolable soit toujours que son individu et son bonheur et vrai plaisir ne peut pas être séparé du bien de toute la monarchie " ; and again, with reference to the necessity of allowing a certain liberty of movement and conduct, especially to strangers : " Je crois que dans tout ce qui s'appelle bagatelles ou choses de propre goût, il faut la liberté plenière aux hommes, surtout exigeant que *dans toutes les affaires concernantes l'État, l'on se soumette aveuglément et voie du même point de vue tout ce que le souverain décide.*" Had he lived he might have given the Monarchy a lasting administrative framework and a definite unitary form. Tragic failure though his reign must be deemed, it served to illustrate, while it lasted, the driving power of the Hapsburg Crown and to prove the thesis, which the reign of Francis Joseph has amply demonstrated, that notwithstanding mistakes and mishaps such as would discredit any uncrowned administrator or statesman, the head of the Hapsburg dynasty possesses, in virtue of his functions and position, an almost inexhaustible influence and invulnerable prestige.

In an epoch when democratic control is generally considered the main guarantee of political welfare, the power retained by the Austrian Crown may well seem anachronistic,

---

[1] Arneth, *Maria Theresia und Joseph II.*, Band iii., pp. 335-361.

but, if "Austria" is to be comprehended, current political notions must be set aside and the special Austrian facts judged on their merits without prepossession. "Austria is just Austria, a neutralization of various elements by and through the dynasty and the power of interests," wrote Krones in the conclusion to his monumental Austrian History,[1] meaning by "Austria" the whole Monarchy. The policy *divide et impera* is the active form of this "neutralization," and is facilitated by the natural divisions between the Hapsburg peoples, divisions that in themselves tend to prevent a serious coalition against the Crown. If one race possesses or acquires predominance, the Monarch acquiesces in it as long as it appears to serve the dynastic purpose, but throws his whole weight against it when it threatens to become overbearing. Hapsburg policy is exalted opportunism in the pursuit of an unchanging dynastic idea. No influence, be it that of a statesman, a party, or a race, is ever suffered long to prevail over the influence of the Crown. Hence perhaps the Hapsburg reputation for ingratitude, a reputation well earned according to normal standards, but one which must strike the Hapsburgs themselves as singularly unjust. Why should the Hapsburgs be grateful? Their statesmen, their officials are their servants, whose duty it is to obey, to execute orders, to offer advice, and to disappear when their period of usefulness is over. Is it not enough that they should have been allowed to collaborate in the fulfilment of the great dynastic purpose? The Emperor Francis, to whom a man was once recommended as a patriot, remarked, "They call him a patriot for Austria, but is he also a patriot for Me?" Among the scores of ministers and statesmen who have served Francis Joseph, few retired without feeling that they had been mere pawns in a dynastic game of which they might guess the rules but could not control the moves. Titles and decorations were lavished upon them while in office; a supreme honour sometimes bestowed with gracious words on their dismissal or retirement,

[1] *Geschichte Oesterreichs*, Band iv. p. 658.

but, after retirement, they disappeared into the twilight
reserved for pensioned officials and were heard of no more,
unless at some moment of temporary embarrassment the
Monarch beckoned them again for a brief space into the
sunshine of his service.   Some vanished as though by magic
in the twinkling of an eye.   The wisest, seeing their hour
to be at hand and estimating aright the value of the
Monarch's flattering assurances, forestalled dismissal by
insisting that their retirement would ease the position of
the Crown.   Such a one was Count Gołuchowski, Minister
of the Imperial and Royal Household and for Foreign
Affairs from 1895 to 1906.   Taught perhaps by the experience of his father who, in 1861, found his resignation
awaiting signature on his desk, Count Gołuchowski the
younger doffed his high office with grace and dignity.
Others, vainer or less circumspect, fared worse.   The tragic
fate of heroes like Benedek belongs to a special category,
but the experience of Austrian Premiers like Badeni and
Koerber, who were abruptly dismissed while believing themselves secure and indispensable ; or of Hungarian Premiers
like Bánffy and Széll, whose successors were designated
while they themselves looked forward to a long lease of
power ; of *hommes à tout faire* like sundry Croatian Bans who
had covered themselves with shame in the service of the
Crown ; nay, even of Andrássy the Elder who, contrary to his
expectation, was never recalled to office, might be paralleled
again and again from the records of Francis Joseph's dealings
with his political agents and advisers.   Little better was the
treatment of those who ventured to cross the Monarch's will
or to protest, albeit mutely, against his action.   Beust, the
only Austrian Imperial Chancellor, found disgrace to be the
price of his triumph over Hohenwart, who had prepared for
the Emperor's Coronation as King of Bohemia at Prague.
A gifted and experienced Austrian nobleman who resigned
the Premiership on finding that declarations he had been
authorized to make to the Chamber had subsequently been
nullified without his knowledge by a clandestine arrangement

between the Crown and Hungary, discovered that an intangible but insuperable obstacle ever afterwards precluded his appointment to any position higher than the governorship of a distant province. In the Hapsburg Monarchy public servants must ever be ready to subordinate their conceptions of patriotism and of political dignity to the exigencies of the dynastic patriotism represented by the will of the Crown. They must be " patriots for Me."

As with individuals so with parties and peoples. The Germans of Austria who, from 1867 onwards, formed the main Austrian pillar of the Dual System, lost favour and were crushed in a general election as soon as they revolted in 1878–79 against the occupation of Bosnia-Herzegovina and the increase of the army which the Monarch held to be indispensable. Thereafter they wandered for thirty years in the wilderness of Imperial disfavour, seeing the influence of the Crown employed to develop their Slav rivals, and were finally obliged in 1906 to accept against their will the Universal Suffrage Bill that placed them for ever in the position of a parliamentary minority. Against universal suffrage they struggled indeed for a while, murmuring threats of obstruction, until at the last moment their leaders were summoned to the Emperor's presence and told that the bill must be passed. And passed it was. The Annexation of Bosnia-Herzegovina in 1908 gave them at last an opportunity to repair their error of 1878–79. They supported the Annexation and voted unhesitatingly the expenditure it entailed. Their reward was Imperial favour. Similarly, the incipient opposition of the Czechs and of some other Austrian Slavs to the Annexation was checked by the fear of incurring the same displeasure with which the Germans had been visited after the occupation of Bosnia-Herzegovina—a displeasure which the Slavs, nevertheless, did not entirely escape.

Nor is this power of the Crown confined to Austria. The Coalition of groups and parties that obtained the majority in the Hungarian general election of January 1905 but declined to take office unless the Monarch should acquiesce in a curtailment of his constitutional military prerogatives, was, after fifteen months' resistance, coerced by the Crown into capitulation. The chief outward means of coercion was the threat that the Crown would break the power of the Magyar oligarchy by substituting, if necessary through a *coup d'état*, universal suffrage for the narrow and tortuous Hungarian franchise ; but the most effective episode in the conflict was the action of the Crown in summoning, on September 23, 1905, the recalcitrant Coalition Leaders *ad audiendum verbum regium*. In this "audience," which lasted five minutes, the Magyar leaders were treated as schoolboys by an irate and masterful dominie, treatment that, despite their subsequent expostulations, went far to convince them that by continuing to challenge the Monarch's authority they would be embarking upon a struggle in which the Constitution and welfare of Hungary might be irremediably compromised. After the dissolution of Parliament *manu militari* in February 1906, they yielded, but not before their conduct had brought into prominence the important truth that, even in Hungary, the Crown is not a mere instrument for the ratification of parliamentary decisions, but is a legislative and governing factor equal, if not superior, in weight to the national representation. The conflict of 1905–6—the first serious trial of strength between the Crown and the Magyars since the Dual Settlement of 1867—raised, moreover, in an acute form the question of the permanence of the Dual System itself.

.   .   .   .

The importance of the Dual System lies less in the details of the Constitutional Settlement (variously termed "Compromise" or *Ausgleich*) of 1867 than in the circumstances from which it sprang. The principle of Dualism, that is, the union of the Lands of the Hungarian Crown with the Hereditary Austrian Lands under a joint Hapsburg Ruler, is at least as old as the Hungarian Pragmatic Sanction of 1722–23 ; but the peculiar significance of the 1867

Settlement can only be appreciated in the light of the events that preceded it and the consequences it has entailed for the dynasty and the Monarchy. It marked an important phase of the process of transformation that began when Francis II., foreseeing the end of the Holy Roman Empire and anxious to preserve Imperial rank for himself and his heirs, assumed in 1804 the title of Emperor of Austria. That title meant "Emperor of all Lands of the House of Austria" and not merely of Austria proper. It implied the development of a specifically "Austrian" policy in the House of Hapsburg, whose attention had until then been chiefly absorbed by the retention and maintenance of the Roman-German Imperial dignity. For centuries the Hapsburgs had sacrificed the strength of Austria to the Roman-German Imperial dream. From Ferdinand I. to Charles VI. their aim had been to exercise universal sway. Maria Theresa, Joseph II., and Leopold recognized the chimerical nature of the dream, but still struggled for undisputed hegemony in Germany. Not until the defeat of Sadowa in 1866, nor, in reality, until the foundation of the new German Empire at Versailles in January 1871, did the Hapsburgs give up their German ambitions and turn their eyes resolutely to their own realms. Though begotten and conceived in 1866 and born in 1867, the Austro-Hungarian Monarchy, as a self-contained individuality among States, acquired a definite conscious existence only after German victories in France had taught the Hapsburgs that the struggle for mastery in Germany had been irrevocably decided against them. The fall in 1871 of Beust, the Bismarck-hating Saxon statesman who, in woful ignorance of Austrian affairs, had negotiated for Austria in 1866–67 the Dual Settlement with Hungary as a prelude to revenge upon Prussia, symbolized the fall of the old Hapsburg policy. Until then the Hapsburgs had looked abroad; Austria had been for them merely the hereditary stronghold from which their influence radiated. If ever they looked to their home Lands it was in order to develop or accumulate resources for the German struggle. Hence, largely, the resistance of the Bohemian and Magyar nations to union with Austria. Such union seemed tantamount to absorption in the Empire of Germany and to servitude to the Crown of Charlemagne. Had the Hapsburgs limited their ambition to the creation of a unified Austrian State, they would doubtless have succeeded. Their strength, insufficient for the German Imperial task, would have availed for the humbler but more essential work of welding Hungary, Bohemia, and the "hereditary dominions" into one solid block. But they perceived too late the true nature of their task, and, when they at last addressed themselves to it, found that their chance of success had been, perhaps irretrievably, compromised by engagements they had contracted towards Hungary in a last vain hope of reversing the verdict of history.

It is essential to comprehension of the Dual System that the Settlement of 1867 should not be regarded as an agreement calmly concluded by two contracting parties after mature consideration of the internal issues it was to regulate, but rather as a snap decision hurriedly taken for dynastic reasons under pressure of events abroad. The Emperor Francis Joseph had, on his accession in December 1848, found the fundamental Dualism established by the Hungarian Pragmatic Sanction of 1722–23 — which stipulated the succession of a single heir, male or eventually female, to all the lands of the Dynasty, and the exercise of inseparable and indivisible sway over Austria and Hungary alike by the reigning Head of the Imperial House — seriously compromised as a result of the ratification of the Hungarian Laws of April 1848 by his predecessor, the feeble-minded Ferdinand. The Hungarian Law III. of 1848 on the formation of a responsible Hungarian ministry was to all intents and purposes a separatist statute. While providing vaguely for the " maintenance of the unity of the Crown and of the association of the Empire," and stipulating that one of the ministers must be " constantly about the Person of His Majesty in order to exercise influence upon all matters concerning the Fatherland (Hungary) and the Hereditary Provinces (Austria) jointly," it only limited, in practice, the independence of Hungary by failing to enumerate a Ministry for Foreign Affairs among the Hungarian Departments of State.   The separatist character of this and other Hungarian Statutes which were sanctioned by the Emperor Ferdinand on April 11, 1848, was enhanced by the promulgation, a fortnight later (April 25), of a Constitution for the Austrian Empire alone without other provision for maintenance of the union with Hungary than a reference in the preamble to the union of the Kingdoms belonging for centuries to the Monarchy.   Though the sanction given to the Hungarian Statutes was subsequently withdrawn, and the Austrian Constitution of April 25, 1848 replaced by the Unitary Constitution of March 1849 for the whole Monarchy, the weakness of Ferdinand had given to the Magyars an undeniably legal basis for their policy of independence.

Francis Joseph therefore took over his inheritance under singularly difficult conditions, juridical and military ; and though the reconquest of Hungary by the Imperial Austrian and Russian forces after the dethronement of Francis Joseph by the Hungarian Diet in 1849 may be held to have destroyed the validity of anterior arrangements, the Magyars, or, at least, the "1848 and Independence Party," have always invoked the Laws of 1848 as an integral portion of the Hungarian Constitution.   Austrian authorities like Professor Tezner maintain, on the other hand, that the fatal blunder of Francis Joseph and his advisers was the destruction, by the Cabinet Order and the Imperial Rescripts of August 1851, of the Unitary Constitution of March 1849, which, they believe, the Magyars could in time have been induced or compelled to accept.   In any case the destruction of this Constitution under the influence of the Ultra-Conservatives, who, like Schwarzenberg, believed absolutism to be the "natural Constitution of the Monarchy," left the Magyars no choice.   Under the oppressive "System," thereafter organized with undeniable technical skill but political short-sightedness by Alexander Bach, no course was open to them but that of passive resistance. Bach's " System," which was maintained with pitiless rigour until 1859, when it and its author were discredited by the defeats of Magenta and Solferino, destroyed all chance of bringing the Magyars to a unitary conception of their position in the Monarchy. Eminent foreign students like Professor Louis Eisenmann, whose work *Le Compromis Austro-Hongrois*[1] is a monument of painstaking research, incline, indeed, to the belief that towards the end of 1860 the Magyar leaders would have been disposed to accept the principle laid down in the Austrian Federal Constitution, or " October Diploma," of that year—the principle that Hungary, while enjoying autonomy, should be represented in a Central Imperial Legislative Council or Reichsrath—had not Schmerling and other German advisers of the Crown induced the Emperor, on February 26, 1861, to substitute for the Federalist " Diploma " a Centralist Germanizing " Patent " of Constitutional government by which Hungary was again reduced to the status of an Austrian Province. Discussion of " what might have been " had Francis Joseph and his Councillors been wiser is now a merely academic exercise. The indisputable fact is that the Constitutional experiments of Francis Joseph's reign after the loss of Lombardy and the collapse of the Bach " System " were not undertaken with a single eye to the good government and welfare of the Monarchy, but were intended chiefly to capture Austrian Liberal and Magyar support for the dynastic policy of overcoming Prussia in the struggle for mastery in Germany. Deák, one of the wisest Magyar statesmen of all time, to whom the Emperor made flattering advances in 1865, resolutely declined to strengthen the hands of the dynasty for a contest in which he thought it certain to be worsted, and from which, should it perchance emerge victorious, he expected it to return with enhanced prestige again to throttle Magyar liberty. He presented to the Crown a

[1] Paris, 1904, Société de Librairie et d'Édition.

memorandum which a special committee of Magyar politicians had endorsed but which the Emperor found unacceptable. Francis Joseph therefore broke with Deák and drifted, without Hungarian support or goodwill, into the final tussle with Prussia. But after Sadowa he hastened to renew relations with Deák, summoned him secretly to Vienna and asked him for a statement of Hungarian terms. Deák, who, like most Magyars, knew how to combine business-like shrewdness with a noble gesture, replied that, notwithstanding Sadowa, Hungary demanded nothing more than before. Touched by such magnanimity and too eager for revenge to haggle over terms that would bring him Hungarian support in the intended war of revenge, Francis Joseph accepted Deák's conditions without perceiving that what the Magyar leader had demanded in 1865 as a maximum, subject to reduction by negotiation, had become a minimum in 1866. Francis Joseph may, indeed, have accepted the Hungarian terms with a mental reservation that, when Prussia should have been overthrown, the inner constitution of the Monarchy would once more be subject to revision ; or he may have lent too ready an ear to Beust, who embodied the policy of revenge and, in preparing it, cared little whether the internal unity of the Monarchy were undermined by over-generosity towards the Magyars. Even Belcredi, the Austrian Premier, who had originally shown indifference towards the negotiations with the Magyars, perceived the dangers to which unity was being exposed, and attempted in vain at the twelfth hour to provide a safeguard in the form of a special Reichsrath for the whole Monarchy. But the Emperor was then, as on some subsequent occasions, seized by a fit of feverish impatience and insisted upon a rapid settlement. Better a bad settlement than none, seems to have been his feeling ; and Beust, who knew how seriously the strength of the Monarchy had been sapped by Magyar resistance since 1848, was equally eager to conclude. As long as military and diplomatic unity were saved, the rest, he thought, would matter little

pending the great squaring of accounts with Prussia.   But
Bismarck, whose military triumph over Austria enabled the
Magyars to make so good a bargain, came once more to
their aid.   The alliance which Beust endeavoured to form in
1869 with France and Italy against Prussia was thwarted
by the attitude of Russia, whose goodwill Bismarck had
assiduously cultivated ; and, before other schemes could be
laid, the German victories over France in 1870–71 saved
the Dual Settlement by relegating the Austrian policy of
revenge for Sadowa to the limbo of hopes unfulfilled.

The Dual System

Thus the Dual System acquired stability.   Its main
features are too well known to require detailed explanation.
It established in Hungary and Austria responsible Ministries,
between which stand three Joint Departments of State, the
War Office, the Foreign Office, and the Joint Ministry of
Finance.   The heads of Joint Departments are responsible
neither to the Austrian nor to the Hungarian Parliament, but
only to Delegations consisting of sixty members chosen from
each Parliament to discuss affairs and sanction estimates
common to both States.   The economic relations of the two
States are regulated by a Customs and Trade Alliance or
Economic Settlement, renewable every ten years and subject
to the proviso that, as the Pragmatic Sanction does not apply
to commercial affairs, Hungary is entitled to regulate her own
commercial interests by special tariffs in case the Customs and
Trade Alliance should lapse.   The Delegations from the Austrian and the Hungarian Parliaments are convoked annually,
at Budapest or Vienna by turns.   They meet simultaneously
in the same city, but sit separately and communicate decisions
to each other in writing, a joint sitting being held only in
case of disagreement, for the purpose of taking a joint vote
without debate.   Grave discrepancies exist between the Hungarian Constitutional Statute XII. of 1867 and the parallel

Austrian Statute of December 21, 1867, which form the
Dual Settlement.   The Hungarian Statute is practically
Deák's memorandum of 1865 hurriedly cast into statute
form.   Its language is involved and vague, its terminology
a fruitful source of dispute.   The Austrian Constitutional
Statute is more precise, but is not recognized by Magyars
as possessing, even by implication, any validity in regard to
the interpretation of the Hungarian Law.   The Magyar conception of the Dual System is that of a constitutional pact
between the King of Hungary and the Magyar Nation, to
which a counterpart was created by the Monarch in his
capacity as Emperor of Austria, who granted to his Austrian
subjects a Constitution containing analogous though by
no means identical provisions.   The Hungarian Statute
stipulates, however, the establishment of " complete constitutionalism in the other Lands and Provinces of His
Majesty, because Hungary can only consent to deal with
the Constitutional Representation of those Lands in regard to
any joint matters whatsoever," and thus recognizes by implication the Constitution of Austria.   Between the Hungarian
Pact and its Austrian counterpart the main links are the
Joint Monarch and the Joint Departments of State.   The
Dual System thus rests upon two parallel arrangements, of
which the one is a bilateral agreement between the Crown
and the Magyar Nation as represented in the Hungarian
Parliament, and the other is a unilateral Constitutional
Statute promulgated by Imperial authority in Austria and
accepted by the Austrian Parliament.   It presents itself as
a kind of doorway consisting of two pillars of unequal
strength with the Crown and the Joint Departments for lintel.
The decennial Customs and Trade Alliance is almost the
only feature of the Settlement that depends upon a direct
understanding between the Austrian and Hungarian Governments as representing their respective Parliaments.   But even
in regard to this, as in regard to nearly every detail of the
working of the Dual Settlement, the influence of the Monarch
makes itself constantly felt.   At moments of tension between

the two States, when, for instance, the question of retaining
the Austro-Hungarian State Bank as a joint institution or
that of maintaining or dissolving the Customs and Trade
Alliance becomes acute, the Monarch is obliged, both personally and through his Joint ministers, to act as moderator and
umpire, sometimes even as dictator.   Yet, thorny and difficult
as are these economic issues, they rarely acquire the same
degree of importance as is attributed to questions affecting
the organization of the army and the Monarch's military
prerogatives.

How fruitful of discord and misunderstanding military
questions may become, can be seen at a glance from the
provisions of the Hungarian Statute and from those of its
Austrian counterpart in regard to the army.   Clause 11 of
the Hungarian Statute says : "In pursuance of the Constitutional princely rights of His Majesty in the sphere of
military affairs, everything appertaining to the unitary
leadership, command, and inner organization of the whole
army, and thus also of the Hungarian Army as an integral
part of the whole army, is recognized as subject to His
Majesty's disposal."   But the next clause, 12, of the same
Statute modifies and confuses the issue as follows : "Nevertheless, on the basis of the previous laws, the country
reserves to itself, both in the spheres of legislation and of
government, the decision concerning the periodical renewal
of the Hungarian Army and the right of granting recruits,
the fixing of the conditions for such granting of recruits
and of the period of service, as also the location and commissariat arrangements of the troops."   Without entering
at this juncture into the precise meaning of the expression
"Hungarian Army,"[1] since no such army exists in the ordinary
sense of the term (the Honvéd troops are not referred to by
Clause 11), it must be noted that whereas Clause 11 recognizes the "constitutional princely right of His Majesty" to
settle everything appertaining to the leadership, command,
and inner organization of the whole army, including the

[1] Cf. p. 69.

" Hungarian Army," Clause 12 declares that " the Country "
reserves its right to lay down the conditions on which it
grants recruits, to fix their period of service, as well as the
location and commissariat arrangements of the troops.   The
contradiction, or, at least, the confusion, is obvious.   Clause
12 limits, if it does not nullify, the provisions of Clause 11.
In point of fact the Hungarian Chamber, taking its stand on
Clause 12, has repeatedly refused to grant the annual levy of
recruits unless the rights of the Crown under Clause 11 were
exercised in accordance with Magyar wishes.   The conflict
of 1903–6 between the Crown and the Magyars turned on
this very point.   The, perhaps wilful, obscurity of the Hungarian Statute is the more striking in the light of the
corresponding Austrian Statute, Clause 5 of which contains
the terse declaration :

" It appertains exclusively to the Emperor to ordain
matters concerning the management, leadership, and inner
organization of the whole army."

No exception has ever been taken by Hungary to this
clear enactment of the Austrian Constitution, which evidently
embraces the " Hungarian Army," inasmuch as it is, by the
Hungarian Clause 11, an "integral part of the whole
army " ; nor can it be objected that the constitutional relations between the Emperor of Austria and his subjects do
not concern Hungary, inasmuch as the Hungarian Statute
expressly stipulates that the Monarch shall establish complete Constitutionalism in his "other Lands and Provinces."
The view of the Crown itself is defined in the Rescript of
February 20, 1867, appointing a responsible Hungarian
Ministry and countersigned by Andrássy, as Premier, by
which Andrássy was provisionally entrusted with the affairs
of National Defence subject to the "undiminished maintenance of my Royal rights relating to the command and
inner organization of the army."   The historical truth is that
the Monarch was, in 1866, disposed to meet Hungarian wishes
on all points save those of military and diplomatic unity.
As long as Count Andrássy (who, with Deák, had been the

chief Magyar architect of the Dual Settlement) remained in charge of its practical working either as Hungarian Premier (1867–71) or as Joint Foreign Minister (1871–79), no question as to its interpretation arose. The Settlement was observed according to the spirit in which the Magyars had concluded it, and not according to the casuistical or perverse interpretations of its letter which the juridical ingenuity of Magyar separatists subsequently devised. But, when Andrássy had retired from office and Deák's voice was hushed, the foundations of the Settlement began to be exposed in Hungary and in Austria to attacks that have progressively undermined its stability.

No greater error can be made in regard to the affairs of the Hapsburg Monarchy than to conceive any of its elements or factors, institutions or Settlements, as entirely known quantities, or as " fixed poles in the flight of phenomena." If there be an exception to this rule, it may perhaps be found in the Pragmatic Sanction with its provision for the indivisibility of the Hapsburg Lands under one and the same Ruler, though, as the Hungarian Revolution of 1848 showed, the Pragmatic Sanction itself has not always been respected. The dynasty is, in theory, a constant factor, but varies in practice according to the individual character of its head, and even, as may be seen from the vicissitudes of Francis Joseph's long reign, according to the circumstances and influences to which its head may at various times be exposed. The Dual System is, by its very nature and by its *vice d'origine*, an oscillating, fluctuating structure, singularly open to attack. It does not and cannot correspond to the permanent interests of the dynasty, nor to those of the non-Magyar and non-German Hapsburg peoples. The Emperor Francis Joseph seems instinctively to have perceived this truth as soon as Beust's policy of revenge upon Prussia was seen to be impracticable. Was it accident or design that made him hold out, in his Rescripts to the Bohemian Diet of August 30 and September 26, 1870, and September 12, 1871, a definite prospect that a Federal Constitution would

be recognized for Bohemia and be sanctioned by solemn
oath on the Emperor's coronation at Prague as King of
Bohemia ?   Austrian-German writers attribute these Rescripts to the baleful influence of Hohenwart, then Austrian
Premier, and of his Slav and Clerical friends; but they have
never frankly faced the question why, within a few weeks
of the first crushing German victories in France, Francis
Joseph should have made a deliberate bid for Austrian-Slav
favour by suggesting the establishment in Bohemia of an
autonomy that could hardly have failed to entail Slav predominance in that kingdom.   Francis Joseph has often
appeared to change his mind, has often yielded to circumstances, has sometimes seemed unreliable to the point of
fickleness, but, underneath his changeability, signs of a
steady dynastic purpose may be detected.   Before 1866
that purpose was German.   As soon as the victorious advance of the German army through the Vosges had convinced him that Hapsburg policy must in future seek its
centre of gravity in its own realms, he seems, however, to
have understood that the predominance of the German
element in Austria must be neutralized by the development
of the Austrian Slavs.   This policy was not compatible
with the Dual System as conceived by Andrássy and Deák,
nor were the Rescripts of 1870–71 to the Bohemian Diet
compatible with the Austrian Constitutional Statute of
December 1867.   Indeed, the German Deputies in the
Bohemian Diet answered the Rescripts by urging that they
transgressed the Constitution of 1867, which does not
recognize the competence of a Provincial Diet to settle the
relationship of that province to the Empire as a whole.
The Rescripts caused, however, such consternation in the
Dualist camp in Hungary and in the German camp in
Austria that adversaries like Andrássy, then Hungarian
Premier, and Beust, the Imperial Chancellor, joined hands
and, with the help of Bismarck, compelled the Emperor
to dismiss the Austrian Premier Hohenwart, who was
nominally responsible for the Rescripts, and to inform the

Bohemian Diet by a further Rescript, on October 30, 1871, that, as the Dual Settlement of 1867 had defined the composition of the two halves of the Monarchy, changes could only be made by agreement between the Austrian and Hungarian Parliaments; and that the Austrian Parliament or Reichsrath was alone competent to regulate the reciprocal relationships of the kingdoms and provinces represented in it.

Hohenwart and Bohemia thus suffered a serious defeat for which the Bohemian Slavs have never quite forgiven the Emperor. He, however, threw the onus of the defeat on to Beust, who was constrained to resign the Imperial Chancellorship within a few weeks of Hohenwart's dismissal, and saw himself replaced, not, indeed, as Imperial Chancellor, but as Minister of the Imperial Household and for Foreign Affairs, by Andrássy, the rival he had most feared. The "Imperial Chancellorship" disappeared, perhaps for ever. Even Metternich had been merely "Chancellor"; but Beust, whose vanity and envy of Bismarck knew no bounds, had obtained for himself titular equality with Bismarck by acquiring the style of Reichskanzler. His record in Austrian and Austro-Hungarian history is not brilliant. Too conceited to understand that in Austrian affairs under Francis Joseph none but "practised Austrians" could hope to work with profit to themselves and the dynasty, he applied a Saxon intelligence to Austrian intricacies, and eked out his ignorance by self-sufficiency. In his blind desire for revenge upon Bismarck, he handed over to the Magyars the keys of the fortress of unity instead of seeking to correct by circumspection the impatience of his Imperial master. " Without you," said Andrássy to him with fine irony, " we should never have made the Dual Settlement "—and Beust was fatuous enough to take the irony for a compliment.

Andrássy's term at the Foreign Office, 1871–79, was the most successful period under the Dual System. In Hungary his prestige was great with all parties; in Austria his action in helping to ward off the blow struck at German predominance by the Hohenwart Rescripts, secured him the enthusiastic support of the German Liberal elements, whose confidence in him was enhanced by the reflection that he, as a Magyar and adversary both of the Hungarian Slav races and of Russian Panslavism, could be relied upon to counteract Austrian Slav influence on the Crown and to maintain cordial relations with the new German Empire. Andrássy believed that the strength of the Dual System depended upon Magyar predominance in Hungary and the parallel predominance of the German Liberals in Austria. As far as Hungary was concerned, Magyar hegemony stood firm. The short-sightedness of Alexander Bach, whose reactionary bureaucracy had, from 1849 to 1859, dragooned and oppressed the loyal non-Magyars of Hungary with the same ruthless severity as the rebellious Magyars themselves, had so cured the non-Magyars of their affection for Austria that when, under the Constitutional Decree or "Patent" of February 1861, an Imperial Parliament was convoked for the whole Monarchy, neither the Croatians nor any non-Magyar race save the Transylvanian Rumanes and Saxons could be induced to attend it ; and even the presence of the Transylvanians was due rather to the influence of the great Rumane Bishop Siaguna and to Transylvanian particularist feeling than to any love for "Vienna." After the reconciliation between the Magyars and the Crown in 1867, the Magyar position in Hungary had been further strengthened by the wise moderation of Deák, his freedom from Magyar Chauvinism, and his conviction that, while not Magyar by race, the non-Magyars could be rendered, by equitable treatment, loyally Hungarian in feeling. In Austria the position of the German Liberals seemed almost equally assured. The dismissal of Hohenwart had removed the danger of a fresh attack upon the Constitution of 1867, and, thanks to the abstention of the Bohemian Slavs, the German Constitutional party held almost undisputed sway in Parliament. The German Liberal Auersperg Cabinet was formed on the basis of an express agreement with the Emperor that he would follow a constitutional policy provided the German majority should grant him all the military credits he might demand. Andrássy therefore began his work as foreign minister under favourable conditions, and had reason to hope that the twin pillars of the Dual System would gain rather than lose strength with lapse of time. The power of the Crown seemed to have been fenced about with Constitutional restrictions, and Austria-Hungary to be developing into a thoroughly limited Monarchy. Free from internal anxieties, Andrássy was therefore able to prepare for the realization of the Monarch's fondest wish —that his territory might be extended in such manner as to compensate the dynasty for the loss of Lombardy and Venetia.

An astute Austrian Slav statesman whose Privy Councillorship was more than a decorative title, once declared that the key to the Hapsburg heart lies in the words, "More acres." Andrássy knew his Sovereign well enough to understand that Francis Joseph's deepest desire must be not to go down to posterity as a lessener of the Empire, and not to appear to deserve the malicious quip of his dethroned uncle Ferdinand, who after Sadowa and the loss of Venetia remarked that it was really unnecessary to have made him abdicate in 1848, because he also could have managed to lose battles and provinces. When, therefore, the insurrection in the Turkish vilayet of Bosnia and the certainty of a Russo-Turkish war offered Austria-Hungary a chance of obtaining compensation for her neutrality, Andrássy and Francis Joseph secured, during a meeting with the Tzar at Reichstadt in 1876, Russian consent to the eventual addition of Bosnia-Herzegovina to Hapsburg territory. The revision of the treaty of San Stefano by the Congress of Berlin brought Andrássy a European mandate to "occupy and administer" the coveted Turkish provinces—but brought to him also the germs of Imperial disfavour and to the Germans of Austria the destruction of their predominance. The Emperor expected that, after so much diplomatic preparation, the Berlin Congress would have sanctioned the annexation of the two provinces outright, and is believed always to have borne Andrássy a grudge for having failed to secure more than an "occupation." However this may be, the mandate to occupy Bosnia-Herzegovina engendered a conflict between the Crown and the German majority in the Austrian Chamber. Relations between them had already been strained by the anti-Clerical policy of the Auersperg Cabinet, whose Bill on Religious Congregations the Emperor had refused to sanction. When he demanded military credits for the operations in Bosnia-Herzegovina, the German majority broke into open revolt and opposed both the credits and the occupation. The Auersperg pact with the Crown having thus been broken, the Emperor was free to visit his displeasure upon the Germans, whom he caused to be crushed by official influence during the general election of 1879. The new Reichsrath showed a majority hostile to the Dualist Constitution of December 1867, but not strong enough to revise it. Under the leadership of Count Taaffe, whom the Emperor then appointed Premier and maintained in office for fourteen years, a majority composed of Conservative-Clerical Germans, Poles, and Bohemian Slavs or Czechs,[1] proceeded to govern in accordance with the Imperial will. Taaffe, indeed, had no other object than to increase the power and prestige of the Emperor, whose friend he had been from boyhood. The renascence of the Monarch's personal influence in Austria dates from 1879.

After the destruction of the German "Constitutional" majority in Austria, it would have been impossible for Andrássy long to remain in office, even had his position not been affected by the vicissitudes of the Berlin Congress and by the falsification of his prophecy that "a band of music" would suffice for the occupation of Bosnia-Herzegovina. One pillar of the Dual System, as he conceived it, had been undermined. His last act before retiring was to conclude

[1] Pronounced Chekhs.

with Bismarck the Austro-German Alliance of October 1879 against Russia.[1] Whether he believed that the Alliance would reinforce the position of the Germans in Austria and create an external prop for the Dual System, or whether he was utilized by the Emperor to give Germany through the Alliance a guarantee of Austro-Hungarian co-operation in foreign policy while in Austria the power of the Crown was being used to diminish German and increase Slav influence, there are as yet no adequate means of judging ; but it is very doubtful whether Bismarck, who had joined Andrássy and Beust in 1871 in thwarting the Slavophil policy of Hohenwart, would have tolerated the resumption of a Slavophil policy under Taaffe, had not the Alliance given Germany a pledge that the Dual Monarchy would not, in foreign politics, side with the adversaries of the German Empire. In later years Bismarck professed himself unable to understand why Andrássy should have been allowed to resign, and why, in a land where statesmen of the first rank are exceptionally rare, he should never have been recalled to office. But Bismarck, whose political fortune was due in great part to the patience and sound sense of a Monarch not jealous of ministerial greatness, knew too little of the inner workings of Hapsburg affairs to comprehend that dynastic interests, real or fancied, neces-

---

[1] The text of the Alliance, which was published on February 3, 1888, at Berlin and Vienna, is as follows :—

Clause 1.—Should, contrary to the hope and against the sincere wish of the two high contracting parties, one of the two Empires be attacked by Russia, the high contracting parties are bound to stand by each other with the whole of the armed forces of their Empires and, in consequence thereof, only to conclude peace jointly and in agreement.

Clause 2.—Should one of the high contracting parties be attacked by another Power, the other high contracting party hereby binds itself, not only not to stand by the aggressor of its high ally, but to observe at least an attitude of benevolent neutrality towards its high co-contractor.

If, however, in such a case, the attacking Power should be supported by Russia, either in the form of active co-operation or by military measures menacing to the party attacked, the obligation defined in Clause 1, of reciprocal help with the entire armed strength, comes immediately into force in this case also, and the war will then also be waged jointly by the two high contracting parties until the joint conclusion of peace.

Clause 3, concerning the secrecy of the treaty, lost its validity on publication.

sarily take such precedence of all other considerations that no minister can long hold office after his usefulness to the dynasty has, or is deemed to have, ceased.

THE DUAL SYSTEM—THE SECOND PHASE

With the fall of Andrássy, the Dual System entered on a new phase. The fundamental condition laid down in the Hungarian Law XII. of 1867 that "complete constitutionalism" should be established in the "other Lands and Provinces of His Majesty," ceased to have practical value after the advent of Taaffe. Hungary was governed Constitutionally by a strong-handed Premier with the help of a compact Parliament; Austria was governed according to the will of the Emperor by a Premier selected *ad hoc* with the help of a Slav and German-Clerical majority known in Austrian political history as the "Iron Ring." In reality, Hungary governed Austria through the Crown. Hungary could resist the Monarch, Austria could not; and the decisions taken by the King of Hungary in agreement with the Hungarian Cabinet were enforced in Austria by the Emperor through the Taaffe Cabinet. Yet it would be a mistake to regard this period as entirely favourable to Hungary. The Crown was gaining time and influence in Austria against the day when it should become necessary to resist Magyar pretensions. Bismarck, in his memoirs, refers to the "ungovernableness" of the Magyar national spirit as introducing an incalculable element into Austro-Hungarian affairs. The late M. de Laveleye made, a month before Sadowa and nearly a year before the Dual Settlement, the profound observation that "les Hongrois n'aperçoivent guère que ce qui est conforme à leurs désirs ; pour ce qui les contrarie, ils sont aveugles." [1] The Magyars have rarely practised the virtue of moderation. Forgetting that the Settlement of 1867 represented a maximum wrested from the dynasty under stress of circumstance, they cultivated

[1] *Revue des Deux Mondes*, June 1, 1866.

assiduously a Magyar Chauvinist spirit of astonishing intensity; and, under Koloman Tisza, who held the Premiership of Hungary from 1875 to 1890, governing for the greater part of that period alongside of Taaffe, they erected Chauvinism into a State policy. Born in 1830, Tisza took no part in the Revolution of 1848, and led, during the years of repression, the life of a country squire. He thus escaped the sobering influence of exile that had convinced Andrássy of the necessity of subordinating Magyar separatist aspirations to the exigencies of the position of the Monarchy as a Great Power. Koloman Tisza lacked also the eminent wisdom of Deák, who had been content to strive for the establishment of a joint Austro-Hungarian Government for common affairs, and had enunciated a tolerant " Hungarian," as distinguished from a narrowly Magyar, policy towards the non-Magyar races that inhabit one half of " Magyarland." [1] Tisza originally desired to limit the tie between Hungary and Austria to a "personal union," that is, to the link formed by the person of the joint Monarch. In the Committee appointed to draft the reply to the Speech from the Throne that opened the Diet of 1865 he, with three others, actually presented a minority report in favour of a merely " personal union "; and, after the Settlement in 1867, he led the anti-Dualist Opposition against Andrássy and the Deák, or Dualist, Party. In 1875, however, Tisza coalesced with the Deákists to form the " Liberal" Party, with whose support he was to govern Hungary for fifteen years. Accepting first the Ministry of the Interior and, a few months later, the Premiership, he discarded all his principles save that of Magyar Chauvinism, and, purchasing the favour of the Crown by pliancy in regard to military and foreign affairs, gained a free hand to deal as he wished with the non-Magyars. Oblivious of his own engagements towards the non-Magyars, and careless of the fact that they had rallied to the Hungarian State in 1867 under the benign influence

---

[1] The Magyar language contains no equivalent for " Hungary "; its only word is *Magyarország*, land or country of the Magyars.

of Deák and Eötvös, Tisza appealed to the passions of the growing Chauvinistic section of his fellow-countrymen by inaugurating a policy of ruthless Magyarization. Thanks to the influence thus obtained, he overcame the opposition to the occupation of Bosnia-Herzegovina and endeared himself to the Monarch, whose gratitude found expression in important concessions to Magyar sentiment in various military questions, and ultimately in regard to the title and style of the Imperial House, the Joint army, and the Ministry for Foreign Affairs.

The attitude frequently taken up by Francis Joseph towards the administrative oppression of various sections of his subjects constitutes a hard psychological problem. While personally unselfish, generous and just, ever ready to redress a private injury or to alleviate private distress, Francis Joseph, as a ruler, has often seemed callous to the point of cynicism and " constitutional " to the point of injustice. Provided that a minister obtained for him the " necessities of the State " in the form of money and recruits, he appeared to care little how heavily the policy of the minister might press in other respects upon whole sections of loyal subjects. Indeed, the bearing of Francis Joseph has sometimes resembled that of the landlord who ignores the petty tyranny exercised by his estate agent and dismisses the agent only when revenue falls off or disturbances occur. Francis Joseph has rarely borrowed trouble or insisted that the political action of his ministers must conform to private ethical standards.

Thus, even at the risk of estranging important races like the Rumanes of Transylvania, he tolerated the Magyarizing tactics of Tisza and of subsequent Hungarian Premiers ; and showed indifference towards the employment of corruption and pressure as means of government while provinces like Croatia were being driven to the verge of revolt. He doubtless thought in generations where ordinary folk think in years or decades ; and felt that the power of the Crown was always in reserve to make good the misdeeds of unscrupulous or incompetent ministers. Deep in his mind there has always lain a semi-fatalistic, semi-religious belief that all things must ultimately work together for the good of the divinely-appointed head of the dynasty, and that, in meeting the necessities of the hour, the Monarch's path need not diverge too widely from the line of least resistance.

Of these necessities the requirements of the army, as the chief prop alike of the dynasty and of its foreign policy, have always been uppermost in his thoughts. Professor Louis Eisenmann shrewdly observes [1] that the system of government adopted in Hungary during the fifteen years of Koloman Tisza's Premiership was based in reality upon an understanding between the Parliamentary majority and the Crown, analogous to the agreement concluded in Austria between the Emperor and the German Liberal majority under the Auersperg Cabinet. The Crown, he adds, has rarely been so powerful in Hungary as during the Tisza period, when the Premier, sure of the majority he had created by official pressure and official favours, obtained from Parliament everything he wanted. But the price paid for the maintenance of so comfortable a system—the development of Magyar Chauvinism—proved presently to be heavier than the Crown may have anticipated, unless indeed it foresaw that, in arousing non-Magyar resentment, Tisza and his successors were weakening the Magyar State and placing in the hands of the dynasty a weapon wherewith to coerce the Magyars whenever their demands should become intolerable. But if Francis Joseph was influenced by a consideration of this kind, Tisza, for his part, adopted tactics hardly less astute. He maintained and nursed a Magyar Nationalist Opposition, whose resistance he used as a corrective to the arrogance of "Vienna," and whose clamour enabled him to ask the Crown for concessions to "Magyar national feeling." Such concessions had repeatedly to be made, the most notable being the issue of Rescripts to the Joint Foreign

[1] *Le Compromis Austro-Hongrois*, p. 585.

Minister, Count Kálnoky, in 1889, ordaining that the Army
and Navy be styled "Imperial *and* Royal" instead of "Imperial" or "Imperial-Royal." The style "Imperial-Royal"
was reserved for Austria alone, the "Royal" referring to the
Emperor's position as King of Bohemia, Dalmatia, Galicia,
etc. ; whereas the new style "Imperial *and* Royal" referred
to the joint character of the Monarch as Emperor of Austria
and Apostolic King of Hungary. True, a first step towards
the titular differentiation of Hungary from Austria had been
taken in 1868, when, in a Rescript to Beust, the Emperor
established his title as "Emperor of Austria, King of
Bohemia, etc., and Apostolic King of Hungary," and prescribed the use of the name "Austro-Hungarian Monarchy"
or "Austro-Hungarian Empire" for "the totality of the
Kingdoms and Lands constitutionally united under My
sceptre," instead of the designation "Austrian Monarchy"
employed by the Austrian Constitution of December 1867.
Nevertheless the Army continued, until 1889, to be styled
"Imperial" or "Imperial-Royal." The Rescripts to Count
Kálnoky removed this Hungarian grievance, but laid down
expressly that the alteration of style could not affect "the
unity and indivisibility of the Joint Army and Navy as
established in principle and definitely by the Austrian and
Hungarian Laws of 1867 on the basis of the fundamental
principles of the Pragmatic Sanction." Yet neither those
titular changes nor those made by the Rescript of October 4,
1895,[1] to Kálnoky's successor, Gołuchowski, in which the
designation "Imperial *and* Royal" was extended to the
Ministry of the Imperial Household and for Foreign Affairs,
revealed so clearly the effect of Tisza's Nationalist policy as
the Magyar demand for the substitution of Magyar for the
German language in the "Hungarian Army"; that is to
say, in the regiments of the Joint army that are recruited
from Hungary. This demand, which the Monarch resented

---

[1] It is a curious, and perhaps a significant fact that none of these Rescripts
have ever been recognized by the Austrian Parliament nor placed upon the
Austrian Statute Book. Cf. Bernatzik, *Oesterreichische Verfassungsgesetze*, p. 16.

as an encroachment on his military prerogatives constitutionally recognized by Clause 11 of the Hungarian Law
XII. of 1867, and defined with absolute precision in the
corresponding Austrian Statute,[1] so alarmed the veteran
Andrássy that in 1889 he devoted one of his last public
utterances in the House of Magnates to a denunciation of
the perils of "national chauvinism." Andrássy's intimate
knowledge of the Monarch's conception of dynastic interests
made him certain that the Crown would defend to the utmost
its military rights, and that Magyar attacks upon those
rights would lead to a conflict in which Hungary might be
worsted. Andrássy's vision was prophetic. Fifteen years
later, by a strange irony of fate, Koloman Tisza's son,
Count Stephen Tisza, was overthrown when attempting,
as Hungarian Premier, to defend the military prerogatives
of the Crown against a chauvinistic coalition ; but after a
struggle of sixteen months the Coalition itself was vanquished
and compelled to yield to the Crown in order to avoid
the establishment, under Royal authority, of a measure of
universal suffrage, which, by enfranchising the non-Magyar
races, would have broken or severely curtailed the power of
the Magyars.

While the Monarch thus showed himself alive to the
importance of maintaining dynastic rights in Hungary, he
succeeded in Austria in reducing the Germans to a position
comparatively commensurate with their numerical strength.
The process of reduction naturally caused race friction, since
almost every advantage obtained by the non-Germans implied some loss to vested German interests and to German
predominance in the Bureaucracy. Taaffe, the Emperor's
chief agent in the execution of this policy, fell in 1893 in
an attempt to fulfil the Imperial wish that, as a means of
curtailing the power of German cliques and corporations, a
certain section of the Austrian Chamber should be elected
by universal suffrage. Three years later Badeni, a Pole, who
succeeded Taaffe, actually introduced a universal suffrage

[1] Cf. pp. 19-20.

section, or Curia, of seventy-two deputies into the Austrian system of franchise—a proceeding which shows how tenaciously the Emperor, as head of the dynasty, clung to the idea of enfranchising and using the masses for dynastic purposes. But Badeni, in his eagerness to strengthen the Slav position, imprudently issued ministerial ordinances to establish the administrative equality of the Czech language with German throughout Bohemia. Thereupon the Germans revolted and obstructed all parliamentary business until the language ordinances were withdrawn. The Emperor, yielding to the pressure of a popular agitation in Vienna, hurriedly dismissed Badeni, and, after German indignation had found vent in a pseudo-Protestant, anti-Hapsburg movement, known by its catchword, " *Los von Rom !* " ultimately sanctioned the withdrawal of the ordinances. The rapidity with which the *Los von Rom !* movement subsided as soon as its Pan-German, anti-Hapsburg character became apparent, and the growth of a loyal German " Christian Social " party under Lueger, speedily demonstrated the power of the dynasty even over its German subjects ; but a not less important feature of the crisis was the gradual establishment of " constitutional absolutism " by the abuse or elastic use of the Clause 14, the " Emergency Paragraph " of the 1867 Constitution.

.   .   .   .

Unspeakably tiresome as were the vicissitudes of the conflict arising out of Badeni's Language Ordinances, they marked a turning-point in Austrian Constitutional history. Under the influence of parliamentary obstruction, carried on by the Germans until the ordinances were withdrawn and, after their withdrawal, by the Slavs of Bohemia, the Government employed with increasing frequency the " Emergency Paragraph " for the despatch of public business. Austrian Parliamentarism was gradually turned into a system under which, on the one hand, the divergent interests of races, groups and parties were exploited by the Government, and the necessities of the Government were, on the other hand, exploited by races, groups and parties at the expense of taxpayers ; and the fact was clearly revealed that no Austrian race or party would hesitate to sell the Constitution at a price. Each party in turn obstructed parliamentary business in order to extort concessions from a government composed mainly of officials. Had the Austrian Constitution been imposed upon the Crown by popular will, the position of parliament might have been stronger, and the respect of political parties for the integrity of the Constitution might have been greater ; but the Constitution of 1867, as well as those of 1849, 1860 and 1861, were gifts of the Crown and were felt to be subject to withdrawal or revision at the Emperor's pleasure. True, the Constitution of 1867 appeared origin-ally to contain a guarantee of stability in the clause of the Hungarian Statute XII. of 1867, which stipulated the existence of complete constitutionalism in Austria as an essential condition of the Dual Settlement. Had the Magyars remained true to the principles of the Settlement, this guarantee might have remained valid, but they, like the Austrian parties themselves, were always ready to sell the Austrian Constitution at a price, and to wink at the intermittent revival of absolutism by the Austrian bureau-cracy or by the Crown. Short-sighted, as they frequently are, the Magyars imagined that the weakening of Austrian parliamentarism would strengthen the influence of the Hungarian State in the Monarchy, and failed to reflect that while the Emperor of Austria was dictating to his Austrian subjects decisions which his immediate interest as King of Hungary had led him to adopt, he was at once increasing the absolutist power of the Austrian Crown and reducing the Austrian Parliament more and more to the position of a tool which, in case of need, might be used against Hungary herself.

Had the Magyars been less absorbed in their own affairs and more careful of the constitutional liberties they affected to prize not only for themselves but also for their Austrian fellow-subjects, they would have kept careful watch against a revival of absolutism in Austria. Watchfulness would have been the more necessary in that the Austrian Constitution of 1867 is so framed as to facilitate an occasional return to absolutism.

The " Emergency Paragraph," the widest of the doors through which the return could be made, runs :—

" Should, at a time when the Reichsrath is not sitting, urgent necessity arise for enactments to which the assent of the Reichsrath is constitutionally requisite, these enactments can be promulgated by Imperial ordinance on the responsibility of the whole Cabinet provided such ordinances aim at effecting no change of the Constitutional Statute itself, at placing no permanent burden upon the Treasury, and concern no sale of State property. Such ordinances possess provisionally the force of law when they are signed by all the Ministers and are promulgated with express reference to this Clause of the Constitution. Their legal validity lapses if the government fails to submit them for approval to the next Reichsrath and, in the first place, to the Chamber of Deputies within three weeks of its meeting ; or if the ordinances fail to receive the assent of either of the two Houses of the Reichsrath. The Cabinet as a whole is responsible for the immediate abrogation of such ordinances when they have lost their provisional validity."

In theory this clause appears sufficiently to safeguard the rights of parliament and to reserve for the popular representatives adequate retrospective control over Ministerial acts, even should a ministry arbitrarily prorogue or dissolve parliament in order to enact by Imperial ordinance measures to which parliamentary assent might not have been given. But, even in theory, the clause presupposes a vigilant parliament, jealous of its rights and ever ready to punish infractions of them. In practice, the Austrian parliament is neither vigilant nor jealous of its rights, though its tendency utterly to subordinate their defence to the promotion of party or race interests was not clearly revealed until parliamentary obstruction began in 1897. Then the Germans, as subsequently the Bohemian Slavs or Czechs, deliberately sacrificed a fundamental guarantee of parliamentary freedom—the granting of supply—in the hope of compelling the government to remove party grievances. This conduct was a gross betrayal of popular rights. Whereas, in Austria, the Crown legislates and parliament ratifies the legislation by its assent, the position is reversed in regard to the budget and the annual contingent of recruits. Here the Crown, through a non-parliamentary Cabinet, asks for the annual supply of money and men which parliament grants or refuses. By directing obstruction against the discussion of the Estimates, the parties of the Austrian parliament therefore made over to the government the protection of popular rights as though they expected the government to be more observant of constitutional precept and practice than the representatives of the people had been —a government armed, moreover, with so formidable a weapon as the Emergency Paragraph. In reality, Austrian parliamentary obstruction is in the nature of an indirect recognition of the supreme power of the Monarch and a tacit confession of the belief that, whatever individual parties may do, the Emperor will carry on the government and look after the main interests of the State. Occasionally also, obstruction acquires the significance of an appeal to the Emperor on the part of a minority against the action of a parliamentary majority composed of other ethnical elements, since the composition of the majority or, rather, the granting of the concessions requisite to purchase for a Cabinet the support of a majority, is largely subject to the Emperor's control.

Juridically and politically the use of the Emergency Paragraph to obtain supply at a time when Parliament was sitting, but was rendered by obstruction incapable of discharging its normal functions, was unquestionably a breach of the Constitution. The emergency was a pseudo-emergency which might have been met by a dissolution, or, as in Hungary, where there is no analogy to the Austrian Clause 14, by allowing the payment of taxes to be merely voluntary until confusion in the public administration should compel parliament to do its duty. But in Austria there is little or no innate constitutional sense. Parliament, theoretically armed with weighty powers, proves in practice too weak to carry the burden of its accoutrement. The Constitution is a respectable cloak for the nakedness of bureaucratic and Imperial absolutism. The Austrian Chamber has never revised or rejected an Imperial ordinance issued under the Emergency Paragraph. It has never seriously called a blameworthy ministry to account for abuse of its powers; and when, under the Koerber Ministry of 1900–1904, obstruction ceased for a time and supply was normally voted, this result was obtained not by any revival of Constitutional feeling on the part of the Chamber of Deputies, but by the announcement of an enormous programme of railway and canal construction, estimated to cost some £40,000,000 and costing in reality as much again. All the chief parties then sank their differences for a time in order to feed at the Government manger. Not even the provision that the Emergency Paragraph may not be used "to place any permanent burden on the Treasury" has been respected in practice. Though no consolidated loan has yet been contracted on the strength of it, Treasury Bills have been issued by ministerial ordinance, and advances secured on current account from private banks pending subsequent conversion into consolidated stock whenever Parliament should be driven or bribed into covering absolutist practice by a fig-leaf vote. Nor have the Imperial Tribunal (*Reichsgericht*) and the Supreme Court of Administration (*Oberster Verwaltungsgerichtshof*) discharged their ostensible functions as the guardians of legality. They declined to examine the validity of the Imperial Ordinances issued under the Emergency Paragraph, and acquiesced in the creation of precedents that allow any cabinet to bring about, during a period of parliamentary obstruction, a financial situation such as no retrospective rejection of Imperial Ordinances by Parliament can remedy. A leading Austrian authority on Constitutional Law, Professor Tezner, claims [1] that it follows from the decisions of these two Courts that Austrian judges would be obliged to recognize as valid even an Imperial Ordinance that should abolish parliamentary control of the Public Debt Administration. Tezner rightly deplores the dangers to which the administration of public finance in Austria is thus exposed, and points out [2] that it would be difficult to find, even in the absolutist epochs of Austrian history, a parallel for the Imperial Ordinance of July 16, 1904, by which suits pending before the Imperial Tribunal against the Treasury, were simply quashed because previous decisions of the Tribunal in similar cases had rendered a condemnation of the Treasury probable. Though this denial of justice was committed by Imperial Ordinance, the absolutist spirit from which it proceeded was rather that of the bureaucracy than that of the Monarch. Between these two absolutisms the difference is considerable, and, of the two, Imperial absolutism is the less insidious. The Emperor Francis Joseph is not unconstitutionally minded, and prefers to work within constitutional forms as long as they serve the supreme interests of State and dynasty ; but it is too much to expect him to be over-respectful of a Parliament of his own making when that Parliament shows itself careless of its rights, and subordinates general issues to local or party considerations.

THE POSITION OF THE EMPEROR

The influence of the Monarch is therefore paramount in Austrian constitutional questions and tends to prevail over that of all other constitutional factors, not always excluding that of the Judiciary. Justice is administered in his name,

---

[1] *Oesterreichisches Staatsrecht : Der Kaiser*, p. 47.
[2] *Op. cit.* p. 48.

though, in the case of ordinary citizens, he is not constitutionally entitled to administer it in person. Judges are appointed by him, and are by the constitution declared to be "independent." The Emperor as Emperor is, however, above the law, and "irresponsible" in the sense that he is not accountable to any organ of the State for his Imperial acts and omissions. *Sedes regia a nemine judicatur.* As a private person he, like other members of the Imperial and Royal Family, is subject to the Office of the Grand Marshal of the Court. He can be prosecuted before this tribunal under the common law, though courtesy requires that a suit against him be directed against his private purse. In other respects also his action as a private person is subject to restrictions. He requires, for instance, municipal permission to erect a building on his private property, and that of the Forestry Authorities to cut his private timber. His private properties and undertakings are subject to State, provincial, and municipal taxation. On the other hand, he possesses many of the rights of a private citizen. He is entitled to vote in political and provincial elections, but is not eligible to any representative body because not subject to the disciplinary regulations of such bodies. His name stands indeed on the electoral register of most Austrian provinces in the class of large landed proprietors ; and though not personally eligible to a municipal council or assembly, his place can be taken by a plenipotentiary representative. His residences, castles and gardens are not his private property, but are registered as belonging to the Court Exchequer unless historical proof can be adduced to show that they are the personal property of the Monarch or of some member of the Imperial and Royal Family. The Austro-Hungarian Court is a State institution, not merely a personal appendage of the Monarch, and some of its departments, notably the Chancery of the Imperial Cabinet and the Grand Court Marshal's Office, are recognized by law. The Chancery of the Imperial Cabinet is specially provided for in the Budget apart from the Civil List. These

Court departments maintain contact between the Crown and the various Departments of State, and deal with the reports, petitions and other documents addressed to the Monarch. Though nominally belonging to the Court, the Heads of these departments therefore perform duties of great political importance. The responsible ministers in the two States are supposed to prevent the personal influence of such officials with the Monarch from transgressing its rightful limits, but some of them have unquestionably played a much larger part in the affairs of State than that to which they were theoretically entitled. Hence, doubtless, the persistence of the belief, especially in Hungary, that a Vienna Court Camarilla exists in defiance of Constitutional Law. If it exists or has existed, its influence, during the later decades of the reign, has frequently been favourable to Hungary rather than the reverse, for some of the most influential Court officials have been patriotic Hungarians. The question whether there exists a separate Austrian and a separate Hungarian Court cannot be answered in the affirmative, though eminent Hungarian authorities claim that the Hungarian Court has never ceased to exist and that under the Constitutional Statute XII. of 1867 the cost of maintaining the Court is not a joint or common affair. Nevertheless, these authorities admit (cf. Marczali, *Ungarisches Verfassungsrecht*, p. 69) that there is now no permanent Hungarian Court. In truth, the Court, like the Monarch, is joint, or common to both States, though the civil list is voted separately by the Austrian and Hungarian parliaments, and though there has been since 1895 a special Court Marshal for Hungary, since 1903 a Hungarian Court Marshal's Office, and since 1905 a special Hungarian bodyguard. A rescript of November 1893 ordained moreover that Hungarian bannerets take the place of the Austrian Court officials at the Coronation of the Hungarian King, the opening and closing of Parliament, and the reception of the Hungarian Delegation.

With the exception of those Court officials whose positions

and functions are constitutionally recognized, the Monarch has absolute control of the Court. He settles all questions of ceremonial and the forms of admission to his presence. Parliament is not entitled to send deputations to him save with his permission. The residence of the Monarch and his Court, as distinguished from his private property, is not subject to any provincial or communal jurisdiction. The Monarch is, moreover, entitled to dispose of the local police as he may wish, and even the State Authorities can only operate within the Court domain with the permission of the Court officials.

THE HAPSBURG FAMILY LAW

Much more complicated than the relationship of the Monarch to the Court is his position in regard to the Imperial and Royal House or Family.[1] There exists a Hapsburg Family Law drawn up on February 3, 1839, of which the provisions are unpublished and secret. Analogies doubtless exist between it and the family laws of other German princely houses, but, in the case of the Hapsburg Family Law, argument from analogy is insufficient. The Pragmatic Sanction,[2] which, with its provision for the

---

[1] The House of Hapsburg consists of the Emperor as Head, his wife, the surviving widows of his predecessors, the Archdukes and Archduchesses descended in male lineage from eligible (*ebenbürtig*) marriages contracted with the consent of the Head of the Family at the time being.

[2] The "Pragmatic Sanction," or Statute endowed with peculiar solemnity, consists mainly of the provisions of the *Pactum mutuae successionis* secretly concluded on September 12, 1703, between the Emperor Leopold and his two sons Joseph and Charles. The *Pactum* was an arrangement for the inheritance of the Lands of the Spanish Throne (which had been assigned to Charles) and of those of the Austrian Throne (reserved for Leopold and his eldest son Joseph) by whomsoever should survive the other parties to the *Pactum*, and by the survivor's heirs in accordance with the right of primogeniture in the male line, or, eventually, in the female line in default of heirs male. When Charles succeeded to the Austrian throne as Emperor Charles VI., and found himself, in consequence of the deaths of Leopold and Joseph, the last male of his line, the Croatian-Slavonian Estates hastened to declare (1712) that, in case of the extinction of the male line, they would recognize as Ruler that Princess of the Arch-House who should possess Austria, Styria, Carinthia, and Carniola, and should reside in Vienna. Charles VI.

indivisible unity of the Hapsburg Lands and their obligation of mutual defence, forms the juridical basis of the Monarchy, establishes the right of succession of that member of the House of Austria whom in the order of primogeniture, with precedence to males, the Family Law shall designate. The question therefore arises whether the Emperor is bound by the Family Law or whether he is superior to it ; further, whether, in case he can alter the Family Law, the alteration can be made single-handed or requires the assent of a Family Council ; and again, whether the validity of the Family Law is subject or superior to that of the Constitutional Law of the State in case of conflict between them. Professor Tezner declares [1] that " the House-Power of the Emperor as ruler of the House of Austria comprises all the elements of the rule of a chieftain or patriarch. . . . As possessor of the House-Power, the Emperor is Lord and therefore not subject to it, though bound by it within the limits of its legal (*i.e.* constitutionally promulgated) provisions. Family and public law are here so merged in each other that it is hard to say where one begins and the other ends. The House-Power expresses itself in all the forms of the power of the State, *i.e.* in legislation, administration and jurisdiction. In the domain of private law it renders requisite the Emperor's assent to the contraction of marriages by members of the Imperial and

---

was of opinion that the solemn proclamation of the secret *Pactum mutuae successionis* of 1703 would suffice to settle the question of the succession to all his hereditary dominions in favour of his daughter Maria Theresa ; and the *Pactum* was consequently proclaimed at Vienna as a *Sanctio Pragmatica* on April 19, 1713. The Hungarians, irritated by the independent action of the Croatian-Slavonian Estates, whom they regarded as subject to the Hungarian Crown, not only declined to recognize the *Sanctio* thus proclaimed, but obliged Charles VI. by the Hungarian Statute III. of the year 1715 expressly to admit the validity of the Leopoldine order of succession. Having thus "saved their faces" by upsetting, as far as Hungary was concerned, the validity of the Vienna proclamation of April 1713, the Hungarians eventually agreed that the Emperor should submit the Pragmatic Sanction to all the Estates of the Lands under his sceptre, with a request that they recognize it as binding upon them for ever. Only when the Sanction had been accepted by the Estates of all these Lands, did the Hungarians consent to enact it as a part of their Constitution by the Statutes I. and II. of the session of 1722–1723.

[1] *Oesterreichisches Staatsrecht : Der Kaiser*, p. 59.

Royal House, and makes the validity of their wills and marriage contracts depend upon his sanction. . . . It is further reserved to the Emperor to appoint a tribunal in every special case for the criminal punishment of members of the Imperial House, or to inflict the punishment in person. In disciplinary matters his decision is also final, and in cases of the banishment or imprisonment of members of the Family, his personal taste settles whether such measures are disciplinary or administrative, as, for instance, expulsion by the police or confinement."

But, adds Tezner, inasmuch as the Imperial Patent of August 11, 1804, which created the Austrian Imperial title, describes the Emperor without limitation as the " Ruler of the House," and since this important Patent was issued also in regard to the Family Law without any reference to a Family Council, the House-Power of the Emperor, so far as it can be proved to reach, must be regarded as absolute. Tezner, however, lays down the principle that, as regards the relationship between the Power of the State and the House-Power of the Monarch, the latter is subject and not accessory to the former. Even in the absolutist State, the Family Law was recognized as subject to the Law of the State by the declaration that the Pragmatic Sanction could not be changed by Family legislation. Family Law can, on the other hand, be raised by Constitutional legislation to the level of State Law, as is shown by the Pragmatic Sanction which, originally a Family Statute, became a law of the State through its recognition by the Estates of the Realms ; and it is conceivable that Constitutional legislation could modify or even abrogate the Family Law.[1] Tezner further advances the somewhat fine-drawn argument that the superiority of Constitutional Law over Family Law is also shown by Clause 16 of the Austrian Constitutional Statute (No. 141) of December 1867, which declares that members of the Reichsrath—to the Upper Chamber of which Princes of the Imperial House belong by birth—can never be called to account for votes

[1] Cf. Tezner, *op. cit.* p. 60.

given in discharge of their functions, and only by the Chamber to which they belong for utterances made in their legislative capacity.   However this may be, it is clear that, in so far as the right of succession to the monarchical position and functions is concerned, the Emperor cannot, with or without a Family Council, so modify the Family Law as to make it override the Law of the State.   A Family Council appears only to have exercised an important influence upon the order of succession at the moment of the abdication of the Emperor Ferdinand and the accession of Francis Joseph in 1848 ; but even the right of abdication is not absolute in regard to the whole Monarchy, for the Hungarian Constitution makes the validity of an abdication contingent upon its ratification by the Hungarian Parliament.

Yet, as in most things Austrian, it is necessary carefully to distinguish between principle and practice, theory and execution.   However clear the superiority of the laws of the State over the Hapsburg Family Law may seem to be, the facts are that, within the framework of the Pragmatic Sanction, the power of the Emperor is practically absolute, and that, were he at any moment to suspend the Fundamental Laws of the Austrian State or radically to revise them, he would meet with little or no resistance, especially if the suspension or revision were made to appear conducive to popular welfare.   Hence the unutterable tiresomeness of most Austrian constitutional questions.   At bottom they are felt to be questions of dynastic expediency.   Francis Joseph was long an absolute ruler.   Defeat abroad and disaster at home were required to convince him in 1859 that absolutism is apt to be both expensive and inefficient ; and financial stress subsequently effected what the revolution of 1848 had failed permanently to assure.   There is, it is true, little likelihood of a return in Austria to naked absolutism, though a suspension or revision of the 1867 Constitution is a possibility if not a probability of the future.   And as regards the authority of the Emperor over the members of the Imperial and Royal House, it seems likely to remain in future as

absolute as in the past. No one who has seen the Emperor
Francis Joseph drill a dozen Archdukes at the reception
of a foreign sovereign, causing them to line up like a
company of recruits, can doubt that his authority over
them is unquestioned. Serious misbehaviour on the part
of an Archduke is sometimes punished by exile to a
distant province, even if the offender be the Emperor's
own brother. Other Archdukes have been brusquely sent
back to their garrison towns for having appeared to
court popularity in the capital. It is indeed conceivable
that some *frondeur* among the Archdukes might avail
himself of his membership of the Upper Chamber of the
Reichsrath and of his constitutionally guaranteed parliamentary immunity to criticise in public, by word or deed,
the policy of the Emperor's government ; but not even
the most insubordinate of Archdukes — and there have
been some whose private reverence for the Emperor left
much to be desired—has hitherto ventured to make public
opposition to the Head of the House. Otherwise, means
would assuredly have been found to prevent him from
repeating the experiment and to deter other Archdukes
from imitating his example.

In one important respect, the question as to the stand-
ing of the Family Law in conjunction or in conflict with
the Law of the State may acquire grave importance. As
in England under the Royal Marriages Act, so in Austria-
Hungary under the Hapsburg Family Law, the validity of
archducal marriages is contingent upon the consent of the
Sovereign. The marriage of the Heir-Presumptive, Archduke
Francis Ferdinand with Countess Sophie Chotek, now
Duchess of Hohenberg, is valid inasmuch as it received
Imperial assent. But that consent was given on condition
that the Heir-Presumptive should solemnly swear and declare
that neither his wife nor their issue should be entitled to
succeed to the Hapsburg throne. The basis of this oath
and declaration was the conception that, in virtue of a
provision of the Hapsburg Family, or House, Law, the

Countess Chotek, though belonging to the ancient nobility of Bohemia, was not as eligible for marriage with a Prince of the Blood-Imperial as if she had belonged to one of the mediatized families whose eligibility was recognized in 1815. The marriage was therefore classed as "morganatic," and the Heir-Presumptive was regarded as having contracted a *mésalliance*. But it is urged by prominent Austrian jurisconsults that the German conception of eligibility or *Ebenbürtigkeit, i.e.* equality of birth-rank with the members of reigning or mediatized houses, has never been recognized by Austrian Law nor admitted by the Bohemian Feudal aristocracy to which the Chotek family belongs ; and that the idea of a morganatic marriage is foreign to the law of the land. The exclusion of the Duchess of Hohenberg and her children from the order of succession to the Hapsburg throne is therefore declared by these jurisconsults to depend, as far as Austria is concerned, upon the validity of whatever provisions the Hapsburg Family Law may contain on the subject of *Ebenbürtigkeit*, and upon the oath and declaration made in pursuance of those provisions by the Heir-Presumptive on his marriage.

In Hungary the case is different. By the Hungarian Pragmatic Sanction (Statute II. of 1722–23) Hungary bound herself to accept as rulers the Archdukes or Archduchesses of the House of Austria in the order of primogeniture recognized by the House. Nevertheless, as regards the marriage of the Archduke Francis Ferdinand the Hungarian Parliament did not accept the Archduke's oath and Declaration as being valid in virtue of the Family Law, but embodied it in a Statute of the Hungarian Realm (Statute XXIV. of 1900), so that its modification or repeal could only be effected by similar legislation.[1] During

---

[1] The Declaration thus enacted as a Hungarian Statute runs :—

"We, Archduke Francis Ferdinand Charles Louis Joseph Maria of Austria-Este, etc., declare it to be our firm and well-considered resolve to unite Ourself in marriage with Countess Sophie Maria Josefine Albina Chotek of Chotowa and Wognin, etc. According to the observance existing from time immemorial in the Most Serene Arch-House, and with the provisions of the Laws of the House

the debate on the Declaration, the Hungarian Opposition urged with cogency that as Hungarian Law recognizes no morganatic marriages, it is inconceivable that the lawful wife of the King of Hungary should not be Queen of Hungary. Whether the adoption of the Declaration in the form of a Statute by the Hungarian Parliament invalidates this thesis as regards the Duchess of Hohenberg, is a question which may presently be fertile in opportunities for political bargaining of the kind so frequent in the history of the relations between the Magyar nation and the House of Austria ; but its reference to the Pragmatic Sanction certainly excludes her children from the order of succession to the Hungarian Throne, inasmuch as, under the Pragmatic Sanction, the Kings of Hungary must be legitimate descendants of Austrian Archdukes and *Archduchesses*. The Duchess

---

which bind Us, We have sought and obtained the consent of His Imperial and Royal Apostolic Majesty the Emperor and King Francis Joseph I. gloriously reigning, Our exalted Uncle, as the Most Serene supreme Head of the Arch-House aforesaid, and His Majesty has deigned graciously to grant Us the same as a new proof of His Most High favour and goodwill. But before we proceed to conclude the marriage bond, We feel Ourself moved to establish—invoking the House Laws aforesaid, the provisions of which We recognize in their entirety and declare binding for Us quite particularly with regard to the present marriage which We are about to contract—that Our marriage with the Countess Chotek is not an eligible (*ebenbürtige*) but a morganatic marriage and is to be considered as such for now and all time, in consequence whereof neither Our wife nor the issue to be hoped for with God's blessing from this Our marriage nor their descendants will possess or be entitled to claim those rights, titles, armorial bearings, privileges, etc., that belong to the eligible wives and to the issue of Archdukes from eligible marriages. And in particular We again expressly recognize and declare that inasmuch as the issue from Our aforesaid marriage and their descendants are not members of the Most High Arch-House, they possess no right to succeed to the Throne in the Kingdoms and Lands represented in the Reichsrath (Austria), nor consequently, in virtue of the Statutes I. and II. (Pragmatic Sanction) of 1723, in the Lands of the Hungarian Crown, and that the same are excluded from the Order of Succession.

"We pledge Our word that we recognize as binding for all time the present declaration, of whose significance and scope We are fully conscious, both for Us and Our wife and for our children by this marriage, and that We will never attempt to revoke this Our present declaration nor undertake anything calculated to enfeeble or to abrogate the binding force thereof."

Though enacted as a Statute in Hungary this declaration was merely communicated to the Reichsrath in Austria and by it "taken note of" in a simple resolution.

of Hohenberg is not an Austrian Archduchess, nor is it certain that her eventual acquisition of the rank of Queen in Hungary could establish retrospectively any claim on her part to be considered an Archduchess.   Her husband's Declaration recognizes indeed the Hapsburg Family Law as binding and, in pursuance thereof, the morganatic character of his marriage ; but the Hungarian Parliament enacted the Declaration as a Statute in virtue of its agreement with Statutes I. and II. of 1722–23, and, in the preamble, omitted express reference to the Family Law.   In adopting the Declaration, the Hungarian Parliament laid down, more- over, the important principle that all questions relating to the succession must be judged in the light of Statutes I. and II. of 1722–23 ; that is to say, in the light of the Pragmatic Sanction and of the Statute introductory to it.   Those Statutes state merely (Statute I. of 1722–23, Clause 3) that the order of succession shall be " regulated, preserved, and assured (in Hungary) in accordance with the order settled, established, promulgated and accepted by his Majesty in the remaining hereditary Kingdoms and Lands of his sacred Majesty inside and outside Germany, without distinction, and giving precedence to the male sex in equal degree of relationship in the same line."   The Hungarian Parliament has, by enacting the Declaration as a Statute and thus embodying it in the Constitution, assured its own right of future decision concerning the compatibility of the provisions of the Family Law in regard to *Ebenbürtigkeit* with the premisses of the order of succes- sion to the Hungarian Crown established by the Pragmatic Sanction.   Therefore the provisions of the Family Law, including those concerning *Ebenbürtigkeit*, or equality of birth-rank, are, as regards Hungary, subject to the control of the Hungarian Parliament and to the extraordinary skill of Magyar political lawyers in the interpretation of constitutional precepts.

If it be imagined for a moment that, upon the accession of the Archduke Francis Ferdinand to the Hapsburg Throne, his wife were to be recognized as rightful Queen of Hungary and that in Austria the conception of *Ebenbürtigkeit* should be maintained with its consequence in the recognition of the Archduke Charles Francis Joseph, nephew of the Archduke Francis Ferdinand and great-nephew of the Emperor Francis Joseph, as Heir-Apparent to the Hapsburg throne, it will be seen that a delicate situation might arise.   True, the Archduke Francis Ferdinand's Declaration binds him absolutely ; but though he has sworn not to seek release from his oath, it is open to the Hungarian Parliament and indeed to the Austrian Parliament, to petition the Pope for a dispensation.   Moreover, the questions have been raised whether the Archduke was entitled to swear away the possible rights of persons unborn ; and whether, if the conception of *Ebenbürtigkeit* can be proved to have no established validity in Austrian or Hungarian Law and, consequently, that the Duchess of Hohenberg ought to have ranked as an Archduchess from the moment of her marriage, their children would always acquiesce in the forfeiture of their conceivable rights by the paternal declaration.   In these circumstances, it is not surprising that voices in Austria should already have called upon the Emperor Francis Joseph to repair, before his death, the error he committed in assenting to the contraction of a morganatic marriage by the Heir-Presumptive.   Either, it has been argued, such assent ought never to have been given since it involves the dynasty in a series of perilous uncertainties, or, when once it was given, the Countess Chotek should have been raised to the rank of Archduchess and the non-Austrian conception of *Ebenbürtigkeit* should not have been invoked as a reason for excluding the children of the marriage from the order of succession.   The Emperor Francis Joseph, it has been claimed, is alone in a position to remedy this error and to remove the obstacles to the recognition of the children of the Archduke Francis Ferdinand and of the Duchess of Hohenberg as Archdukes of Austria.   But the marriage of the second Heir-Presumptive, the Archduke Charles Francis Joseph, to Princess Zita of Bourbon-Parma in 1911, and the birth of their son, the infant Archduke Francis Joseph, have presumably settled in the negative all question of raising the Duchess of Hohenberg and her children to archducal rank ; and though she may be recognized as Queen of Hungary and even, by courtesy, as Empress of Austria should her husband survive the Emperor Francis Joseph and succeed to the throne, it now appears improbable that the graver issues concerning her children will be added to the preoccupations of Austro-Hungarian statesmen.

Of these issues the gravest was undoubtedly the lever which the Declaration of the Heir-Presumptive placed in the hands of the Hungarian Parliament. Ever since the growth of the Magyar Nationalist conception of the Dual System, the tendency of Magyar jurisconsults and politicians has been to whittle away every feature of the Settlement indicative of the " indissoluble unity " of the Hapsburg dominions as laid down in the Hungarian as well as in the Austrian Pragmatic Sanction. The Dual System reposes upon the conception of the Monarch as three juridical personalities in one physical person,—to wit, the Emperor of Austria ruling over the " Kingdoms and Lands represented in the Reichsrath " ; the King of Hungary ruling over the Lands of the Crown of St. Stephen ; and the Joint Monarch representing the joint interests of a polity, unitary in its relations with foreign countries though dual, save in regard to the main aspects of military matters, in its internal arrangements. The Magyars have consistently striven for at least a generation to deny the existence of the Joint Monarch, and have put forward the contention, both in theory and practice, that in dealing with foreign countries he is merely a dual person simultaneously Emperor of Austria and King of Hungary, but not a unitary Austro-Hungarian Monarch. They have tried to exclude " the Emperor " from any relationship to Hungarian affairs, and when obliged to refer to him in his joint capacity have constantly preferred the designation " His Majesty " to the correct constitutional style

"His Imperial and Royal Apostolic Majesty." Similarly in regard to other features of constitutional terminology. The expression "Empire,"[1] meaning the whole Monarchy, which Deák and Andrássy accepted without difficulty and included in the Hungarian Statute XII. of 1867, has disappeared from modern Hungarian political literature or has been confiscated for the sole use of the Kingdom of Hungary. Objection has even been taken to the term "Austro-Hungarian" and the use of "Austrian *and* Hungarian" demanded. The Emperor Francis Joseph as joint monarch has made concession after concession to this separatist tendency, partly out of a desire for a quiet life and partly out of a feeling, very widespread in Austria, that, despite titular niceties and legal chicane, the future relationship of Austria to Hungary and *vice versa* will be settled by the respective strengths of the two countries and by the power of the one to impose its will on the other. In Hungary, no less than in Austria, public opinion has come increasingly to regard the question as destined one day to be settled by a trial of strength, and for this reason also the Magyars have sought to extend their control over the Hungarian regiments of the joint army. The Crown, for its part, appears to have been less than prudent in not perceiving the use that can be made of titular concessions in working up a body of politico-juridical doctrine which, in case of need, could be made to command the passionate support of a masterful people.

In no recent development has the fundamental divergence of the Austrian and the Magyar tendencies—the one unitary, the other separatist—been so clearly revealed as in connexion with the annexation of Bosnia-Herzegovina. The juridical title to the possession of those provinces is based upon the European mandate given to Austria-Hungary by the Congress of Berlin to "occupy and administer" them; and upon the assent of the Great Powers, in the spring of 1909, to the extension of Austro-Hungarian sovereignty to

[1] In Magyar "*birodalom.*"

the provinces.   In the rescript of annexation dated October 5, 1908, and addressed to Baron von Aehrenthal, Joint Minister of the Imperial and Royal House and for Foreign Affairs, the Emperor Francis Joseph wrote, " I extend the rights of my sovereignty to Bosnia and Herzegovina, and at the same time put into force for these Lands also the order of succession of my House." The sovereignty thus extended was undifferentiated.   Under the Austrian Law of February 1880 and the Hungarian Statute VI. of the same year it is requisite that any change in the relationship of these provinces to the Monarchy should receive the *concordant* assent of the legislatures of both parts of the Monarchy.   Despite this provision, the Hungarian Bill which registers the annexation differs essentially from the Austrian Bill.   Whereas the latter simply accepts the extension of sovereignty and of the order of succession, the former " takes note " that his Imperial and Royal Apostolic Majesty has extended his Sovereign rights to those lands " out of regard for the ancient ties that united those lands to his glorious predecessors on the Hungarian throne."   Further, the Hungarian Bill does not " take note " of the extension of the Hapsburg order of succession to Bosnia-Herzegovina, but ordains independently that " the provisions of Statutes I. and II. (Hungarian Pragmatic Sanction) of the year 1723 come into force in respect of these Lands also."   The object of this independent legislative provision on the part of Hungary is to deny, by implication, the right of the Monarch to extend the order of succession of his House to new territories by an act of undifferentiated sovereignty ; and at the same time to reiterate the principle enunciated in the preamble to the enactment of the marriage declaration of the Archduke Francis Ferdinand that " the settlement of the order of succession contained in Statutes I. and II. of the year 1723 is, as regards its origin, conditions, and contents, an entirely independent settlement, and that all questions appertaining to the succession are to be judged in accordance with the provisions " of those Statutes.   This Hungarian attitude has a double if not a triple purpose. As regards the actual possession of Bosnia-Herzegovina, it seeks, by referring to the ancient ties which bound those provinces to the glorious predecessors of Francis Joseph on the Hungarian Throne, to establish a special Hungarian claim to the eventual incorporation of the provinces in the Kingdom of Hungary ; and, by citing the Hungarian Pragmatic Sanction, of which Clause 5 deals with the "succession to the Kingdom and Crown of Hungary and to the Lands and Kingdoms thereto belonging which with God's help have been won back (from the Turks) and may be won back in future," to make it appear as though special provision had been made in 1723 for the reservation of Hungarian rights to Bosnia - Herzegovina, which Hungarian historians identify with the legendary Kingdom of Rama, that is reputed once to have been subject for a brief period to the Hungarian Crown. But the special purpose of the Hungarian attitude is to reject the pretension that the Act of Annexation was an act of the joint Austro-Hungarian Monarch, or the sovereignty he extended the joint Austro-Hungarian Sovereignty, and thus to counteract as far as possible the Austrian claim that Bosnia-Herzegovina are provinces belonging to the Monarchy as a whole and a kind of Dual Reichsland.

In point of fact the Hungarian claim to special rights to the possession of Bosnia-Herzegovina is very nebulous, although the banners and emblems of the "Kingdom of Rama" figure at the coronation of the Kings of Hungary. The Turkish title to the possession of Bosnia-Herzegovina was repeatedly recognized by Austro-Hungarian monarchs, particularly by the peace of Sistovo (August 4, 1791) ; and the occupation of the provinces in 1878–79 was undertaken on the strength of a mandate given by Europe to "Austria-Hungary," and effected by Austro-Hungarian troops. But in order to appreciate Hungarian doctrine in regard to territories once connected with the Hungarian Crown it should be observed that even so cautious a Hungarian authority as

Professor Henrik Marczali writes [1] that Hungary has never renounced her right to the possession of the Kingdoms of Bosnia, Galicia, and Lodomeria, although Galicia and Lodomeria were recognized in 1867 as Austrian Crown Lands !

The conflicting standpoints in regard to the possession of Bosnia-Herzegovina and the existence of a joint Austro-Hungarian Sovereignty, the leverage acquired by the peculiar position of Hungary in regard to the marriage declaration of the Archduke Francis Ferdinand, and the tendency of Hungary towards political and economic separation from Austria, are signs that a radical readjustment of the relationship between Austria and Hungary may become indispensable.   The present relationship, with its ambiguities and friction, its unfulfilled premisses and its restrictions of the political development of various Hapsburg peoples, is a product of the chequered history of Francis Joseph's reign, and to some extent a reflection of Francis Joseph's own individuality.   Years, perhaps decades, may pass even after he has been gathered to his fathers before his political portrait can be faithfully drawn, and before his personal action during the great crises of his reign can be accurately determined.   No modern ruler has lived through so many changes as he, and none has passed through trials so cruel. Historically, he is not one but several personalities ; psychologically, he is a compound of them all.   The youth, not illiberally educated, who in 1848 succeeded to the throne of an Empire in revolt and learned to distrust constitutionalism, liberalism, and all forms of progressive political aspiration ; the absolutist ruler, led by stress of circumstance and reactionary advisers to believe that the Army, the Church, the Police, and the Bureaucracy are the only reliable pillars of a throne, and induced on his twenty-fifth birthday to present his peoples with a Concordat involving an abject capitulation of the State to the Church ; the defeated commander-in-chief at Solferino, whom the loss of Lombardy and the imminence

[1] *Ungarisches Verfassungsrecht,* p. 29.

of State bankruptcy caused to doubt the wisdom of his reactionary counsellors ; the semi-constitutional Emperor of
1860–65, who, anxious to save his leadership among German
princes but, being out-manœuvred by Bismarck at the Frank-
furt Diet of Princes in 1863 and by Moltke at Sadowa in
1866, was compelled to fall back on his hereditary peoples,
to bargain with Hungary and to bedizen Austria with Constitutional robes in the vain hope that what was irrevocably
lost might yet be retrieved ; the Dual Monarch of 1870–71,
convinced at last that in Austria and Hungary alone lay the
guarantees of a prosperous dynastic future, but too conscious
of the changeability of human affairs to neglect threads of
policy that might lead to fresh avenues of home and foreign
development ; and, finally, the Constitutional King of
Hungary and Constitutionally-absolutist Emperor of Austria,
working from dawn to dark as one dynastic person in pursuit of a perennial dynastic aim and persuaded by innate
conviction, religious sentiment, and family tradition that,
despite bickerings and struggles, race feuds and ethnic rival-
ries, the power of the monarchical function and the prestige
of the dynasty would bring him and his House triumphantly
into a better future.

Such a man or some such man is Francis Joseph of
Hapsburg-Lorraine. None would call him "great" as
greatness is judged in Monarchs ; those who call him "good"
think chiefly of his private characteristics ; but all call him
venerable, some call him wise, and few feel deep enmity
towards him. It has yet to be proved that the Hapsburg
Monarchy can be governed on a "system." Joseph II. tried
and failed ; Metternich tried, and ended his career in flight
before a revolution ; Alexander Bach tried, and found his
nemesis at Solferino; Schmerling tried, and prepared Sadowa.
These were unitary "systems." Then came the Dual System,
which has lasted, well and ill, some forty-six years, but has
not proved a panacea. Francis Joseph has lived through or
under all these "systems," save that of Joseph, and has
reigned over most of them. He has acquired by experience

the feeling that systems are made for the moment and for the public men who seek to apply them, but that the monarchical function is more than they, however completely the Monarch may seem at times to be identified with them. It may be doubted whether Francis Joseph ever sanctioned, in Home Affairs at least, any project or policy without having considered two or more alternatives which a slight change of circumstance might render feasible. Hence much of his vacillation, opportunism, and apparent inconsistency. Had he been endowed with creative statesmanship, he might perhaps, during his long reign, have used the power of the Crown to stamp his dominions with a permanent impress. Who can say what the Austrian Monarchy, and, indeed, Central Europe, might not have become, had Joseph II. been granted the years of Francis Joseph, and had he controlled the fortunes of the House of Hapsburg from 1790 to 1830; or had Francis Joseph been endowed with the qualities of his ancestor! True, he might have wrecked his realms in the process; and those who argue that "whatever is, is right" will find little difficulty in proving that during an era of economic transition, acute race-consciousness and democratic aspirations, the temporizing caution and cynically good-natured adaptability of Francis Joseph may have been the qualities requisite for the preservation of the Hapsburg patrimony. " En théorie, en théorie, peut-être; mais, en pratique, il faut avoir été Empereur soixante ans," he replied smilingly to an ardent adviser who laid before him some new scheme for the reorganization and regeneration of the Monarchy. Whatever the verdict of history may be, it cannot fail to acquit him of base motives and narrowness of mind; and it must recognize that he brought to the discharge of his task a never-flagging sense of duty, a spirit of self-denial and an ever-present feeling that an account of his stewardship would one day be required of him. Though he followed more than he directed the course of events, there is hardly an episode in the development of his peoples that would not have been otherwise but for the touch of his hand.

Francis Joseph will bequeath to his successor a rich store of dynastic prestige and a perennial example of the truth that, high above the internal struggles and vicissitudes of the Monarchy, stands, or may stand, the all but indestructible influence of the wearer of the Crown.

CHAPTER II

THE STATE

STRICTLY speaking, there is no Hapsburg State save in the sense that a Hapsburg monarch can, without serious exaggeration, say : " L'État c'est moi ! "   There is an Austrian State, a Hungarian State, and there are joint Austro-Hungarian Departments of State.   But the essential things in the Hapsburg polity can no more be expressed in terms of political or administrative organization than the fighting value of an army can be indicated by a military handbook.   In the Dual Monarchy it is more important to ascertain whence impulses proceed or weaknesses derive than to catalogue the vertebræ of the body-politic.   A list of State departments, tribunals, and public institutions would shed little light upon the spirit that animates them or the manner in which they work.   Classification needs to be broad and sparing of detail.   In this sense it may be said that the State consists of the Army, the Bureaucracy, the Police, and the Church, for these are the main instruments of government.   The people exists for the State rather than the State for it ;—it is there to be governed.   Parliamentary institutions through which " the will of the people " is supposed to be expressed, fulfil, especially in Austria, functions ranging from those of a legislative registry office to those of a political market-place.   They rarely serve as a means of imposing popular demands upon the Government, though they are sometimes valuable as a safety-valve.   On paper, most things in Austria-Hungary are regulated by ordinance or by law.   Spheres of administrative and political competence are accurately defined, disputed points being settled by administrative tribunals.   But, in practice, few institutions discharge precisely the functions theoretically assigned to them.   Hence in some cases a complication and in others a simplification of issues which are in theory rigidly regulated by rule and compass.   The influence of tradition, the arbitrary personal element, the ingrained belief that human motives are usually other than they are professed to be, the sense of authority (mitigated by an easy-going disposition), contribute to form an atmosphere that Kürnberger satirized as " Asiatic," and which is, in many respects, semi-oriental.   To comprehend Austria it is necessary therefore to discard preconceived notions and prejudices, and to take things as they are.   Names count for little, but the facts behind the names may count for much.   This is the secret of the Hapsburg Monarchy, a secret not to be divined by study or thought, but to be penetrated by dint of experience.

THE ARMY

The institution that corresponds most nearly to its professed purpose is the Army.   " In deinem Lager ist Oesterreich," wrote Grillparzer of Radetzky in the days before the Dual System ; and though the re-establishment of the Hungarian Constitution in 1867 and the doctrine of " parity " between Hungary and Austria have not remained without effect upon the Army, there is much force in the perpetual complaint of Magyar separatists that the Army is a school of unitary sentiment and constant corrective of particularist ambitions.   Above all, the Army is a nursery of dynastic feeling.   It is the Imperial and Royal Army, constitutionally subject, as regards organization and leadership, to the exclusive control of the Monarch.   Within its framework, politics have no place except in so far as the military spirit naturally tends to influence Austro-Hungarian policy in an aggressive and military sense.   Yet it cannot fairly be said that, in Austria-Hungary, "militarism" presents the objectionable features noticeable in Germany. Though many officers are drawn from the nobility and even from the high aristocracy, the bulk of the officers' corps is recruited from the middle and lower-middle classes and is composed of men of slender means. The noble has, in such circumstances, to accommodate himself to the unpretentious life of his brother officers, who are, as a rule, hard-working, hard-living men, obliged, in their turn, by the special composition of their regiments, to stand in close personal relationship to their men. Of the excellent fighting qualities of the Austrian soldier it is superfluous to speak. They have been shown on a hundred battlefields. They won the unstinted admiration of Napoleon himself, who suffered at Austrian hands at Aspern his first serious defeat in the field; but it would be idle to dogmatize upon the value, as a fighting machine, of an army that has not been seriously tested for nearly half a century. The effective value of the Austro-Hungarian Army must always depend largely upon the quality of its corps of officers, and, under the conditions of modern warfare, upon the quality of the non-commissioned officers and upon the nature of the cause to be fought for. On these points expert opinion alone can carry weight. As far as impartial expert opinion is available, it is flattering to the quality of the Austro-Hungarian officer, who is, as a rule, held to be the superior of the average German officer. He is more intelligent, more readily adaptable to circumstances, in closer touch with his men, less given to dissipation, and remarkably free from arrogance. He is a good fellow and a lovable being. Though sometimes of apparently inferior physique, he is tough and wiry, equally accustomed to stiff climbing in the Alps and to dreary marches on dusty or snow-covered plains. Given intelligence and unity of direction in the higher regions of the Army, the Austro-Hungarian officer should do himself justice in case of war. He did himself justice during the partial mobilizations in 1908–1909 and 1912–13, when the General Staff showed both intelligence and unity of direction. Whether the machine-like smoothness of those experiments justifies the positive conclusion that the Army would be fully equal to its task in war, is a question not lightly to be answered. Recent manœuvres have revealed some palpable defects in commissariat arrangements and in the handling of large masses of troops in the field; the artillery is stated to be below the highest level both as regards *matériel* and men; the non-commissioned officer is believed to be inferior to the task, likely to devolve upon him in war, of replacing temporarily the subaltern or even the company officer. There is, besides, considerable shortage of non-commissioned officers. Special care is now being given to the improvement of the non-commissioned officers, and efforts are being made to induce them to serve long enough to acquire real efficiency. Some years must pass before these efforts, even if successful, can bear fruit, and, in the meantime, the Austro-Hungarian Army will be at a corresponding disadvantage.

In the higher grades of the Army the conditions are good. Birth alone carries few or no privileges. To pass successfully through the War School into the General Staff a man must have brains, aptitude for work, and fitness for command. Among the names of well-known Austro-Hungarian officers few have an aristocratic sound, especially if it be remembered that a patent of nobility, as indicated by the particle "von," is usually granted to officers after thirty-five years of service. There exists in Austria a military nobility, a kind of Samurai caste, just as there exists a bureaucratic nobility; many families of modest fortune have been "military" for generations, sending all or most of their sons into the Army and Navy. This stock of military families is one of the great assets of the dynasty. The wearing of the Emperor's Coat has become to them a second nature, and they are not only intensely "black and yellow,"[1] but are also what the Emperor Francis called "patriots for me." Their spirit leavens the whole military

[1] The Austrian colours.

lump, affects their comrades devoid of family traditions, and penetrates the rank and file. In their camp is " Austria."

Unitary though its spirit is, in the main, the Austro-Hungarian Army is divided into several distinct organizations, which are co-ordinated for action in war by the Emperor, under advice from the military ministers and the Chief of General Staff. These organizations are—(*a*) the Joint or Common Austro-Hungarian Army ; (*b*) the Austrian Defence Army or Landwehr ; and (*c*) the Hungarian Defence or Honvéd Army. In addition to these regular organizations there is the Landsturm or general levy of the able-bodied male population not liable for service in the Joint, Landwehr, or Honvéd armies. The Landsturm may, however, be regarded as the supreme reserve, and scarcely comes into consideration as an active military force except in so far as it completes the general military organization of the people, and helps to maintain the idea of liability to military service for the defence of the common Monarchy.

Austria-Hungary thus possesses three regular armies. Neither the Austrian Landwehr nor the Hungarian Honvéd are Reserve formations in the ordinary sense, but have, like the Joint or Common Army, their own levies of recruits, their own cadres, and their own reserve formations. Practically the Landwehr and Honvéd regiments are regiments of the Line, not quite so fully equipped or quite so accurately trained, perhaps, as the regiments of the Joint Army, but fit, nevertheless, to take their place alongside of the joint troops without weakening the efficiency of the Line to anything like the same extent as the German Army would be weakened were it ever to be obliged to send its Landwehr troops to the front. Three Military Departments, with a large measure of independence, but always subject to the Emperor and the General Staff, control the working of the three armies, each Department being placed under a separate Minister. Thus the Joint Austro-Hungarian Army is administered by the Imperial and Royal War Office under the

Joint Minister of War, who is hierarchically the superior of the Chief of General Staff, and is responsible in theory to the Austrian and Hungarian Delegations which sanction the Joint military estimates. The Austrian Landwehr Army is administered by the Austrian Department for National Defence under the Austrian Minister for National Defence, who is responsible to the Reichsrath. Likewise the Hungarian Honvéd Army is subject to the Hungarian Honvéd Minister, who is responsible to the Hungarian Parliament. The levy of recruits for the three armies is granted annually by the Austrian and Hungarian Parliaments according to population, the Austrian Parliament granting the Austrian quota of the recruits for the Joint Army and the levy for the Landwehr, while the Hungarian Parliament grants the recruits for the Hungarian quota of the Joint Army and the levy for the Honvéd. Save as regards some features of military judicial procedure in Hungarian regiments, German is used throughout the Joint Army and in the Austrian Landwehr Army as the official language, and also as the language of command and service, though the "regimental languages" differ according to the racial composition of the various regiments. The purely Polish, Czech, Ruthene, and Serbo-Croatian regiments are instructed in their respective languages, though commanded in German ; the mixed regiments are, as nearly as possible, instructed in the several languages spoken by the men, minorities above 20 per cent of the whole regiment being entitled to instruction in their own tongue. In the six or seven purely Magyar regiments of the Hungarian part of the Joint Army, Magyar is the language of instruction. In the remainder the same principle is observed as in the ethnically mixed Austrian regiments of the Joint Army, though attempts are constantly made artificially to increase the percentage of Magyar-speaking recruits, and thus to make the Hungarian regiments of the Joint Army instruments of magyarization. In the Honvéd regiments recruited from Hungary proper, Magyar is the official language and the language of command, and also, as far as practicable, the language of instruction ; but in the Honvéd regiments recruited from Croatia-Slavonia, Magyar gives place (under the Hungaro-Croatian Settlement of 1868) to Serbo-Croatian.

The maintenance of unitary sentiment and of efficient organization in this maze of languages and races is a dynastic and military miracle—a miracle accomplished by the devotion of the corps of officers to its task and by the intelligent elasticity of its members. How efficient the army, particularly the joint army, remains as an element of unity may be judged by the attacks of racial extremists upon it. The most frequent charge against it is that it works as an instrument of Germanization—a charge both well and ill founded. German is necessarily the language of intercourse throughout the Hapsburg Monarchy, for the simple reason that it is indispensable. But the days when German was used as the one official language are past and gone. To-day German is not even the official language of the Austrian State, though by force of circumstances it remains the leading language. In Hungary, on the contrary, Magyar is the official State language, though half the population is non-Magyar. A glance at an Austro-Hungarian bank-note reveals the veritable characters of the Austrian and the Hungarian " State Ideas." On the Austrian side the value of the note is printed in German, Czech, Polish, Serbo - Croatian (in Latin and Cyrillic characters), Ruthene or Little Russian, Slovene, Italian, and Rumanian ; on the Hungarian side the value is given in Magyar alone, although Hungary comprises as many "nationalities" as Austria. The Austrian "State Idea" thus stands for equality of ethnic right, the Hungarian, or rather the Magyar, "State Idea" for the hegemony of a governing race. Against this Magyar tendency, which, if restricted to the Lands of the Hungarian Crown, may be historically explicable and practically defensible, the influence of German, working through the joint army, is a valuable set-off. Its leading position in the Monarchy as a whole is far more justifiable than the exclusive position of the Magyar language in Hungary.

When the non-Magyar recruit has acquired a smattering of the Magyar State language, he has learned nothing likely to be of value to him save in his intercourse with the local and State authorities. When, however, the non-German recruit has picked up a smattering of German, he has acquired the means of making himself understood throughout Central Europe and in a great part of the civilized world. The Austrian and Hungarian Slavs recognize the value of German as a medium of intercourse, and use it constantly for verbal if not for written communications between themselves. Few Austrian Slavs are familiar enough with Czech, Polish, Slovene, Little Russian, and Serbo-Croatian to use all these idioms with equal facility. They therefore fall back on German as a *lingua franca*, and can have no interest to see German ousted from its preeminent position, however much and however justly they resent and resist the Germanizing spirit that used to prevail, and still lingers, in some high administrative quarters.

The Austro-Hungarian Army, and especially the joint army, is thus a symbol of unity, a school of unitary sentiment, and the main support of the dynasty. Although the Emperor Francis Joseph has allowed the Hungarian regiments of the joint army to be differentiated from the Austrian regiments in some details of uniform and facings, he has repeatedly declared, and has proved by his action, that he will never allow the unitary organization of the army to be seriously impaired. In one of his most famous enunciations, the Army Order dated from Chlopy in Galicia, on September 16, 1903, during the constitutional crisis in Hungary, he wrote: "The better founded my favourable judgment of the military value, the self-sacrificing delight in service, and the single-minded co-operation of all parts of my total Defensive Forces, the more must and will I hold fast to their existing and well-tried organizations. My Army, in particular, must know that I will never relinquish the rights

and privileges guaranteed to its supreme War-Lord—my
Army, whose stout bonds of union are threatened by one-
sided aspirations proceeding from misapprehension of the
exalted mission the Army has to fulfil for the weal of both
States of the Monarchy. Joint and unitary as it is shall my
Army remain, the strong power to defend the Austro-
Hungarian Monarchy against every foe. True to its oath,
my whole Defensive Force will continue to tread the path of
earnest fulfilment of duty, permeated by that spirit of union
and harmony which respects every national characteristic
and solves all antagonisms by utilizing the special qualities of
each race for the welfare of the great whole." The storm of
protest which this Army Order raised among the Magyars
—then engaged in an assault upon the constitutional military
prerogatives of the Crown—alters nothing in its fundamental
significance as a statement of the dynastic standpoint.
Magyar opposition, indeed, took rather the form of protests
against the absence of a ministerial counter-signature to the
Army Order, and against expressions such as "my total
Defensive Forces" (*Gesamtwehrmacht*), than against the
Monarch's resolve to maintain military unity at all costs ;
and, in reply to the protests, the Crown addressed a
Rescript to the Hungarian Premier declaring that just
as he had been careful to fulfil the obligations laid
down in the Hungarian Statute XII. of 1867, so " I am
determined to maintain undiminished my rights and to
transmit them untouched to my successors." Of these
rights, as defined by Clause 11 of that Statute, mention has
been made in the previous chapter.[1] The only change in
regard to their interpretation which the Monarch has ever
sanctioned, was contained in the programme drawn up in
October 1903 by a Hungarian commission of nine members
and accepted by the Crown as the basis for the formation of
the Tisza Cabinet of that year. This programme, known in
Hungarian Constitutional history as the " Programme of the
Nine," included the introduction of a military penal code

[1] Cf. pp. 17-20.

providing for the use of the Magyar language by courts-martial in Hungarian regiments ; the transfer to Hungarian regiments of officers of Hungarian nationality but serving in non-Hungarian regiments ; the establishment of Hungarian Cadet schools ; and, in regard to the Constitutional military prerogatives of the Crown, the recognition of the Monarch's right to fix the language of command and service in the Hungarian regiments.   The programme added, however : " The political responsibility of the Cabinet extends to this act as to every act of the Crown, and the lawful influence of Parliament remains intact in this respect also as in respect of every constitutional right.   This condition of things can be changed by legislation, that is to say, by the Crown and Parliament jointly.   While emphasizing the rights of the country, the Liberal (ministerial) Party does not raise the question of the Magyar language of command and service, because weighty political reasons affecting great interests of the nation make it appear undesirable to do so."

Though not a law this " Programme of the Nine " is regarded in Hungary as fixing the interpretation of the word " constitutional " in Clause 11 of Statute XII. of 1867. Whereas that word undoubtedly meant, in the eyes of Deák and Andrássy, that the right of the Monarch to settle everything relating to the leadership, command, and inner organization of the Army was " constitutional " in the sense of being recognized by the Constitution, the " Programme of the Nine " makes it " constitutional " in the sense that the Cabinet is responsible for all acts of the Monarch undertaken in virtue of this right, and that " lawful " Parliamentary influence exists also in regard to such acts.   This is the only positive constitutional outcome of the conflict between the Magyars and the Crown that lasted from the end of 1902 until April 1906, since the demand for the Magyar language of command which figured so prominently in the conflict was omitted from the settlement of April 8, 1906, between the Magyar Coalition Leaders and the Crown.   It is, however, a result eloquent of the

Magyar tendency to undermine the unity both of the Army and of the Monarchy that may presently involve the Magyars in serious and not unmerited misfortunes. The Magyar argument that the attempts to differentiate the " Hungarian Army " from the Austrian Army are legitimate inasmuch as Clause 11 of Law XII. recognizes the existence of a "Hungarian Army as an integral part of the whole Army," is specious. Since 1526, when Hungary was crushed by the Turks at Mohács, there has never existed a " Hungarian Army " save during the revolution of 1848–49, when the Kossuthist forces were fighting against Austria. The words " Hungarian Army " employed in the Statute of 1867 are an echo of the expression *exercitus hungaricus* employed in the Hungarian Law I. of 1802, in which it was used in the sense of " Hungarian Regiments " or *legiones*. In the Hungarian Chamber in 1868 Deák insisted that though the Law of 1802 and a Law of 1846 refer in this sense to a " Hungarian Army " they make no allusion to it as a separate or independent force ; and he added, " I remind the members of the House that an independent and special Hungarian Army came into existence in 1848 when our troops were not fighting in the sense of the Pragmatic Sanction by the side of His Majesty's troops, but against them ; and, if any one cares to inquire why the Estates of the Realm did not press for a separate and independent Army, he would probably find that they omitted to do so because they were convinced that it would have been impossible to defend either the Fatherland, or the Throne, or the other Lands of His Majesty as required by the Pragmatic Sanction, had there been two separate, special, and independent Armies." Deák, who well knew that the Settlement of 1867 embodied the most generous conditions Hungary could hope to obtain without risking her very existence, realized the danger of provoking in Austria and in the mind of the Monarch a reaction against the constitutional liberties then so recently restored. The developments of the last ten years, and the growth in Austria of a feeling that accounts will sooner or later have to be settled afresh with the Magyars, have shown how far-sighted was Deák's view of the position of Hungary, and how clear his perception of the inevitable consequences of attempts to encroach upon the military rights of the Crown.[1]

The danger involved in Magyar attacks upon the unitary character of the joint Army is therefore rather a danger for the Magyars themselves than for the institution they have sought to undermine. The Austro-Hungarian Army is likely to remain, next to the Crown, the most popular and powerful prop of the State. It lends a helping hand in cases of disaster, exercises an educational influence on the bulk of the population, and is rarely guilty of brutality even in the repression of disorder. The spirit in which it is administered is, on the whole, tolerant and non-aggressive— at its best (to repeat the words of the Chlopy Army Order) a spirit " which respects every national characteristic and solves all antagonisms by utilizing the special qualities of every race for the welfare of the great whole."

It stands to reason that this high spirit cannot be evinced in every detail of military organization, nor in the working of all military departments. Red tape and mandarinism, to which Austro-Hungarian officials are more prone than those of any Continental people except, perhaps, the Russian *tchinovniks*, flourish exceedingly in the Austro-Hungarian War Office, the Ministries for National Defence, and in the Commands of the various Army Corps. But, in the Army, the personal control of the Monarch, or of the Archdukes representing him, sometimes places a check upon officialism, whereas in a civilian bureaucracy the wheels of the bureaucratic machine would go on unhindered in crushing the life and the individuality out of men. One typical case was that of General Galgotzy, a splendid old

---

[1] As a consequence of the recent Balkan wars and of the encouragement derived from them by the Austrian and Hungarian Slavs, the Magyars and the Austrian-Germans have tended to draw nearer each other for the purpose of defending the Dual System against Slav attack ; but it is an open question whether this *rapprochement* will survive the new military demands which the Austro-Hungarian Army authorities are about to make upon the two Parliaments.

soldier who was for many years the idol of the Army and whose name recurs in a hundred anecdotes. During the occupation of Bosnia-Herzegovina a road had to be built in haste. The work was difficult, funds were short, and time pressed. Galgotzy undertook the work and did it for a trifling sum, thanks to the devotion of his men. Then he reported: " Road built. Twenty thousand florins received, twenty thousand florins spent, remains nothing. Galgotzy." Shocked by so terse a statement, the military audit officials demanded of Galgotzy a detailed account of florin and kreutzer, with vouchers. Galgotzy ignored the demand, which was presently repeated in peremptory tone. Then he rejoined: " Twenty thousand florins received, twenty thousand florins spent. Whoever doubts it, is an ass." Thereupon the chief audit official solemnly drew the Emperor's attention to Galgotzy's irreverent reply and suggested a reprimand. The Emperor blandly inquired, " Do you then doubt it ? "

To his best officers the Emperor has usually stood in the relationship of an elder to younger comrades, and has generally, though not invariably, given them loyal support. He has rewarded their services, comforted them in misfortune, paid their debts in some instances, and " fathered " them with affectionate solicitude. But there have been exceptions. The case of Benedek, the commander defeated at Sadowa, affords tragic proof that the real or supposed interests of the dynasty are apt to take precedence of all other considerations.

After the death of Radetzky, Benedek was the ablest and most popular general in the Army ; and when, in 1866, an Italian attack threatened from the South and a Prussian attack from the North, Benedek was placed, against his will, in command of the Northern army, because, it was argued, the popularity of his name would be worth an additional army corps. The real reason for the appointment was another. Defeat at the hands of Prussia was foreseen, or at least apprehended, and it was thought undesirable that the Archduke

Albert, the only other general of sufficient standing, should be exposed to discomfiture. Benedek was called from Verona and told of his appointment to the Bohemian command. He protested and refused it, because, he said, he knew every stick and stone in Lombardy, but nothing whatever of Bohemia, not even the course of the Elbe. He prepared to return South but was roused at night by the Emperor's aide-de-camp and urged to make the sacrifice for the dynasty which could not afford to have a member of the Imperial House beaten in the field. Benedek bowed to this appeal, handed over to the Archduke Albert the victory he had organized in the South, and went to crown his brilliant career by discomfiture at Sadowa. He stipulated only that he should have a free hand in Bohemia. This was granted him verbally and refused him in practice, for his plan of campaign was constantly interfered with by the Imperial Council of War sitting in Vienna. After defeat he was made the object of public odium. His wish to report in person to the Emperor upon the vicissitudes of the campaign was never granted. The Archduke Albert, returning victorious from Lombardy, appealed to him not to reply to public attacks nor to attempt any kind of self-justification. Benedek pledged his word in writing (November 19, 1866) to bear all in silence —and read on the following December 8, in the official *Wiener Zeitung*, an article belittling his former services and declaring that the loss of Imperial confidence, the destruction of his military reputation in the eyes of his contemporaries and of posterity, the knowledge of the immeasurable disaster which the Army, and, through his defeat, the whole Monarchy, had suffered under his leadership, must be for him a severer punishment than condemnation by court-martial could have been! The responsibility for this article seems to have lain between the Archduke Albert himself and the War Minister, General John, both of whom corrected the proof-sheets. In his will, Benedek described their conduct as "surpassing my ideas of right, justice, and respectability. I have taken this also in silence," he added,

" and have, with philosophy and self-denial, borne for seven years my hard soldier's lot. I think I am lucky that, in spite of all, I have not lost my reason and that I bear no one a grudge. I have done with myself and with the world and have a completely clear conscience—only, all the poetry of my soldier's life has been lost in the process." And, as a sign of his lost " soldier's poetry," Benedek forbade the commander of the garrison of Gratz to render any kind of military honours to his remains.

Admiral Tegetthoff, the victor of Lissa, was treated with scarcely more regard than the unfortunate Benedek. For some mysterious reason he was removed from the command of the Fleet within a few weeks of his victory, and was sent into a kind of exile on the pretext that he needed to study foreign navies. The mystery that surrounds the battle of Lissa may perhaps one day be cleared up, and it may become known whether Tegetthoff was punished because of a petty difference with audit officials over the cost of a banquet given to celebrate the victory, or because he had taken too seriously a part assigned to him in an international tragi-comedy. One thing may be affirmed with certainty— that the contemporary records and published versions of the circumstances attending the battle of Lissa are not worthy of entire confidence. No one who knows approximately the truth concerning the circumstances that preceded and followed the annexation of Bosnia-Herzegovina, and is aware how carefully the truth was hidden from the Austro-Hungarian public by the press under official influence, will readily accept as authentic any contemporary Austrian official version of a given occurrence.

THE BUREAUCRACY

In every organized State the question of the relationship between the State officials and the public which supports them is acquiring increasing importance, but nowhere is it so urgent as in the Hapsburg Monarchy.

Though the Monarch is imbued with a sense of his divinely constituted Imperial authority and of his dynastic mission, his rule over matters coming under his immediate control is just and clement when compared with the anonymous tyranny exercised through a dozen Departments and a hundred divisions of State by thousands of hierarchical potentates. Experience of and reflection upon the nature of bureaucratic rule in Austria and other countries leads to the conclusion that it possesses four main characteristics : The sense of authority and of superiority over those who are administered or governed, a sense formerly existing in the shape of a corporate bureaucratic consciousness, but now atomized and individualized ; the dislike of responsibility, and, consequently, a disposition to clothe administrative action in elusive forms elaborated by the practice of generations ; the hierarchical spirit which renders every official of a certain rank an object of respect for officials of lower rank and makes the attainment of higher rank the main object of bureaucratic endeavour ; and the tendency to resent, as a sort of *lèse-majesté*, all attempts to criticize the working, to curtail the power, or to reform the organization of the bureaucracy itself. This last-named characteristic is perhaps the strongest tie between Austrian officials to-day. A curious instance may be cited. Not long ago the manager of a Court Theatre wished to revive a comedy by a well-known Austrian-German author which one of his predecessors had produced with success. On being consulted, the author expressed doubt whether the Court authorities would sanction the revival, since a chapter in one of his subsequent non-dramatic works had been suppressed by the public prosecutor on the plea that it contained passages offensive to the dynasty. The manager, on inquiry, ascertained that this doubt was unfounded and that neither the Court authorities nor the Emperor had any objection to the revival of the comedy. He therefore decided to revive it, but received a hint that it would be well to consult the archives of the theatre before taking further steps. In the archives he discovered a letter from a former Austrian Premier, an official, to the previous manager of the theatre asking that no further plays by that author might be produced at the Court Theatre, in view of the strictures which the author had passed upon the bureaucracy. The manager thereupon applied to the Premier of the day, another official, for a removal of the ban, but was informed that nothing could be done. Ferdinand Kürnberger, whose collected essays are an indispensable guide to the comprehension of things Austrian, devoted one of his most brilliant satires to the illustration of this bureaucratic spirit. It was inspired by the difficulty which he and an ex-officer named Schöffel experienced in bringing to justice sundry corrupt officials who were attempting to sell to Jewish speculators the girdle of meadow and forest that renders the environs of Vienna the most beautiful of any European capital. Schöffel and Kürnberger saved the forest girdle, and a modest monument at Mödling bears witness to their merits. Kürnberger's satire " Dishonesty is the Best Policy "[1] deals with the terror of a thieving " Moroccan " official whose depredations in the forests of his master had been discovered. By a Frankish friend the thief was encouraged to redouble his depredations and at the same time to have himself and the official caste publicly denounced in the " Moroccan " press. This having been done, the thief flourished exceedingly, and escaped punishment because the fact that an official had been publicly denounced was enough to ensure him the protection of his fellow-officials, all of whom swore by the mystic formula, *Justament nöt !*

The *justament* spirit, and what is known as *Justament-politik*, play a large part in Austrian affairs. It is an inverted spirit of authority, a consciousness of power to obstruct that may perhaps be rendered in English by the phrase, " You just shan't ! " The Bureaucracy has immense powers of obstruction, and uses them when its authority is ignored or its importance questioned. Otherwise it is inoffensive, or

[1] *Siegelringe*, original edition, p. 271, " Dieb-Sein währt am längsten."

at least non-aggressive. Austrian officials are, as a rule, well-educated, well-mannered men of easy disposition and devoid of stiffness. They are often willing to show the private citizen a short-cut through a law or a way round an apparently insuperable obstacle. But the private citizen must recognize, at least by implication, their power and authority. He must, so to speak, sue *in formâ pauperis* for their help, without insistence upon what he may consider his rights. Under the "architectural police regulations" in Austria it is, for instance, technically impossible to build a theatre so as to make it a profitable undertaking. Yet new theatres are built and flourish, while old theatres that violate the main principles of the regulations are maintained. The good-natured authorities are willing to close one eye to illegalities, on the tacit understanding that he who profits by such indulgence will not be recalcitrant should the convenience of the State require pliancy on his part. The manager of a theatre who should refuse to remove from the playbill a play displeasing to the authorities, or should insist upon the circumstance that the play had been authorized by the censor, might find the sanitary arrangements of his theatre declared to be insufficient by a special commission, or the condition of the ceiling perilous, or the fire exits much too narrow. If he were wise he would speedily understand the impropriety of the play. A singular case occurred some three years ago in connexion with a military "skit" written by an ex-officer of literary proclivities. It was produced, with the consent of the censor, and played nineteen times, not only without objection but to the great amusement of the civilian and military public. Then some officious prig discovered that one of the personages was a caricature of an important military dignitary. The manager, who was bound by contract to the author, failed to withdraw the play when gently pressed to do so by the authorities. He was therefore summoned to the police headquarters and recommended to announce that the chief actor was ill; otherwise, he was reminded, his licence, which had only been granted for

musical comedy, would need revision. Too old a hand to
think of resistance, the manager prepared to capitulate, but
the Stage Society and the Authors' Society intervened, and
unkindly threatened to boycott him if he gave way. He
therefore begged the authorities to prohibit the play ; but
they, ever chary of incurring responsibility, answered that he
must petition for a prohibition. The manager demurred,
and offered to make "cuts" and other alterations. The
authorities claimed that before this offer could be accepted
the Auxiliary Council of the censorship must be consulted.
The Council thereupon saved the situation by refusing to
sanction the alterations and by forbidding a harmless farce
which the censor had originally sanctioned.

Kürnberger would call this state of things "Asiatic." It
is simpler to call it bureaucratically Austrian. The bureaucracy feels itself to be the State ; and, for the public at
large, it is the State. So instinctively is this truth recognized that the "race struggle" in Austria, of which so much
has been said and written, is largely a struggle for bureaucratic appointments. Germans and Czechs have striven for
years to increase on the one hand and defend on the other
their patrimony of official positions. The essence of the
language struggle is that it is a struggle for bureaucratic
influence. Similarly, the demands for new Universities or
High Schools put forward by Czechs, Ruthenes, Slovenes,
and Italians but resisted by the Germans, Poles, or other
races, as the case may be, are demands for the creation of new
machines to turn out potential officials whom the political
influence of Parliamentary parties may then be trusted to
hoist into bureaucratic appointments. In the Austrian Parliament the Government, which consists mainly of officials,
sometimes purchases the support of political leaders by giving
State appointments to their kindred or *protégés*, or by promoting *protégés* already appointed. One hand washes the
other, and service is rendered for service. On occasion the
votes of a whole party can be bought by the appointment
of one of its prominent members to a permanent Under-

Secretaryship in a Department of State. Once appointed, he is able to facilitate the appointment of other officials of his own race or party. Each position thus conquered forms part of the political patrimony of the race or party by whom it has been secured, and is defended stoutly against attack. Appointments are thus multiplied exceedingly— to the cost of the taxpayer and to the complication of public business.

Joseph II., who made a gallant attempt to reform and simplify the bureaucracy, wrote in his memorandum of 1765 on the state of the Monarchy : " Il arrive que personne ne travaille, et qu'entre cent rames de papier qui se consument bien en huit jours dans les dicastères de Vienne, il n'y a pas quatre feuillets d'esprit, ou de choses nouvelles ou de propres idées. Le préambule, une longue récapitulation, et deux mots d'opinion composent nos référats, qui se réduisent toujours à peu près au même." [1] Though it would be untrue and unjust to say that nowadays *personne ne travaille*, it would be easy to prove that of every hundred reams of paper consumed in the Austrian Departments of State, ninety are wasted in superfluities. Red tape exists the world over, but the extent to which it impedes freedom of movement in the Hapsburg Monarchy should be a warning to all countries that lightly propose to add new wheels to the bureaucratic machine. Professor Joseph Redlich, a prominent member of the Reichsrath and a competent critic of the Austrian administrative system, seems indeed to agree with Joseph II. More work must be done, he writes.[2] Our officials in Vienna do not work enough. There are Departments in which one is astonished at the number of officials, and asks what all these people do. It is, for instance, incomprehensible why an Audit Office should need so many hands as are to be found in our audit offices. What is called " bureaucratism " proceeds from this plethora. Bureaucratism is form without

[1] *Maria Theresia und Joseph II.*, herausgegeben von Alfred Ritter von Arneth. Vienna, 1868.
[2] *Zustand und Reform der österreichischen Verwaltung*, pp. 35-37.

substance, appearance without reality, careful maintenance of appearances coupled with indifference towards results. The multiplication of officials is naturally a consequence of the multiplication of departments and authorities. Let me, continues Professor Redlich, give an instance taken from practical life. What happens in Austria when the caretaker in an Industrial Education Extension School asks the schoolmaster for a special remuneration of twenty Kronen (16s. 8d.)? The master transmits the request with a favourable note to the Provincial Schools Council. There the request is registered and submitted to a superior official of the audit department of the Council. This department emits an opinion, on the basis of which the Provincial Council reports to the Ministry of Public Works, after the report has been duly drawn up, approved, and revised by three separate officials. In the Ministry the report is registered and numbered, and is handed by the chief of a department to a special official for consideration, and eventually an opinion is obtained from the audit department of the Ministry. An understanding with the Ministry of Finance may also be requisite. In this case the request is sent to the Finance Ministry, accompanied by a ministerial document from the Ministry of Public Works. In the Finance Ministry this document is reported upon, approved by one official, and revised by his superior, after having been registered, numbered, fair-copied, collated, and transmitted from one department to another. Finally a decision is taken, communicated to the Ministry for Public Works, which communicates it to the Provincial Schools Council, where it is again registered and reported upon. Ultimately the Provincial Council informs the master of the school that the special remuneration for the caretaker cannot be granted !

Lest it be imagined that this example is exaggerated, the procedure in another instance may be given. A doctor wishes to found a Sanatorium and applies for a licence. The application goes to the Juridical Department, and after due registration, examination, fair-copying, approval, and revision is transmitted thence to the technical departments, of which there are two. These departments deal with it after the same fashion, and ultimately send it back, with their opinions, to the Juridical Department which orders a local investigation. The local investigation having been made, the report upon it goes once more to the Juridical Department and is by it again submitted, with due observance of bureaucratic procedure, to the two technical departments. Here it is subjected to expert examination, and unless— which is rarely the case—the first local investigation is considered to have been exhaustive, the Juridical Department is advised by the technical departments to instruct the local authorities to make a supplementary local investigation, the report on which is sent by the local authorities back to the Juridical Department and by the latter to the two technical departments. Then, if no objection has been discovered, the licence may be granted and its happy possessor may begin his struggle with the provincial and municipal officials who have jurisdiction over building and other regulations. If it be remembered that at every stage of this complicated procedure each document is subjected to half a dozen bureaucratic processes, and requires, as the untranslatable bureaucratic jargon runs, to be *präsentiert, exhibiert, indiziert, prioriert, konzipiert, revidiert, approbiert, mundiert, kollationiert, expediert,* and *registriert,* it will be seen how large is the field for the employment of talent in the service of the State. A former Papal Nuncio in Vienna, experienced in the slow and roundabout ways of the Roman Curia, expressed some years ago to the writer his indignation at the delays of Austrian bureaucracy. "One knows when a document is handed in to an Austrian Department of State," he said ; "but a young man may grow old before knowing when he will see it again. Accustomed as I am to the business-like methods of the Vatican, I find these eternal delays exasperating"!

It should not be supposed that the public and the business world do not writhe under such an administrative system. But no one has much hope of real reform. Every official appointed becomes a kind of vested interest. A new Joseph II., or a new Lueger, and a new popular movement would be required to reduce the bureaucracy and to simplify its procedure. It is therefore wiser for those who have dealings with the official world to cultivate a good personal relationship with influential officials and to obtain, by favour, the application of what is known as "short procedure" in their particular case. This wisdom is much practised. It is astonishing how rapidly the cumbrous bureaucratic machine can work when its wheels are greased by good-will. But where good-will is absent, or ill-will exists, the portals of a ministry might bear the inscription : *Lasciate ogni speranza, voi ch' entrate!* Not even the direct personal command of the Emperor is always of avail to overcome the resistance of obdurate officials who seem, at times, determined to chasten the Monarch's sense of authority and to prove to him that *L'État, c'est nous!* Some years ago a merchant, much esteemed but ill-advised, became involved in difficulties. A rascally lawyer, and an equally rascally relative, contrived to give to these difficulties a fraudulent appearance and to secure the condemnation of the merchant to a term of imprisonment. Indignant at such injustice, the friends of the family obtained for the victim's young daughter whom these machinations had reduced from affluence to shameful penury, a private audience of the Emperor, who, touched by the girl's story, gave her an order for her father's immediate release. The order was delivered to the competent official, but the merchant remained in prison and fell seriously ill. Anxious to save him from the shame of dying in prison, friends obtained a second audience for the daughter, to whom the Emperor, astonished that his first order should not have been obeyed, gave another and more peremptory command. Again the girl repaired to the competent official, who again, with disparaging remarks, showed a disposition to obstruct the course of Imperial clemency. Luckily the girl, though scarcely more than a child, had the courage so vigorously to scold the official and so to threaten him with exposure, that he countersigned the order of release. The merchant was set free—to die a few weeks later among his impoverished family. The details of this singular instance of bureaucratic obstruction and the names of the persons concerned are known to the writer and can be vouched for.

When a State Department sets itself to obstruct either the course of justice or a claim against itself which, if admitted, might imply the existence of some culpability or negligence on the part of its officials, the resistance it can offer is almost insuperable. Early in 1911, at a level crossing on one of the ʉState Railway lines in Bohemia, a waggon laden with wood stuck fast between the rails on account of the rottenness of a sleeper. A passing train smashed the waggon, killed one of the horses and injured another. The local tribunal acquitted the waggon-driver of blame and recognized that the fault lay with the railway administration. The waggon-driver consequently demanded from the State £50 indemnity. The first step of the State Railway Administration was to forbid the use of the horse that had been injured but had in the meantime recovered. Then seven different commissions, some of them consisting of eight persons, made "local investigations." The commissions were composed of officials from Pilsen, Eger, and Karlsbad, and included veterinary surgeons from Prague, Eger, and Karlsbad to enquire into the condition of the injured horse. The accident was "reconstructed"—a waggon loaded with wood was placed between the rails and a locomotive driven to within a foot of it. The repair of the defective sleeper was forbidden lest the *de facto* situation be changed pending the reports of the commissions. Presently, a local manufacturer, whose drays repeatedly stuck fast at the same crossing and had to be lifted out of it by main force, offered to repair the defective spot at his own expense. The railway traffic managing department at Pilsen forbade him to do so—doubtless lest the case be prejudiced against the State Railway by his action. On March 6, 1912, more than a year after the occurrence, a member of Parliament brought the matter to the notice of the Minister for Railways and pressed him to have it settled, but received from the Minister on July 3, 1912, the following notification : "The matter at issue is in the stage of probative procedure, and the management of the State Railways at Pilsen cannot therefore take up any attitude in regard to it until the procedure is terminated. Investigation on the spot, together with the examination of witnesses and experts, has already taken place and now the reports of the expert and the examination of several railway servants are awaited." The sequel is unknown, save that the unfortunate waggoner was ruined by the loss of his waggon and by the prohibition to use or sell his surviving horse.

The bureaucracy, whose power of obstruction such instances illustrate, is fast becoming the greatest Austrian problem. The nationalization of railways has increased the number of officials by leaps and bounds and has rendered reform imperative. State Railway servants are at once in the position of officials and of workmen. If the travelling public insults them, the insult comes within the category of " offences against State officials in the discharge of their functions." Yet, if railway servants are discontented, they can victimize the travelling public by striking work, or by " passive resistance," which consists in over-punctilious observation of the regulations. Austria has not yet ventured to imitate the Prussian system of dividing State officials into three broad categories—the superior officials with University or Technical High School education, the medium officials with a secondary school education, and the subaltern officials with lower educational qualifications ; nor is it certain that Austria, which is in many ways a more elastic State than Prussia, would do well merely to copy Prussian models. Austrian officials are divided into eleven ranks cr classes. Though a university education is usually requisite for the attainment of the highest ranks, some favoured individuals spring rapidly from rank to rank and obtain increased position and emoluments. But the mass have often to wait ten or twelve years before passing from a lower rank to a higher. Emoluments and advancement are fixed by law but an infinity of ordinances and special allowances leave room for favouritism and arbitrary treatment. Increases of salaries and allowances have repeatedly been voted by Parliament, but no statesman has yet had the courage to grapple with the problem as a whole.

The times, maybe, are not yet ripe for the drastic measures needed to effect a real improvement. Dynastic interest does not seem to demand immediate reform, nor has the people, in Carlyle's phrase, yet quite " got its eye on the knot that is strangling it." Lueger's attempts to defend the " small man " against the monopolistic organization of trade and industry led, and were bound to lead, to an increase of State and Municipal departments. The true defence against bureaucracy of all sorts—the cultivation of a spirit of political independence and of economic self-reliance among private individuals, and the treatment of bureaucrats as veritable servants, not as privileged masters of the commonwealth—is singularly difficult in Austria, where public acquiescence in the superiority of the State and its servants to the community at large is so general as to impede vigilant public control of bureaucratic doings. Reform, if reform be feasible, must come from above, or from within the bureaucracy itself, whose more intelligent members may presently perceive the dangers to which the overgrowth of departments and the multiplication of appointments are exposing the State and themselves. In Austria, changes of bureaucratic system have, since the middle of the eighteenth century, usually accompanied or preceded political metamorphosis. The process of transforming the old feudal State into a centralized polity began under the semi-enlightened autocracy of Maria Theresa who, with the help of Haugwitz and under the influence of French Mercantilism, strove to absorb into the State the independent administrations of the great nobles, the municipalities, the monasteries and the ecclesiastical sees. At the same time, the Police System, which was afterwards to become a synonym for Austrian rule, was gradually developed. When, on the death of his father in 1765, Joseph II. became co-regent with his mother, Maria Theresa, the transforming tendency was accelerated. Little by little the power and jurisdiction of the feudal nobles were curtailed, the population began to perceive that the new bureaucrats were more influential than the old lords, the fiscal and military systems were reorganized and the juridico-administrative power of the Church broken. A special body of politico-economic doctrine was formulated by writers and professors like Martini and Sonnenfels, the latter a savant of Jewish extraction. Sonnenfels enunciated the theory that, in the interest of the State, the Police must control all manifestations of public life. The "Era of Enlightenment" had dawned. The Jesuits, formerly omnipotent, had been abolished and expelled ; the Freemasons and other secret societies took their place and flourished exceedingly. The new bureaucracy was permeated by the lay spirit and by secular notions of the relationship between Church and State, of the nature of the marriage contract and of the lay character of education. The clergy itself accepted in part the new ideas and, like the nobility, acquiesced in the extension of the functions and attributes of the State. At first, the progressive centralization of public business caused delays and confusion, but when, in 1780, Joseph II. succeeded entirely to Maria Theresa, his capacity for hard work made the new system as nearly a success as it could possibly become. He worked from dawn to dark and made his officials work likewise ; but he established "conduct lists" for officials that made promotion depend upon secret reports and engendered a spirit of prying and delation. Deft manipulation of reports and of "conduct lists" enabled the Freemasons and other partisans of "enlightenment" to secure important appointments for their own nominees. The Jews, whom Maria Theresa

had detested,[1] but whom Joseph had partially emanci-
pated,[2] made rapid headway, and Protestants found themselves tolerated and encouraged. The spirit of the age was
Encyclopedist and Jansenist, but the channels through
which it spread were German. Joseph's object was to
create an Austrian nation out of the heterogeneous elements
constituting the Hapsburg inheritance under the Pragmatic
Sanction. Hence his attempt to establish German as a
single State language for the whole Monarchy and his
ordinance that none but officials knowing German could be
eligible for appointment in Hungary. The inherent impossibility of transforming in so short a time his diversified feudal
realms into a centralized State, the pertinacious resistance
of the Magyars and his own declining health, doomed his
work to formal failure. But the centralized bureaucracy survived him and remained the chief instrument of government
throughout the nineteenth century.

When, upon Joseph's death in 1790, Leopold came from
Tuscany and brought with him precise ideas concerning the
secret police as a means of government, and a disposition
less radical than that of his brother, the reaction that was to
last till 1848, and from 1849 to 1867, gradually set in.
The excesses of the French Revolution strengthened the
reactionary tendency and enabled Leopold's successor,
Francis, and his Ministers, Colloredo and Metternich, to
transform the police and the bureaucracy into the instrument
of oppression under which Northern Italy and the greater

---

[1] Three years before her death, Maria Theresa replied as follows to a private
petition presented by her Chief Chancellor, Count Blümegen (June 19, 1777):
" In future shall no Jew be allowed to stay here (in Vienna) without my written
permission. I know of no worse plague for the State than this race on account
of deceit, usury and money,management, to bring people to beggary, to do all
evil deeds which other honest folk abhor ; therefore, as much as possible, to be
kept away and avoided " (cf. Krones, *Geschichte Oesterreichs*, vol. iv. p. 501).

[2] Joseph allowed the Jews (1785) to hire and subsequently to own land,
subject, however, to the condition that it be worked by "Jewish hands," not
exploited indirectly. This condition was successfully evaded. Joseph was as
little able to overcome the Jewish dislike of agricultural labour and to keep them
from speculation as he was to solve the Gipsy question in Hungary and Bohemia
(*op. cit.* pp. 489-490).

part of Germany groaned for decades. Colloredo, the omnipotent Minister of the Emperor Francis, had seen that in the French Revolution, as in the earlier disturbances in Belgium and Holland, an important part had been played by lawyers, doctors, literary men, small capitalists and the lower clergy, whereas most of the monarchical counter-movements had been led by members of the nobility and supported by the common people. Hence, he concluded that danger to Thrones proceeded principally from the educated middle classes. His "system," subsequently taken over and developed by Metternich, sought, consequently, to curtail and circumscribe the development of the middle classes by means of bureaucratic and police control. A severe censorship impeded the publication of scientific or literary works. The centralized administration established by Joseph naturally became clogged when monarchs less energetic than he ascended the throne and when officials were no longer kept up to their duty by his example and martinet discipline. Matters which Joseph would have settled in a few days or weeks lingered under Francis and Colloredo from three to ten years. Francis, moreover, resembling in this his successors, distrusted men of talent. He regarded them as ambitious and prone to innovation. Mediocrity was preferred. This tendency remained strong in Austria throughout the nineteenth century and has not yet disappeared. It has been well defined as "the principle of inverted selection," the application of which guarantees Monarchs and Ministers tranquillity in ordinary times and leaves them without a reliable counsellor at moments of crisis. The bureaucracy was schooled to bow its head, obey and not interfere. Officials were forbidden to point out the defects of the working of laws and ordinances, and soon came to understand that when their opinion as "experts" was asked, flattering acquiescence rather than criticism was desired. In these circumstances the men of the "Party of Enlightenment" that had grown up under Joseph and was still strong in the lower bureaucracy were fain to hide their heads and

dissemble their existence. The word "Culture" was substituted for "Enlightenment," "virtue" was much talked of,
and abject loyalty was professed towards the established
order of things. This pliancy saved the party from destruction and preserved, at least in spirit, many of Joseph's minor
ordinances. In later decades when milder breezes blew,
Austrian "Liberalism" blossomed upon the old Josephine
stock—an anæmic blossom, bearing traces of the means by
which the stock had been kept alive. Austrian "Liberalism"
was ever a hot-house plant. It had its roots in the bureaucracy and in financial and industrial capitalism, not in the
people. Yet, between 1867 and 1879, it served a useful
purpose until superseded by Lueger's Christian Socialism on
the one hand, and by Social Democracy on the other. The disappearance of "Liberalism" and the degeneration of Austrian
parliamentarianism into a system under which cabinets
composed of officials purchase the support of parliamentary
groups or of influential deputies by means of bureaucratic
concessions, have tended at once to demoralize the bureaucracy
itself and to increase its numbers. Now the community is
confronted with a problem of the first magnitude for which
no solution is yet in sight—the problem presented by the maintenance of an immense army of officials possessing executive
authority and great obstructive but little creative power, an
army whose maintenance eats up nearly one-third of the public
revenues without contributing notably to them. The growing complexity of social and economic organization naturally
implies an increase of the administrative and regulative elements
and a decrease of the productive elements in a community.
But in Austria the increase has been disproportionate and
needs to be checked. Unless means are found to reduce the
number and to increase the efficiency of offices and officials,
the bureaucracy itself will fall into discredit and will become
at once a class of privileged drones and educated paupers.
The cost of living has risen far more rapidly than the salaries
of officials; progressive impoverishment and indebtedness
are resulting. From time to time, Parliament is induced to

grant an extra dole of a few pounds per head per annum, but so great is the number of officials that, though the dole in the aggregate runs into millions of pounds and adds seriously to the burdens of the Exchequer, it brings no appreciable relief to those whom it is intended to benefit. Meanwhile the universities continue to train year by year thousands of youths for an official career. Formerly the training was almost exclusively legal and was calculated to unfit those who received it for practical comprehension of the needs of the people. These legally trained officials, or "jurists," still predominate in the Austrian bureaucracy ; there are nearly two hundred of them in the Lord Lieutenancy of Lower Austria alone. But latterly the Technical High Schools have turned out engineers and other "experts" who have gone to swell the army of bureaucrats without greatly increasing its efficiency. As the supply is greater than the legitimate demand, political influences and "protection" of all kinds are called into play to secure appointments for qualified but unemployed candidates. Thus the evil grows, and the taxpayer is annually burdened with the maintenance of more and more officials who would have been better employed in trade, industry, agriculture, or even in skilled labour. Sooner or later the feeling that the bureaucracy, like the monasteries of the middle ages, are eating up the land will inevitably find expression in a demand for drastic retrenchment and reform.

Signs of change are already noticeable, though not of a change for the better. While hundreds of aspiring, artificially-trained youths crowd into the bureaucracy from below, some of the high officials, particularly those of Jewish extraction, are forsaking the service of the State for that of private or semi-private banks and business undertakings. Others claim their pensions at the earliest moment and increase their incomes by joining the boards of banks and industrial companies to which their former official connexions enable them to render valuable service. The points of subterranean contact between the bureaucracy and the private enterprises which it ought in theory to control are thus increased, and new wheels are added to the wheels within wheels that complicate the working of Austrian affairs.

THE POLICE

Scarcely less important than the Bureaucracy in action and influence is the Police. Those who have never lived and worked in a *Polizeistaat* or police-ridden country can hardly comprehend the extent to which the whole life of the community is, or may be, influenced by the police. The Anglo-Saxon conception of the police as an organization created to serve the public and to protect society and individuals from evil-doers is singularly at variance with the conception of the functions of the police that prevails in most Continental States. The police are a direct emanation of the theory of Divine right. The Sovereign in ruling over "his" peoples requires a "State" to administer or exploit them, an Army to keep them in subjection, a Church to direct their religious aspirations into salutary channels, and a Police to watch over, spy upon, denounce, arrest and guide them. The police are thus not the servants but the drill-sergeants of the public. They may perform their functions roughly and rudely as in Prussia, corruptly and stealthily as in Russia, or politely and unobtrusively as in Austria, but in their essence the functions are the same. Even in France and Italy the police spirit still exists and is frequently utilized by "democratic" Governments. In Austria the spirit is at least as old as the Counter-Reformation. It came with the Jesuits and was elaborated by the Inquisition but, by the irony of Destiny, it was reserved for Joseph II. the "reformer" and "enlightener" to infuse the police spirit into the whole State.

A monarch of Joseph's energetic, not to say tyrannical, disposition who, for all his enlightened principles, could brook no opposition to his policy, was naturally tempted to develop and apply a police system. Sonnenfels, the ex-Jewish

economist and savant, had written a work on the *Principles
of Police and Financial Science.* Its arrogance and sophistry
did not prevent it from exercising considerable influence
upon Joseph. By "police," Sonnenfels understood everything pertaining to the arrangements for the internal
safety of the State, and laid down the principle that
the Church, the Schools, the Charitable Institutions and
the censorship of books and of the press must be subject
to police control. "Among the most efficacious means of
maintaining good morals and manners," wrote Sonnenfels,[1]
"Religion undoubtedly deserves the first place. Religion
supplies the deficiencies of legislation. Wherever the eye
of the Legislator and the penalty of the Judge cannot reach,
Religion is present to check by her threats the evil enterprises of the individual. Therefore the Ruler must not
neglect this rein and must carefully see that every citizen
has Religion." For this reason, Sonnenfels enjoined upon
the Ruler to organize parishes, pay the parish priests, and
regulate Divine service, since the "control of the clergy is
an essential feature of the policing of Religion." Similarly,
he claimed, the police could not remain indifferent to education, which is too closely connected with general welfare to
be allowed to remain in private hands. Therefore the
police must decide the curriculum of the schools, the teachings of the clergy, and censorize "not only books, maxims,
newspapers, public speeches, pictures and etchings but everything whatsoever that is in any way of a public nature."[2]
The registration of citizens, police passes, domiciliary visits
and other measures, he recommended as valuable means of
control. Cleanliness must be enforced, and child murder
checked "by loving treatment of fallen girls,"[3] and duels
must be made subject to criminal penalties. The objection
that such a system would stifle civil freedom was met by
Sonnenfels with the claim that veritable freedom is freedom
to act in a manner not contrary to civil laws.

[1] *Polizeiwissenschaft*, p. 90.   [2] *Polizeiwissenschaft*, pp. 146-147.
[3] *Polizeiwissenschaft*, p. 213.

Under Maria Theresa, District Offices had been established to watch over the execution of the laws. Under Joseph II. these Offices were transformed into offices of public surveillance and were themselves controlled by the police. Priests, doctors, officials and lawyers whom the police suspected were prevented from receiving promotion. Despite the ordinance of June 1771, in which Joseph authorized " criticism in so far as it is not merely abuse," a simultaneous ordinance made all publications subject to the official *imprimatur* which, in practice, proved to mean the suppression of everything distasteful to the police. Joseph II. used the press and even the theatre freely for the propagation of his ideas, and suffered no contradiction. In proportion as discontent grew he extended the institution of secret " conduct lists " for officials, favoured secret informers and utilized the clergy to praise all Government measures. In 1785 he established in every provincial capital a director of police who, in some respects, was dependent upon the Governor of the Province but was in other respects independent of him. In practice, the police was used to spy upon the local officials. Alongside of the uniformed constables, a host of " plain clothes " men and women were engaged under the names of " friends," " correspondents," and *confidents*. The *confidents* were coffee-house and hotel-keepers, theatre servants, cab drivers, house porters, and prostitutes. They permeated the civil administration and even the Army, spreading distrust and suspicion. The evils inseparable from their activity were mitigated, however, by the good nature and easy-going disposition characteristic of most Austrians, even when clothed with official authority—provided always that their authority be not called in question. Upon the death of Joseph little change occurred, save that the police also was affected by the general slackening of tension which characterized Leopold's short reign of transition. Leopold, indeed, maintained and developed the secret police, though in some parts of the Empire the number of regular police officials was diminished. But, upon the accession of Francis, the Josephine system was revived in all its rigour and was brought by Count Colloredo to a pitch of perfection unequalled before or since in any large State, save perhaps in the Ottoman Empire under Abdul Hamid. The principles of Sonnenfels were extended by Colloredo in the light of the lessons taught by the French Revolution. While in the provinces some freedom of opinion persisted despite police pressure, the intellectual life of the cities was completely blighted. The objects of the police were to prevent the dissemination of "dangerous knowledge," to impede conversations disagreeable to the Government, and secretly to spread news, opinions, and principles favourable to the Government. Violent means of oppression and repression were rarely employed. Imprisonment and the gallows were reserved for political rebels ; their employment for "crimes of opinion" might have caused an undesirable sensation ! Police "warnings," slight restrictions of personal freedom, constant surveillance, and, in the case of individuals in Government employ, degradations, transfers and "isolation" were felt to be preferable and more efficacious.[1] In a word the employment of subterranean methods became a maxim of Government—a maxim which has not lost currency even to-day.

A graphic description, by a contemporary British observer, of the condition of Austria and of Vienna in particular during the reign of the Emperor Francis, may be found in a book entitled *A Tour in Germany and some of the Southern Provinces of the Austrian Empire in the years 1820, 1821, and 1822*, by John Russell, Esq. (Edinburgh : Archibald Constable & Co., 1825). " But," he writes, " though the Austrians have no great capacity for thinking, and a very great capacity for immorality and superstition, much of both must be ascribed to that total prostration of intellect which their government inflicts upon them, a prostration which can never last long, in the degree in which it exists in Vienna,

---

[1] Cf. *Geschichte der österreichischen Staatsverwaltung*, 1740–1848 ; von Dr. Ignaz Beidtel, Innsbruck, 1898, vol. ii. pp. 77-131.

without producing some degradation of the moral principle. The whole political principle is directed, with prying and persecuting jealousy, to keep people in ignorance of all that goes on in the world, except what it suits the Cabinet to make known, and to prevent people from thinking on what is known differently from the way in which the Cabinet thinks. All the modes of education are arranged on the same depressing principle of keeping the mind in such a state that it shall neither feel the temptation, nor possess the ability, to resist power. During the Congress of Laybach, the Emperor said to the teachers of a public seminary, ' I want no learned men ; I need no learned men ; I want men who will do what I bid them,' or something to the same purpose,—the most unfortunate words for the honour of his throne that could be put into the mouth of a monarch. The principle is fully acted on in Vienna ; over all knowledge, and all thinking, on everything public, and on everything relating to the political events and institutions not only of the Empire but of all other countries there broods a 'darkness that may be felt' ; nowhere will you find a more lamentable ignorance, or a more melancholy horror of being suspected of a desire to be wise above what is written down by the editor of the Austrian *Observer*. Nothing is known but to official men ; and the first official duty is to confine all knowledge within the official circle. . . .

" The Austrian police,—*monstrum horrendum, ingens* ;— it cannot be added, *cui lumen ademptum*, for it has the eyes of an Argus, though no Mercury has yet been found to charm them to sleep, while he rescued manly thought and intellectual exertion from the brute form into which political jealousy has metamorphosed them. The French police under Napoleon was reckoned perfect ; in efficiency, it could not possibly surpass that of Vienna, which successfully represses every expression of thought, by forcing on all the deadening conviction that the eyes and ears of spies are everywhere. The consequences of a denunciation are, secret arrest, secret imprisonment, and an unknown punishment. . . .

The efficiency of such a system depends upon those who are its instruments being unknown."[1]

Despite the changes and reforms that have marked the reign of the Emperor Francis Joseph, practical acquaintance with the daily life of Austria soon convinces observers that the Austrian police remains, at least potentially, much what it was a hundred years ago. Its portrait, posthumously painted by experienced officials like Dr. Ignaz Beidtel, whose *History of the Austrian State Administration,* 1740–1848, has been laid under contribution in the foregoing pages, is still true to the life, though the colours, like those of ancient frescoes, have grown paler with time. At moments of crisis, the colours revive automatically and render the resemblance or rather the identity more apparent. In normal circumstances, however, the action of the police is not obtrusive. The stranger is unaware that the porter of his house is a *confident* of the police, and that his goings and comings, his manner of life, the number and names of his friends and all personal details are carefully communicated by the porter to the police which preserves them in a *dossier* ready for communication to the political or to the fiscal authorities as occasion may require. Unless warned from some friendly quarter, he may not know that his correspondence is being watched, his telephone " tapped " and his intercourse noted. On settling in Austria he must, as in Germany, fill up a registration form for the police, and is thereupon invited to visit personally the police commissioner of his district who examines his papers and questions him as to the purpose of his residence in the country. Then, if explanations be satisfactory, he is troubled no more except by the income-tax authorities who sometimes display quite uncanny knowledge of the number of dinner parties he has given, how often he has driven out in a two-horse cab or motor-car and whether he is addicted to expensive amusements. Here his direct knowledge of the action of the police will probably end unless, having declined to certify, as the Regulations in

[1] Cf. Russell, *op. cit.* vol. ii. pp. 296-299.

regard to Domestic Servants require, that a dishonest servant is "industrious, honest, and faithful," or having otherwise resisted exactions, he finds that advantage has been taken of his ignorance of laws and customs to invoke the aid of the police against him.   In such cases the police is, as a rule, conciliatory and patient.   Its tendency as, indeed, the tendency of the lower tribunals, is to protect the servant against the master, and the lower against the middle class. The readiness with which the lower classes appeal to the police is remarkable and indicates the success of the systematic endeavours on the part of the authorities to make the common people feel that the State is on their side.   There are doubtless exceptions, as when powerful nobles or high officials are involved in disputes with some member of the lower classes.   Then the influence of the police or of the district tribunals may not so readily favour the "small man."   But it is when political interests are directly at stake that the police and the courts appear most clearly as instruments of Government.   Political disturbances and rioting are dealt with as official interests are supposed to require.   In the autumn of 1905 a Socialist manifestation in favour of universal suffrage was violently suppressed ; blood was shed and arrests were made.   But within a week the wind in the higher regions had changed, and the Government had veered round in favour of universal suffrage.   A huge Socialist demonstration was organized in agreement with the police which was instructed by the Government to evacuate the main thoroughfare of Vienna, the Ringstrasse, and to leave it for several hours entirely to the Socialists.   The police guarded only the Hofburg or Imperial Palace.   In the autumn of 1911, a Socialist agitation of which the Government did not approve was directed against the Agrarians and the rise in the prices of food for which the Agrarians were held responsible. The police and the military suppressed it with vigour, a number of lives being lost.   On this occasion the Courts inflicted severe sentences upon boys not out of

their teens, and punished with long terms of imprisonment any culprit who confessed that he had thrown a
stone.

In general, however, the relationship between the public,
nay, even between the criminal classes, and the police is
reciprocally amicable. The harsh angularity noticeable in
Prussia and the gratuitous brutality that sometimes char-
acterizes the Paris police are alike unknown in Austria.
Without being the friend of the public like the British police-
man, the Austrian constable is not a terrorist. Toleration
and moderate control seem to be preferred to drastic action.
Even the police officials are artistically minded and prone
to make allowances for human nature. There is an easy-
going *Gemütlichkeit* in their methods that would scarcely be
conceivable in other countries and is not always laudable,
even in Austria. But on occasion the police is intractable
—whenever its professional vanity or the personal ambition
of its chiefs is involved. Then it can be ruthless and tyrannical, browbeating or inspiring the press, disseminating de-
famatory information concerning the objects of its suspicions,
and appearing to be persuaded that the condemnation of a
possibly innocent man would be a lesser evil than a police
fiasco. The case of Lieutenant Hofrichter, who was convicted of poisoning a brother officer belonging to the
General Staff, is a case in point. Hofrichter was doubtless guilty, but the methods employed by the police to
hound him down and discredit him long before any but
the most imperfect circumstantial evidence had been
obtained, would have ruined him had he been a hundred
times innocent. Other criminal cases have thrown singular
light upon Austrian police psychology. In the autumn of
1911 a vagabond named Voigt was tried for outrage and
murder. The murderer, who had made a confession to the
police, changed his version of the circumstances during the
trial. The presiding Judge reminded him that his first
account had been different, as his confession to the police
showed. The accused asserted that the confession had only

been made in order to give pleasure to the police commissioner, who had begged Voigt "not to grudge him this success." "That," returned the Judge, "sounds very improbable." Voigt : "It is very probable. . . . The commissioner begged me and tormented me saying, 'Don't grudge me the success.' I repeat it. I answered, ' Good ; if you want a success, let us make a confession.'" (Loud laughter in Court.) Presently the police commissioner in question was called as a witness and asked by the Judge whether he had put any moral pressure upon the prisoner to make him confess. The Judge added that, according to the prisoner, the commissioner had asked the prisoner "not to grudge him the success." The commissioner replied, " I was convinced that Voigt was the murderer and, as he would not ease his conscience by confessing, I said to him, ' If you will not confess of your own accord, give me the personal satisfaction of doing it as a pleasure to me.' That I readily admit." Voigt rose and said, " This evidence of the police commissioner commands my entire respect. Although the commissioner said in taking leave of me, ' We may never see each other again,' I have nevertheless (with an elegant bow to the commissioner) the honour and pleasure of seeing him again." The Public Prosecutor : " A humorous fellow ! " This scene is characteristic not only of the attitude of the Austrian police towards criminals but also of the tone that frequently prevails in court.

JUSTICE

The administration of Justice in Austria is naturally affected by the conditions under which it has developed and the public atmosphere of the country. The judges are not priests of the Veiled Goddess, applying the law with a single eye to equity, but are State officials, dependent for appointment upon the Minister of Justice and, in the higher ranks, upon the pleasure of the Crown. The Emperor Francis in-

scribed, indeed, the words " Justitia Regnorum Fundamentum"
upon the outer gateway of the Hofburg, but his conception
of Justice, like that of patriotism, was apt to be, "Justice
for Me." Judges are, theoretically and practically, officials
delegated to discharge the judicial functions of the Crown.
They are appointed by the Emperor, or in his name,
for life, and can only be removed or punished in accordance with regular procedure. By the Constitution of
1867 they are independent in the exercise of their office.
They are not allowed to question the validity of the laws
they administer, though the Higher Courts are entitled
to decide upon the validity of Ministerial Ordinances.
Like the administrative functions of the State, the judicial
functions were originally exercised by or in the name
of the Feudal Nobles and landed proprietors who had,
in most cases, power of life and death. Maria Theresa
centralized the higher instances of civil and penal justice,
leaving only the District Courts in the hands of the local
magnates and landlords. After the Revolution of 1848 the
whole system of justice was "nationalized" and reformed by
Alexander Bach. It was further reformed by the Constitution of 1867 and the competence of the various courts
defined by law. But the independence of Judges (of whom
there are some 7000 as compared with 160 in England) is
an independence *sui generis*. As a body of officials, the
Austrian judges are as incorruptible and upright as any
similar body of 7000 ill-paid men in any country in the
world ; but the very conditions that regulate the appointment and promotion of judges ensure that a judge shall not
be undesirably independent of State interests. Promotion is
entirely in the hands of the Minister of Justice and, in the
last resort, of the Crown. A judge whose attitude dis-
pleases the Minister, or the Crown, is apt to wait in vain for
advancement. Before a judge of a District Court can hope
for promotion to a Provincial or to the Supreme Provincial
Court, he must acquire "protection" from some influential
quarter or have distinguished himself by publishing a learned

treatise on jurisprudence or have rendered services to the Government by special pliancy or skill. Moreover, the higher judges are usually chosen from among the State Attorneys or public prosecutors. The careers of these men have tended to unfit them for the exercise of judicial functions. The best years of their lives have been passed in executing instructions received from the Government or in instituting judicial proceedings against tendencies and persons displeasing to the Government, in the hope that zeal may be rewarded by a judgeship. Consequently they are apt to remain, after appointment to the judicial bench, rather the executors of instructions and servants of the Government than veritable custodians of law and equity.

The tendency of Judges to accommodate their attitude to the supposed exigencies of the State has rarely been more strikingly illustrated than during the famous Friedjung trial of December 1909.[1] The trial arose out of the prosecution of the Austrian historian, Dr. Friedjung, by the Serbo-Croatian Coalition majority in the Croatian Diet for calumnious assertions made by Dr. Friedjung in an article contributed to the *Neue Freie Presse* of March 25, 1909. The article was based on secret documents supplied to Dr. Friedjung by the Austro-Hungarian Foreign Office, and was intended by the Foreign Minister, Count Aehrenthal, to be at once a fanfare of war against Servia and an indictment of sundry Serbo-Croatian politicians for alleged treasonable commerce with Servia. Had war broken out, it is unquestionable that, on the strength of these secret documents, the leading Croatian and Serb politicians of the Monarchy would have been court-martialled and shot ; but Russian acceptance of the German " ultimatum " presented at St. Petersburg on March 24, 1909, removed the danger of war and made Dr. Friedjung's article on March 25 a work of supererogation. Otherwise the article would have passed

---

[1] An accurate and detailed account of this important trial is given in Mr. R. W. Seton-Watson's *Southern Slav Question*. London : Constable & Co.

as a patriotic utterance and the authenticity of the documents underlying it would have been the less open to question in that most of the personages against whom it was directed would have been shot or compelled to flee the country. But, as peace was preserved, these very personages were at liberty to examine the charges brought against them and to demonstrate their baselessness. The Serbo-Croatian Coalition, as a body, therefore prosecuted Dr. Friedjung, while its leader, M. Supilo, and other members whom Dr. Friedjung had accused by name of treasonable corruption, prosecuted him separately. The question at issue was whether a Serbo-Croatian conspiracy against the Monarchy had been organized with the help of the Servian Government through a Servian student society called the *Slovenski-Jug* (the Slav South), and whether the documents supplied by the Austro-Hungarian Foreign Office to Dr. Friedjung, which purported to be minutes of the secret sittings of the Slovenski-Jug Society, were or were not authentic. Great interest attached to the trial, both because of the light it was expected to throw upon Austro-Hungarian policy towards Servia and the Serbo-Croatians, or Southern Slavs, in general, and because Austro-Hungarian Ambassadors abroad had been instructed to inform foreign governments that the Monarchy had been driven by this alleged Serbo-Croatian Conspiracy to annex the provinces of Bosnia and Herzegovina. In point of fact, the real defendants in the action were not so much Dr. Friedjung and his associates as the Austro-Hungarian Foreign Office and its secret service. Dr. Friedjung was a figurehead and a tool whose reputation as a historian had been used by Count Aehrenthal to lend weight and an appearance of respectability to an unscrupulous piece of political denunciation. Had Austria possessed a judiciary trained to place the interests of Justice above the supposed interests of the State, the Friedjung trial would have redounded to the credit of the Monarchy and have increased its prestige in the Southern Slav world. Some minor diplomatists and their dubious agents would have been punished, the Austro-Hungarian Foreign Office would have stood convicted of light-minded carelessness, but the impartiality of Austrian Justice would have been so vindicated that its name would have rung sympathetically throughout Europe and the Balkans. Unfortunately this was not to be, nor could it be. A judiciary trained to be an instrument of Ministers cannot undertake overnight the protection of the State's highest interests. The presiding Judge was chosen for his " reliability," the Jury was packed with "patriots" of the most narrow-minded "black and yellow" school, and a plan of campaign was arranged in advance with the defendants for the purpose of overwhelming the plaintiffs. The Judge lost no time in revealing his attitude. He allowed the defendants to harangue the Jury in an ultra-patriotic strain for two days and to lay before the Court printed copies — but no originals — of their secret "documents," before the plaintiffs or their counsel were given an opportunity of stating their case or of cross-examining the defendants. False witnesses having been called with the object of discrediting the Serbo-Croatian Coalition in the person of its leader, M. Supilo, the semi-official press was let loose, before he could be heard in self-defence, to describe him as a " political corpse hanging, with shattered bones, from the tree of Justice." But in Austria, as elsewhere, the best-laid plans are apt to go awry. The publication in the press of Dr. Friedjung's " documents," purporting to be the minutes of the Slovenski-Jug Society, brought suddenly from Belgrade a University professor, Dr. Bozo Markovitch, the president of the Slovenski-Jug itself. Seeing his name appended to a number of fantastical secret " minutes " and accounts of money payments to M. Supilo and others, he came unbidden to Vienna to inform the Court that during the weeks when, according to these " documents," he was presiding over meetings of conspirators at Belgrade, he had been in reality at Berlin attending lectures on juris-prudence and frequenting the houses of eminent German professors of Law. This *alibi*, which the Berlin police

unkindly confirmed in every particular, tore a grievous
hole in Dr. Friedjung's case. Further rents were made
by the demonstration, undertaken by the Servian Under-
Secretary of State for Foreign Affairs, M. Spalaikovitch,
whom Dr. Friedjung had likewise denounced, that the
numbers, dates, and language of secret despatches alleged
by Dr. Friedjung to have been purloined by Austro-
Hungarian agents from the Servian Foreign Office Archives
and replaced after having been photographed, were false
and fantastical ; and by proof that all the circumstances
mentioned in the false evidence adduced against M. Supilo
were malicious inventions. Supported by the Judge and
Jury, Dr. Friedjung, whose vanity as a " scientific historian "
got the better of his good sense, struggled for days against
this weight of misfortune ; until the Judge, who had obtained
an inkling of the effect produced in Government spheres by
the collapse of the "documents," suddenly changed his
attitude and promoted an "honourable settlement." He
transformed himself from a prejudiced browbeater into a
benevolent peacemaker, allowed the plaintiffs full latitude
to state their case and to prove both the inherent im-
probability and the actual baselessness of the charges
brought against them. Finally, under pressure from the
Government, the case was "arranged" by an exchange
of declarations between defendants and plaintiffs ; Count
Aehrenthal informed a visitor that he had never believed
in the authenticity of the documents ; and the official
organ of the Foreign Office astounded the diplomatic
world by stating that Austro-Hungarian Foreign Policy
had never been influenced by any belief in the existence
of a Serbo-Croatian Conspiracy ! The effect upon Austro-
Hungarian prestige in the Southern Slav world may be
imagined.

The Serbo-Croatian leaders, who felt that they owed
their lives to chance and their reputations to the intrepid
honesty of a young Servian Professor, worked nevertheless
to discover the veritable source of the notorious " documents."

With the help of Professor Masaryk, a Czech, or rather Slovak, savant of the highest scientific and moral standing, they succeeded in proving, a twelvemonth later, that most if not all of the "documents" had been fabricated and photographed at the instance and in the house of a member of the Austro-Hungarian Legation at Belgrade, and sent thence to the Austro-Hungarian Foreign Office and other influential quarters. The original of one such fabrication, found in the possession of the forger, a ne'er-do-well Servian named Vasitch, proved to be a yard long by fifteen inches broad—a singularly unwieldy size for the "minutes" of a conspiring student society, but well adapted for photographic purposes and corresponding exactly to the holes made by drawing-pins in the door of the Austro-Hungarian Legation servant's room, to which the "documents" had been affixed after fabrication in order to be photographed. Vasitch, the forger, who had been employed by a member of the Austro-Hungarian Legation at Belgrade, was prosecuted by the Servian Government for high treason and condemned to fifteen years' penal servitude.

.   .   .   .

It is characteristic of Austrian public affairs that so resounding a fiasco as the Friedjung trial and so discreditable a scandal as its sequel, should not have led to changes and reforms. No public punishment of officials followed the trial. The Judge, whose conduct would, in most other countries, have been felt to have compromised the reputation of the Bench, was shortly afterwards promoted and presently died amid general esteem. The position of the Foreign Minister, Count Aehrenthal, was not appreciably shaken either by the course of the trial or by Professor Masaryk's exposure in the Delegations of the source of the forged documents. The validity of Kürnberger's principle that the best way to consolidate the position of culpable officials is to expose them publicly, because exposure engages the *amour propre* of the whole bureaucratic caste and makes it a point of honour that unofficial influences shall not triumph, was once again vindicated. True, some bureaucratic changes were eventually made. The official in charge of the Foreign Office Press Bureau, who is alleged to have expressed doubts as to the authenticity of the documents from the beginning, was placed on the retired list, ostensibly for having failed to stop the publication of Dr. Friedjung's article in the *Neue Freie Presse* at the last moment when events had rendered its publication inopportune ; and the Austro-Hungarian Minister at Belgrade was transferred to a minor German capital.[1] These measures, however, escaped the notice of the general public, which was and is too indifferent towards such matters or, perhaps, too conscious of its own impotence, to trouble greatly about original causes and ulterior effects. As one satirical writer remarked, "When the press cried, ' Austria is menaced by the Serbo-Croatian conspiracy,' the crowd answered ' Indeed !' and when the press presently declared, ' Austria was not at all in danger !' the crowd answered ' Really ; Indeed !' "

THE CHURCH

As a matter of fact, the Austrian State system fits the character of the people as an old shoe fits the foot, and, like an old shoe, reveals its defects only when the weather is bad. The Austrians, and especially the Viennese, prefer to jog along comfortably and to let the State manage their affairs for them. They grumble and carp, but their grumbling is rarely serious. Earnestness bores them. The artistic temperament of the people and the efforts long and consistently made by the Government to encourage " amusements " and to discourage interest in intellectual pursuits and in questions of public import, have combined to produce a sceptical indifference that still seems to preclude sustained effort or action. Yet one feeling lies deep in Austrian hearts—the old Imperial pride that has never quite lost faith in Austrian

[1] He has since been given high employment at the Austro-Hungarian Foreign Office.

destinies, and only awaits some real or apparent success to blaze forth again in all its ancient intensity. For the same reason, insults and disparagement are rarely forgotten or forgiven. Criticism on the part of foreign and even of Austrian writers is apt to be regarded as hostility. True, Austrians are wont to answer inquiries why this or that has not been done in Austria by saying, "Wir sind in Öster-reich; wir sind noch nicht so weit" (We are in Austria; we are not yet so far advanced); but the prudent foreigner who demurs to this self-depreciation, and praises, as he can do with sincerity, the many virtues of the Austrian character, will soon strike a responsive chord and get a glimpse into the recesses of the Austrian heart. Humility and self-depreciation will then be recognized as *de l'orgueil rentré*, and the force of the saying of a shrewd Frenchwoman, "Les Autrichiens n'ont jamais tort," will be realized. The general fear of ridicule, or of what is called *Blamage* or "loss of face," proceeds from this source, as does much of the reluctance in private individuals and officials to own to a mistake or publicly to redress an injury. The superior moral courage that admits an error and repairs it spontaneously is little appreciated. While physically brave and often accustomed to effort and hardship, the average Austrian is singularly lacking in moral hardihood and in steadfastness of moral purpose. Nor is it easy to see how the defect can be removed. The Church, which might be an instrument for the moral elevation of the people, uses its influence partly in the service of the State and partly to promote its own political objects. Despite the increase of Ultramontane clericalism since the days of Joseph and Leopold, the spirit that inspired Leopold's decree of March 3, 1792, is still strong: "Though the priest be a shepherd of souls, as he should always be, yet he must be regarded not only as a priest and a citizen but also as an official of the State in the Church, since the administration of the care of souls has unlimited influence upon the sentiments of the people, and participates directly or indirectly in the most important political matters." The

Church in Austria is less a State Church than an ecclesiastical department of the State, working like the army, the bureaucracy, and the police in the interests of "government." When the Church contrives to capture the reigning monarch and to make him subordinate the influence of the dynasty to priestly ends, it becomes all-powerful. Such a monarch was Ferdinand II. (1619–37), who was mainly an instrument of the Jesuit Counter-Reformation. Monarchs like Maria Theresa and Joseph II., on the other hand, reduced the Church to the position of a dynastic tool, kept Rome at arm's length, and organized the "religious police." Even under the Emperors Francis and Ferdinand (1792–1848) Ultramontanism made little progress, despite the return of the expelled Jesuits and of their "straw men" the Redemptorists. Ultramontane clerics were simply denied promotion, and Bishops and Archbishops were chosen for their dynastic sentiments. Notwithstanding Metternich's predilection for the Roman Curia, the police, in the later 'forties, once sent back to Rome a whole boxful of Roman breviaries, because one of Joseph II.'s ordinances had forbidden their use in Austria. Indeed, the influence of Joseph's ecclesiastical reforms lasted until the dynasty and the State capitulated to Rome in 1855 by the conclusion of the Concordat, the Emperor Francis Joseph's twenty-fifth birthday gift to his peoples. Francis Joseph lived, however, to sanction the destruction of the Concordat and to restrict Clerical influence over education which the Concordat had made supreme. During the later 'sixties and the 'seventies he re-established the supremacy of the State and reduced the Church once more to a position of dependence. In the Conclave of 1903 he commanded Cardinal Puzyna, Archbishop of Cracow, to pronounce the Imperial Veto against the election of Cardinal Rampolla, who had incurred the political displeasure of the Triple Alliance, and whose elevation to the chair of St. Peter as successor of Leo XIII. was thought politically undesirable —a proceeding unspeakably offensive to the consciences of devout Catholics who believe the selection of the Vicar of

Christ to be inspired by the Holy Spirit. Despite Cardinal Rampolla's dignified protest, the Princes of the Church nevertheless bowed to the Hapsburg dictate, though Pope Pius X. felt moved to ordain that any Cardinal who may in future attempt to repeat the veto shall be placed under the major ban. Cardinal Puzyna is credibly reported to have been astounded that the Sacred College should have resented the violence done to it in the exercise of its highest functions —so profoundly is the Austro-Hungarian Episcopacy penetrated by the spirit of subservience to the dynasty! Something like a revolt against State and dynastic control of the Church was noticeable during the earlier phases of the Christian Social movement. The minor clergy broke away from the political domination of the Bishops and developed a semi-Socialist, semi-Ultramontane spirit. But in 1907 the Conservative-Clerical or "Bishop's" party amalgamated with the Christian Social party in the Reichsrath and, stooping to conquer, accepted the Christian Social name in order to leaven the whole lump with the old conservative sentiment. Even the Eucharistic Congress held at Vienna in September 1912 bore witness to the predominance of dynastic over ecclesiastical feeling in Austria. The Emperor and the Imperial family associated themselves intimately with the Congress, which gradually became an apotheosis of Hapsburg Catholicism; and, during the Eucharistic procession that closed the proceedings, far greater homage was done by the people of Vienna to the Emperor and to the Imperial family than to the Host which the Emperor and the Heir-Apparent followed, sitting bareheaded in their State Coach, through the streets of the Capital.

The Austrian ideal would therefore seem to be far removed from Cavour's formula, "A free Church in a free State," which the Roman Curia has lately come to regard as a lesser evil than that of a subservient Church in an omnipotent State. When Joseph II. claimed to have established the "freedom of the Church," he meant the freedom of the

Church from Rome. He severed, indeed, all regular communication between the Austrian episcopate and the Pope, and, while proclaiming religious toleration and removing many of the disabilities previously imposed on Protestants and Jews, he placed the Roman Catholic clergy under a system of State control that set an indelible mark upon them. No definite solution has ever been found nor will, perhaps, ever be found for the problem of regulating the relationship between the Roman Church and the political authorities of the countries in which it works; but, of all possible relationships, the worst is that which makes of the clergy the spiritual gendarmes of the State. A cultured and philosophical Austrian statesman, profoundly religious in temperament, used to argue that the Lutheran Reformation had vitiated the whole position of the Church by inspiring her with such fear of destruction that, in order to save what could yet be saved, she sold her soul to Temporal Powers. Whereas, prior to the Reformation, the Church was never entirely subjugated by the Emperors and Kings with whom she was now at variance and now in alliance, and was always in a position to fulfil, well or ill, her mission of protecting the weak and the lowly against the tyranny of feudal monarchs and lords, she became, after the Reformation, the handmaid of Emperors and Kings on condition that they should lend her their aid in extirpating heresy. Since then she has too often appeared to be the ally of the oppressor against the oppressed, and to care less for the saving of souls by the power of the Gospel than for the crushing of heresy by the power of the State. As far as Austria and Spain are concerned this theory holds good. The Jesuits, who were the apostles of the Counter-Reformation, strove successfully to inspire and control the actions of fanatical monarchs, careless whether in so doing they inflicted suffering and misery upon millions of human beings. Despite their many admirable qualities and exemplary discipline, the Jesuits, who, in this as in other respects, bear a strong mental resemblance to the Jews, seem incapable of understanding that, beyond a certain point, the friction engendered by aggressive action must not only check their advance, but end by creating a resistance which is apt to develop into violent reaction. Their spirit of domination provokes revolt, their casuistical methods tend to produce scepticism even among their adepts, and the overweening confidence that comes of initial success and of faith in their own superiority produces a short-sightedness fatal to the most carefully laid plans. To speak of the Jesuits *en bloc* is to court the reproach of uncritical generalization. There are numerous varieties of Jesuit, each entrusted with some special work, and appearing rarely to justify the accusations frequently directed against the Company of Jesus as a whole. Many Jesuits whose exemplary lives and earnest faith attract to or retain within the Roman fold souls that would otherwise look in vain for a spiritual refuge, are themselves unaware of the policy of the Order to which they belong and of the principles on which it is based. Nothing is more tragic than when such Jesuits awaken to the veritable situation and are confronted with the alternatives of suffering in silence or of severing themselves from the body to which they had hoped to devote their lives. One such wrote to the present writer shortly after making his choice : " I had come to the conclusion and had presented it to the General (of the Jesuits) that ' Jesuitism ' summed up all the maladies from which the Roman Church is slowly dying—Jesuitism in the Society of Jesus and outside it ; for it stands for a set of principles rather than for the Society which is specially devoted to their propagation." In Austria it is a fact that the personal moral standard and the individual efficiency of Jesuits are considerably higher than those of the members of other religious orders, and it is, to say the least, a singular circumstance that the Jesuits and Redemptorists in Austria, unlike the members of other Orders, are not as a rule Austrian subjects, but natives of the Rhine Provinces, Alsace-Lorraine, or Bavaria. They would therefore be unhampered by any patriotic or dynastic loyalty, even had not the training to

which they are subjected removed from their minds the
sentiment of patriotism or, at least, substituted for it the
feeling, *Ubi Ecclesia ibi Patria.* They are, in a special sense,
the missionaries of Rome and the apostles of Ultramontanism;
that is to say, of the subordination of local patriotic considerations to the dictates of the Pope who, in his turn, is
usually subject to the influence of the Regular Clergy, and
more often than not to that of the Jesuits. In Austria,
Jesuit influence has been steadily directed towards the propagation of the Ultramontane spirit. Two of the best
educational institutions—Kalksburg and Feldkirch—are in
their hands. Their pupils are invariably polished, well-
mannered youths whose natural aptitudes have been developed in " desirable " directions, and who are, as a rule,
capable of filling with distinction any post to which they
may be appointed—but incapable of taking any independent
decision on matters of moment. Jesuit education tends to
develop talent, not character ; to fashion efficient and un-
obtrusive instruments, not autonomous individualities ; the
young men trained are never lost sight of, and, so long
as they remain obedient and useful, enjoy protection and
rapid advancement. By these means Jesuit influence in
State affairs is rendered far greater than it appears to be on
the surface, and is, in fact, comparable only to the surreptitious influence exercised by the Jews. A French historian
whose theoretical knowledge of Europe is incomparable
declared not long since that " l'Autriche est entièrement
gâtée, d'abord par les Jesuites, ensuite par des Juifs."
Whether Austria is in reality " totally spoiled " is a very
open question ; but, could the learned historian obtain closer
experience of Austrian affairs, he might indeed see the Jesuit
and the Jewish influences apparently paramount, now opposing, now supplementing, but always comprehending each
other in virtue of a singular psychological affinity. Both
are supremely teleological, or, to employ a less technical
expression, both have their eye constantly fixed on the
main chance," the immediate object, be it money, power,

or the two in conjunction. But neither can count upon lasting success unless they can control the State and, in the last resort, the mind of the reigning Monarch.

With few exceptions, Hapsburg monarchs have, however, tended to revolt against attempts to control their action. While munificent towards the clergy and apparently subservient to the Church, the Hapsburgs have, since the reign of Maximilian I., held fast to their right of controlling ecclesiastical appointments and enunciations. Even Ferdinand II., the creature and instrument of the Jesuits, was obliged in several instances to place his duties as monarch above his inclinations as a fanatic. Leopold I., Joseph I., and also Charles VI., utilized the *Placetum Regium* in a manner not always agreeable to Rome. In Maria Theresa the " State idea " gradually prevailed over obedience to Rome though she remained, in all private respects, a devoted daughter of the Church. The starting-point of the predominance of State over Church in Austria was the appearance of the veritably epoch-making book of " Justus Febronius " (Johann von Hontheim, Bishop-Suffragan of Treves), *Concerning the Ecclesiastical State and the Rightful Power of the Roman Pope.* In 1764 Kaunitz induced Maria Theresa and the Council of State to forbid the publication in Austria of Clement XIII.'s Bull in favour of the Jesuits, whose position was then threatened in France ; and in 1770 the Cardinal-Bishop of Constance reported to Clement XIV. that, in Austria, opposition to the prevailing Constitution and administration of the Church extended from the lowest classes up to the Ministers of State. Whether or not there be truth in the statements of some historians that Maria Theresa was finally turned against the Jesuits by the chance discovery that her confessions had been written out and sent to Rome by her Jesuit confessor, it is certain that her attention had been attracted from 1757 onwards to the insubordination of the Company of Jesus, its progressive monopolization of education, and its influence over the secular clergy. The Jesuits had, moreover, bitter enemies in the Benedictines and, among the younger orders, in the Piarists, no less than in the Freemasons whose secret influence began to make itself felt. Therefore when in 1773 Pope Ganganelli (Clement XIV.) suppressed the Jesuits, the Austrian Government lost no time in sanctioning the publication of the Papal decree. The Archbishop of Vienna, Migazzi, informed the Viennese Jesuits of their suppression in the presence of an Imperial commissioner and, in the following year, the Jesuit property was seized. A militant "Apology" for the Jesuits, published in Hungary, was burned. The blow thus struck at the Company of Jesus was heavy. In Hungary alone it possessed twenty-three colleges and residences while in Vienna it had six institutes apart from its control of the University. But it was the less able to withstand the blow in that it had gradually become an intolerant, arrogant organization as devoid of mental elasticity as of spiritual earnestness and caring only to maintain its own domination and the outward form of respect for the Church.

Before the Jesuits could return to Austria under the Emperor Francis and begin again the work of extending their influence during the era of the Holy Alliance, the ecclesiastical and administrative reforms of Joseph II. had radically changed the internal conditions of the Monarchy. Joseph's Toleration Edict of 1781 and his further edicts of 1784–85 had curtailed the power of the Church, cut off the Bishops from Rome and restricted their authority over their sees and their clergy. More than six hundred religious houses had been dissolved and the number of monks reduced to about two thousand. The Religious Orders had been placed under strict surveillance, remittances of money to Rome had been forbidden and no Austrian was allowed to study at the German College in Rome. The *Placetum Regium* was vigorously enforced and the Papal Bulls *In Coena Domini* and *Unigenitus*, defining the prerogatives of the Holy See, were not allowed to be published in Austria or taught. With the revenue of the ecclesiastical property that had been seized Joseph formed a *Religionsfonds* for the maintenance of the clergy. This fund still contributes nearly 9 per cent to ecclesiastical revenue in Austria. Like his administrative reforms, the ecclesiastical reforms of Joseph survived him and remained in many respects unchanged till after the Revolution of 1848.

Few institutions in modern Austria can be understood without reference 'at once to the reign of Joseph II. and to the Revolution of 1848. The effect of the Revolution upon the not illiberal mind of Francis Joseph, who ascended the throne on December 2, 1848, has never been quite obliterated ; and the reaction against the influences that were believed to have caused the Revolution or, at least, to have failed to prevent it, was largely a conscious reaction against " Josephinism." In no sphere was this reaction so successful as in ecclesiastical affairs. The view was propagated, and was strongly held by some members of the Imperial family, that, if the Church as well as the Army, the Police and the Bureaucracy had failed to avert the Revolution, it was mainly because religion had been made for seventy years an instrument of Government and had, in consequence, lost its hold upon the people. This view, encouraged by Jesuit and other Ultramontane influences, found acceptance also with the Austrian Minister, Count Leo Thun, who, with the help of the Archbishop of Vienna, Mgr. Rauscher, one of the Emperor's tutors, and with the acquiescence of Alexander Bach, concluded in 1855 a Concordat with Rome by which education, marriage and numerous other matters were placed under the control of the Church. The *Placetum Regium* was abolished, the Bishops were allowed free intercourse with Rome, their right was recognized to enforce their authority over the diocesan Clergy with the help of the State, and the Church was rendered, for the first time since the reign of Ferdinand II., the mistress of the whole body-politic. The Concordat proceeded from a conference of Bishops held at Vienna in May and June 1849 and was, in fact, virtually in force for some years before its actual conclusion. In 1852

the territory of the Monarchy was once more officially
opened to the Jesuits who had been allowed to return
surreptitiously and had been tolerated since the reign of
Francis.   Signed on August 18, 1855, the twenty-fifth
birthday of the Emperor Francis Joseph who, under the
influence of Mgr. Rauscher, had taken a considerable part in
its conclusion, the Concordat was hailed by the official press
as "the veritable Constitution of Austria and much better
than any other Constitution."   Abroad, and by the more
enlightened subjects of Francis Joseph, it was regarded as
an absolute capitulation of the State to the Church and, in
commenting upon it, the *Times* declared that "a Crown
worn under such conditions is not worth the metal of which
it is made."   The Austrian police strove to prevent any
echo of foreign opinion from reaching Austrian ears and
sought to propagate the official view that the Concordat was
"an act of exalted State wisdom."   But, in point of fact, the
Concordat, like so many apparent changes in Austria, affected
rather the form than the substance of things.   Bach, the
former revolutionary and now a deliberately Clerical minister,
was convinced that the conclusion of the Concordat was an
excellent police expedient which would give to the State a
spiritual gendarmerie, more numerous and more devoted than
that organized by Joseph II. and less discredited because
working with apparent freedom in the interests of religion
and of the Church.   The State doubtless incurred greater
risks under the Concordat than under the system of Joseph
II., but never felt itself to have lost its power again to
curtail the privileges of its spiritual police in case the clergy
should exceed the functions they were meant to perform.
The recognition by the State in the Concordat of the
"imprescriptible rights proceeding from the Divine origin of
the Church" formed merely a clause in a contract which—
despite its "perpetual" nature and its promulgation as a
Constitutional Law—the State, that is to say the Monarch,
felt free to denounce and discard at any moment as he had
discarded the various civil Constitutions of 1848–49.

Thus even at the moment of its apparent omnipotence, the Church in Austria never ceased to be the handmaid of the Crown. The Vatican which may have deluded itself into believing that it had acquired complete control of Austrian affairs was rudely undeceived when, twelve years later, on the establishment of the Dual System in 1867, the German Liberal party gained ascendency and destroyed one by one the provisions of the Concordat. On July 30, 1870, the Emperor addressed to his Chancellor, Count Beust, a rescript declaring that the dogma of Papal Infallibility had destroyed the Concordat since the Infallible Head of the Church could not be bound by a contract. Four years later this ordinance was supplemented by laws formally annulling the Concordat, regulating ecclesiastical autonomy and determining the limits beyond which ecclesiastical interference would be an encroachment upon the inviolable rights of the State. Not until the later 'nineties did the Church begin to recover the ground it thus lost. The " Los von Rom," or rather " Los von Habsburg " movement which was organized among the Pan-Germans and Liberal Germans of Austria as a protest against Badeni's ordinances placing the Czech on a footing of equality with the German language in Bohemia, led to the formation of clerical societies, notably the Societies of St. Boniface and St. Raphael, to combat anti-Catholic and anti-Hapsburg tendencies and to support a German race-movement on Catholic lines. The Heir-Presumptive, Archduke Francis Ferdinand, accepted the protectorship of a Catholic *Schulverein* or Schools Association ; Dr. Lueger and his Christian Social followers attacked the preponderance of anti-Clerical and Jewish influence in the Universities ; and subsequently the *Piusverein* was founded to support the Catholic anti-Jewish press, several of whose organs gradually acquired considerable circulation and influence.

But here again, it was evident that the Church was fulfilling rather the functions of voluntary police in the interest of the dynasty than ecclesiastical functions proper. The

" Los von Rom " peril having been warded off, the Clerical
organizations engaged in a violent and sometimes thoroughly
unscrupulous campaign against Social Democracy whose
progress had inspired uneasiness in the highest quarters.
The greatest achievement of these organizations was undoubtedly the arrangement of the Eucharist Congress
at Vienna in September 1912, which was rendered an
apotheosis for the Emperor and the Imperial family. Those
foreign Churchmen who saw only the enthusiastic devotion
of masses of Hapsburg subjects to the Dynasty under the
ægis of the Church departed, as it was intended they should
depart, with the impression that in the Hapsburg Monarchy
the Church lives and thrives under the best of conceivable
conditions ; but foreign priests and prelates who knew more
of the workaday life of Austria and of the true position of
the Church, shook their heads sadly at the thought that
religious organizations had once more been utilized to promote the mundane ends of an ancient dynasty which keeps
the Church in leash. In few countries has the Church so
little grip upon the daily lives of the people as in Austria-
Hungary. The condition of the clergy itself in many
provinces would be considered scandalous had it not come
to be regarded as normal. The system of Joseph II. which
tended to transform the clergy into a body of civil servants,
and the enormous revenues still enjoyed by many bishops,
archbishops and religious houses, have combined to produce a type of ecclesiastic bent rather on securing lucrative
appointments than on fulfilling a spiritual vocation—a type
not unlike that which existed throughout Central Europe in
the fourteenth and fifteenth centuries. Laxity of morals is
widespread. Practically only the Jesuits and the Redemptorists are above any general reproach on this score, but the
Augustinian Canons of Klosterneuburg, St. Florian and
Vorau ; the Cistercians of Heiligenkreuz, Lilienfeld and other
monasteries, the Premonstratensians of Tepl and Wilten ;
the Benedictines of Melk, Kremsmünster and Admont ; the
teaching order of the Piarists and the Barnabites are all, in

greater or less degree, open to well-founded suspicion of interpreting their vows with self-indulgent latitude. Moreover, a large number of parishes are served by members of these Orders—with results the reverse of edifying. The monasteries themselves remain principally in the hands of elderly monks whose lives are rather those of "holy friars" in the sense of the old English song, than monastic in the veritable sense of the term. If the influence of the clergy upon the morals of a people can be tested by the illegitimate birth-rate—a test not invariably reliable—it would show the influence of the Austrian clergy to be extremely defective. In cities like Vienna it is estimated to be 20 per cent, in thoroughly Clerical centres like Brixen in the Tyrol it is so high as to shock foreign ecclesiastical visitors, and in Carinthia it is 41 per cent. In Croatia and in some parts of Hungary the clergy seem to consider the vow of celibacy to be alone valid. But, at the same time, outward respect for religion is strong, men almost invariably raise their hats and women cross themselves on passing a Church, and when, some years ago, a petition in favour of divorce obtained 70,000 signatures, the clergy had no difficulty in presenting a counter petition with 4,500,000 signatures.

The supreme test of the vitality of a religious organization—that of being thrown entirely on its own resources and of being obliged to hold its own or conquer new ground by the power of its doctrine without the support or despite the hostility of the civil authorities—is unlikely to be applied to the Church in Austria. Despite admirable work done here and there by some categories of the clergy, notably the parish priests in congested urban and in sparsely populated mountain districts, the Church seems likely to remain what it has been for centuries—an institution fulfilling semi-political functions and, in many respects, subordinating its evangelical mission to the maintenance of its privileges ; enjoying fat revenues (the Archbishop of Olmütz, for instance, has an income of £60,000 a year and some Hungarian Sees are equally well endowed) and serving at best to counteract the disintegrating tendencies of Jewish and pseudo-Liberal elements. It, like the Army, the Bureaucracy and the Police, to which in many respects it is allied and akin, works as an instrument of the State and an appendix of the Dynasty.

CHAPTER III

THE title of this chapter should be understood in its broadest sense. There is, in reality, no Austrian, Hungarian or Austro-Hungarian "people." There are the peoples that inhabit the Monarchy, Hapsburg peoples, but no Hapsburg people. Whenever the Monarch addresses his subjects collectively, as on his accession or on the outbreak of war or in connexion with some festival or bereavement, the form of address is always " To my Peoples." In a sense there is nevertheless a " people " in the Monarchy. It consists of the governed as distinct from the apparatus of government, the administered as distinguished from the administration. It is supposed to be represented in Parliament, Diets and Municipal Councils, and to possess a means of utterance in the public press. But the press is largely an instrument of Government and is far more careful of its official connexions than of its duty to the people ; while the functions veritably discharged by Parliament differ strangely from those laid down by Constitutional Law and defined in treatises on popular representation. In Austria, at least, Parliament is an immense club where representatives of all nationalities meet, jostle and sometimes make acquaintance with each other. In the work of committees and commissions, party conventicles and " national," i.e. racial associations, members of Parliament gain a practical consciousness that Austria is a strange medley of peoples under one dynastic head and an all-powerful bureaucracy; and, despite the particularist standpoints and individual interests frequently thrust into prominence, they gradually acquire a feeling of *Zusammengehörigkeit* or "belonging together." In Parliament, the provincial and racial views of Czechs and Germans from Bohemia, Germans from the Alpine lands, Slovenes from Carniola, Croats or Italians from Istria, Rumanes from the Bukowina, Poles or Ruthenes from Galicia and Slovaks from Moravia, lose something of their angularity in contact with the mass of their fellow-deputies. Parliament, in this sense, is an institute for political education.

In another sense it is an institute for political corruption. The Government, composed of officials appointed by the Emperor, purchases majorities by concessions to the interests which parties represent or which individual party leaders wish to further. Railways, canals, bridges, tobacco licences for constituents, government appointments for *protégés*, and a hundred other objects of local or individual solicitude, form the object of the *Kuhhandel*,[1] constantly carried on between an Austrian Cabinet and the members not only of its majority but also of the opposition. The opposition of to-day may form part of the majority of to-morrow and, in stormy places like the Austrian Chamber, it is always well to cast an anchor to windward. The Government thus corrupts the political consciences, such as they are, of members of Parliament; and the latter, profiting by instruction, hasten, both as individuals and as parties, to extort political blackmail from the Government and the permanent officials. Apologists of the Austrian bureaucracy ascribe many of its shortcomings to the constant interference of members of Parliament with the regular work of administration; and defenders of parliamentarism in its purity, ascribe many of the defects of Austrian parliamentarism to official intrigue and to the little favours habitually bestowed by the Government upon the "well-disposed." In any case, the present system is a circle all the more vicious because there

---

[1] Literally, "cow-dealing."

are no strong traditions to keep officials and deputies on the hither side of the line beyond which complaisance becomes complicity.

Parliament, nevertheless, justifies its existence by providing an outlet for feelings which might otherwise remain pent up and potentially explosive. Every Austrian race is able to bring its desires and grievances to public notice through the parliamentary channel. The public prosecutor, the police and the bureaucracy are powerless to prevent such utterances which, having been made under parliamentary privilege, may be reproduced by the press from the official report of parliamentary proceedings without danger of confiscation or prosecution. The utility of this safeguard is unquestionable. A public prosecutor, inspired by zeal for his conception of public welfare or anxious to improve by subserviency towards his superiors his chances of promotion to a judgeship, may order the confiscation of a journal whose opinions or allegations appear to him obnoxious. The confiscation is rarely followed by a prosecution. The object of inflicting pecuniary loss upon the journal is attained without the troublesome procedure and the chances of discredit that would be involved in a public trial. If, however, the confiscated journal has the ear of a member of Parliament, it is able to secure privilege by persuading him to embody the confiscated matter in a parliamentary interpellation. The journal is then able to reproduce its confiscated article from the parliamentary reports and to wave it under the nose of the public prosecutor and the police. One of the most striking instances of this procedure was furnished some years ago by the confiscation of the remarkable booklet *Wien*, by Hermann Bahr, an Austrian-German writer too independently patriotic to find favour in the eyes of a public prosecutor. A well-known deputy promptly interpellated the Government upon the confiscation and read aloud to the Chamber the whole of the confiscated matter. Bahr was consequently able to issue another edition of his booklet *minus* the confiscated chapter but *plus* the text of the interpellation. In a country where officials regard themselves less as the guardians of popular rights than as the executive instruments of State or dynastic authority, such a check upon petty tyranny is wholesome.

Nevertheless the value of Parliament for the defence of public interests and liberties is often limited by the subtle control which the Government and its agents exercise over parties and individual members. A deputy who acquires undesirable prominence as a critic of official acts or whose conduct the "well-disposed" are able to represent as "unpatriotic," is apt to find his opportunities for public usefulness circumscribed in every quarter within the reach of the Government's long arm. The larger journals, most of which are accessible to "influence," fail to report his speeches. Less able men are preferred to him when parliamentary committees have to be selected ; his own party is made to feel that the Government will be well pleased if he is kept in the background ; and on important occasions, as during the choice of party nominees for the Delegations, direct official pressure or indirect official intrigue may be employed to exclude him. In no country are members of Parliament invariably men of moral courage. In Austria the percentage of heroes is perhaps lower than elsewhere, not necessarily because Austrian politicians are peculiarly deficient in moral stamina, but because — with the exception of some of the Slav races — their constituents and the public at large are disinclined long to support "unpopular" deputies. The Austrian public is, moreover, prone to suspect that politicians who "fly in the face of Providence" are merely trying to advertise themselves and to screw up the political price that must eventually be paid for their silence or support.

To all these rules there are exceptions, the most notable during recent years having been that of Dr. Lueger who was forced upon the Emperor as Burgomaster of Vienna by a powerful and well-organized popular movement after the Emperor had repeatedly declined to sanction his election.

Lueger's strength lay in his ability to appeal to the rank and file of his fellow-citizens and in their well-founded conviction that he was personally disinterested. The Social Democratic party has also produced and borne aloft men upon whom the Court and official circles frowned ; though it became clear, during the Universal Suffrage movement of 1905–7, that the Court and the Government are willing to accept as allies any party or person that may serve, for the time being, dynastic ends. Austria is essentially a land of compromise where ideals are reserved for party programmes and public declarations but where the working principle is so to arrange matters that, in the words of the Italian proverb, both the goats and the cabbages may be saved. If, as a result, the goats are only half fed and the cabbage leaves nibbled, the Government has no cause for dissatisfaction. Equilibrium of discontent often seems to be its object. It knows that, among the discontented, jealousy will thrive, and that when claims for further concessions are advanced they can be partly met by pointing out that rival claimants are no better off. There is much truth in the contention that Austrian statecraft has brought matters to so fine a point that each race or party accepts, as partial consolation for its own unfulfilled desires, the consideration that the plight of its rivals is no better or still worse.

It follows that no greater misdemeanour can be committed by a political leader than to join together those whom the State has elected to keep asunder. When in October 1905 the Serbs and Croats of Dalmatia, Croatia and Slavonia formed a Coalition and proceeded, on the basis of a Resolution adopted in conference at Fiume, to make an alliance with the Hungarian Opposition then in conflict with the Crown, the wrath and dismay of government circles at Vienna and Budapest were extreme. Had it not been for decades the aim of " Vienna " to keep Serbs and Croats apart and at the same time to maintain the feud between Hungary and the Southern Slavs by allowing the Magyars to oppress and exploit Croatia-Slavonia ?

Much that seems mysterious in the Annexation Crisis of 1908–9, including the false documents exposed during the Friedjung trial, becomes explicable in the light of "Viennese" resentment towards the authors of the Fiume Resolution ; and the animosity against M. Supilo, chief author of the Resolution, who was suspected of being a Croatian Kossuth *in posse*, proceeded from the well-founded belief that he had been the promoter of Serbo-Croatian brotherhood. "Brotherhood" and, indeed, any generous impulse not sanctioned and approved of by "the authorities," is apt to be regarded with suspicion in Austria-Hungary. The State is, *ex hypothesi*, the best judge of what is good for the peoples that exist in order to be governed by it ; and as long as they recognize that their only hope of welfare lies in the State, their lot is tolerable. But when they revolt or oppose the State they may fare badly unless they are strong or clever enough to embarrass it by their action and to convince it that the safest course is to pay blackmail with a good grace under the cloak of some "face-saving" formula. An Austrian people need never despair as long as it can find means, in case of need, to frighten the Government. The impotent, or those for whom the State has "no use," are alone in a hopeless position. The case of the Italians of Dalmatia is eloquent of this truth. As long as Austria held her Italian provinces and needed home-grown officials of Italian culture to govern them, the Italians of Dalmatia were pampered and petted. The authorities were always on their side, education was placed under their control, and their economic interests were taken into account. But after the loss of Lombardy in 1859 and of Venetia in 1866, the demand for Italian officials decreased and with it the "usefulness" of the Italian element. The authorities discovered that the Italians in Dalmatia formed an insignificant proportion (little more than 3 per cent) of an overwhelmingly Slav population—a population then pitifully ignorant, uncultured and backward in every respect. It was therefore decided to let this population loose upon the highly civilized minority, and the bitter struggle between Slavs and Italians began, the Government supporting and encouraging the Slavs and at the same time doing its utmost to foment discord between them and the Italians. Unfortunately the Italians, proud of their heritage of Venetian culture, failed to perceive until too late whither the policy of the Government was tending. The Slavs were leaderless save for a handful of fanatical priests and half-educated peasants. Had the Italians, who originally possessed a monopoly of culture, aided Slav development instead of opposing it, they might have become the natural leaders of a bilingual province and, by uniting with the Slavs, have compelled the Government to do something for Dalmatia as a whole. But they elected to play the Government's game and were, little by little, driven from their favoured position. Commune after commune fell into Slav hands until only Zara, the capital, remained under Italian control. In their bitterness of heart the Italians cast longing eyes across the Adriatic and invoked the moral support of Italy—conduct which enabled the Austrian authorities to denounce them as "unpatriotic," and to take measures against the danger of "Irredentism." At last a sense of reality seems to be dawning in the minds of the more perspicacious Dalmatian Italians, some of whom now see that their only hope lies in an understanding with the Slavs whose interest it is to join the Italians in opposing the present efforts of the Government to Germanize the Austrian Adriatic.

The case of Trieste offers another instance of the need for co-operation between Slavs and Italians. Save to the South and along the Istrian coast the territory around Trieste is entirely Slav. On the hills above the city nothing but Slovene is to be heard. The struggle between the Italian municipality and the Slav organizations has been fierce and has, as in Dalmatia, facilitated the penetration of German and Germanizing agencies. Until recently the Triestine Italians had always a supreme resource whenever they wished to extort concessions from the central Government. An explosion of " Irredentist" sentiment or the hoisting of the Italian tricolor upon some municipal building by stealth sufficed seriously to frighten the authorities and to procure for the city—after the inevitable prelude of threats and punishments—a douceur in the form of a new wharf or some other material concession. Now, however, the authorities are steadily making war on the Italian element. Subjects of the Kingdom of Italy are being expelled one by one, as many as ninety expulsions taking place in a month. Italian applications for Austrian citizenship are almost invariably refused, even when the applicants are natives of Trieste. The Government has, moreover, steadily declined to sanction the establishment of an Italian Law School at Trieste. The School was formerly lodged at Innsbruck, but was in 1904 looted and wrecked by the German populace, led by Pan-German deputies. Any Government with a sense of equity would have chastized the wreckers and have given satisfaction to the Italians. Not so the Austrian Government. The Germans were powerful and in a position to embarrass it in a hundred ways. The Italians were weak and tending to grow weaker. Hence they were put off again and again, until, after years of agitation, they secured a promise that the Italian Law School would be established at Vienna—a long day's railway journey from the nearest Italian centre, one of the most expensive cities in Europe, a city, moreover, thoroughly out of sympathy with Italian ideals. For which mercy Austrian-Italian youths and their families are expected to be grateful !

Ab uno disce omnes. The Czechs, whose power of blackmailing the Government is considerable, have hitherto failed to obtain a second university at Brünn, the capital of Moravia, although the Czech University at Prague is crowded to overflowing. The Germans, who have universities at Vienna, Innsbruck, Prague and Graz, block the way. The Ruthenes or Little Russians, of whom there are nearly four million in Austria and more than half a million in

Hungary, found no hearing for their demand for a separate Ruthene University at Lemberg, until it appeared to the Government that the university might become a powerful centre of attraction for the 25,000,000 Ruthenes or Little Russians of Russia, and might serve to spread Austrian and Catholic influence among them. Fear was, as usual, the motive of the change. Russian agitators had begun in Eastern Galicia and the Bukovina a campaign of propaganda in favour of the conversion to Orthodoxy of the Ruthenes belonging to the Greek United Church. The campaign appears to have been in part a response to the activity of the Greek United Archbishop of Lemberg, Mgr. Count Szeptycki, who was suspected of working with the object of bringing the Little Russians more and more under Austrian and Roman control. The Russian reply to the Austrian movement caused alarm and led to the adoption of repressive measures—which Russians denounced as political persecution on the part of the Austro-Polish authorities in Galicia and of the Austrian authorities in the Bukovina. Under the influence of the alarm the Austrian Government suddenly changed its bearing towards the demand for a separate Ruthene University at Lemberg and the Emperor was induced to favour the idea and to put pressure upon the Poles who had, until then, opposed it vigorously. A crisis ensued in which all the personal influence of the Emperor had to be employed to tranquillize the Poles. At last the idea of the Ruthene University was accepted "in principle," that is to say it was shelved pending further developments. The nature of these developments will probably depend upon the political relationship between Austria-Hungary and Russia.[1] If the relationship improves, the Ruthenes may have to wait many a long year for their University because the University would be conceived not only as a means of spreading higher education among the Ruthenes but as the instrument of an aggressive "cultural" policy against Russia. The University would not be "Ruthene" or "Little Russian" but "Ukraine,"

[1] Cf. pp. 288-292.

that is to say it would represent the tendency to Austrianize and Catholicize the Little Russians on both sides of the border and to detach the Little Russian mass from its Great Russian allegiance. If, on the contrary, Austro-Russian relations improve, this aggressive Austrian policy will be likely to remain in abeyance, and the Ruthenes or Little Russians of Austria may have to content themselves with the satisfaction of a small fragment of their demands—unless Russia turns the tables on Austria by establishing a Little Russian University at Kieff.

It will thus be seen that university questions in Austria, of which the outer world hears so much at moments of parliamentary crisis, are by no means simple questions of promoting or refusing to promote the culture and enlightenment of given races. The Government tends to regard them primarily from the standpoint of political utility, and secondarily, perhaps, from the standpoint of financial outlay. The races and parties which demand universities regard them also mainly from political standpoints. Apart from the circumstance that the concession of a university by the Government represents a marked political success for the party which manages to extort it, there is always the underlying consideration that a university is a fresh key to open the door leading to bureaucratic appointments and consequently to participation in the government of the State. The higher officials require a university degree, usually a Law degree. Latterly, technical degrees have been recognized as qualifications for certain branches of the civil service. But a Law degree is the principal passport into the bureaucracy. Consequently the law schools of Austrian Universities are crowded to overflowing, and young " Doctors of Law " are turned out annually by the thousand. Of these only a small proportion elect to follow the legal profession. The majority aspire to Government appointments ; and when no vacancies exist, political pressure is often used by parties and individual politicians to obtain the creation of fresh offices. The results are remarkable. In some of the State Railway administrations "jurists," as these Doctors of Law are styled, do work which in private administrations would be left to office boys or typewriting clerks.   In certain State and Provincial departments the overcrowding by jurists is a crying evil.   It has been previously mentioned [1] that in the Lord Lieutenancy of Lower Austria alone there were recently nearly two hundred of them.   In Bohemia, Galicia, Moravia and other provinces matters are little better.   In the Ministry of the Interior and even in the Ministries of Finance "jurists" swarm.   It is comprehensible that the Government should therefore resist the tendency towards the creation of new Universities with new Law Schools, which would produce new batches of jurists devoid of all practical experience or training. A remedy for the evil is hard to descry, unless some courageous Government suspends for a term of years the appointment of fresh officials, and, by regulating the conditions of future employment, strives to correct the assumption, general among the peoples of Austria, that the State is able to confer upon private citizens dignity and rank superior to those attainable by individual effort.   The root of the evil lies naturally in the conception that the State is something higher than the people and that private persons, in so far as they are not nobles, are necessarily inferior to government servants.   But the State itself is unwilling to undermine this idea lest it lay the axe at the root of its own authority. The growth of trade and industry, now largely in Jewish hands, and the rise of a powerful middle class might help to break through the vicious circle.   But at present the middle class feels itself to be dependent on the State on which it bases its hopes of attaining higher social rank.   It supplies the Army with officers, the State Departments with officials and the universities with professors.   To hope for relief from this quarter seems therefore to be vain.

The peasant class, which is the backbone of Austria and especially of Hungary, stands by itself and exercises little direct influence upon the State or the other elements of the

[1] P. 89.

community. Its position varies considerably from province to province. Except for the broad circumstance that the German peasants of Lower and Upper Austria, the mountaineers of the Tyrol, the Polish and Little Russian peasants of Galicia, the Czech and Slovak peasants of Bohemia, Moravia and North-Eastern Hungary, not to mention the sturdy Magyar peasants of the Hungarian Lowland, are all engaged in agricultural pursuits, there is between them no common bond or special sympathy. A monograph on each province and race would be requisite to portray their various characteristics or to describe their conditions of life. Politically, they enter only into the calculations of the State as the electors who return Agrarian or Clerical deputies to Parliament ; fiscally, they come into consideration as taxpayers ; from the military point of view they are important as supplying the bulk of the recruits for the army ; socially, they are stationary except in so far as they may send their sons into the Church or seek to fit them by higher education for bureaucratic appointments. The peasantry is not collectively articulate, nor is its political horizon such as to fit it to play an important political part.

The aristocracy, on the contrary, still exercises an influence disproportionate to the duties it discharges. By " aristocracy " the great nobles are meant, some of whom stand in a special relationship to the throne and enjoy special privileges. Others wield immense influence by reason of their vast landed estates and their large revenues which would bear comparison with those of the wealthiest London landlords and of all save the very wealthiest American milliardaires. Their revenues are derived partly from their rent-rolls, partly from the direct management of their estates and partly from trade. The name of many a princely house is to be seen above milk-shops, as indicating that the produce sold is derived from their dairies. Others are engaged in forestry and the timber trade, others in the production of coal, others again in horse-breeding, while not a few have large inland fisheries. The best side of the Austrian noble is his care for the development of his estates. As a result he is usually a healthy, open-air being, not over-burdened with intellect nor troubled with fastidious tastes save in regard to music and sport, but a "good fellow," without over-weening pride though conscious of his privileged position and rank. He is, as a rule, related in some degree to the rest of his caste. The "first society" of Austria is a "society of cousins," a society, that is to say, interested mainly in its own affairs and attributing to them greater importance than to public affairs in general. Such knowledge of the outside world as its members may possess has usually been acquired by travel and hearsay rather than by study. Big-game shooting or interest in other forms of sport frequently leads them far afield and adds knowledge and experience to their innate courtesy. But with few exceptions the Austrian and particularly the Austrian-German nobleman remains a decorative rather than a useful member of society. Hungarian and, to some extent, Polish and Bohemian noblemen belong to a different category. Their interest in public affairs is often keen and their action constant. The Austrian-German nobleman knows, however, that it will be difficult for him to play a leading part in politics, and is inclined therefore to restrict his political activity to occasional attendance at the sittings of the Upper Chamber or of the Delegations. In the Army he has long ceased to aspire to the most responsible commands. Diplomacy offers him a larger field for activity ; though the gibe of a Prussian diplomatist, that in most Austro-Hungarian Embassies and Legations is to be found an aristocrat with good manners and few brains to do the honours, while behind a screen in the Chancery sits the son of a baptized Jew who does the work, is more malicious than accurate. The diplomatic service, even in its higher grades, is by no means an aristocratic monopoly. If it be not exactly *une carrière ouverte aux talents*, there are enough instances in the diplomatic history of the Monarchy to prove that non-aristocratic birth is by no means an insuperable obstacle to advancement.

The careers of the late Counts Hübner and Calice and of some ambassadors and retired ambassadors still living are cases in point. The Hapsburg dynasty has often seemed to prefer servants of lower to those of higher extraction, and has at times exhibited positive distrust of the independent spirit which great nobles are apt to display. True, the Emperor Francis Joseph has usually reserved the chief Court appointments for scions of great houses, though, here again, the most confidential and influential positions about the person of the Monarch have frequently been held by men of comparatively low birth. It is in the bureaucracy that noblemen of minor fortune and sometimes those of wealth find their principal opportunity of serving the State. The annual private revenues of Count Andrew Potocki, the late Lord Lieutenant of Galicia, who was assassinated some years since by a Ruthene student, could be counted by hundreds of thousands of pounds. He spent, nevertheless, the greater part of his maturer years in assiduous administrative work. The present Lord Lieutenants of two important provinces hold princely rank while the title of Count is by no means uncommon among their colleagues and subordinates. Yet the general rule holds good that the Austrian aristocracy takes less part in public affairs than the aristocracy of England or Prussia. Shooting seems often to be its chief object in life, and many a nobleman laughingly recognizes the symbolical truth of an anecdote told of a Count Czernin who, when on the point of death, was heard by his faithful servant to mutter, " And when the Lord inquires of me, 'What hast thou done with thy life?' I must answer 'Oh! Lord. I have shot hares, shot hares, shot hares.' It is really very little." But, as a *vis inertiae*, the influence of the aristocracy is great. The saying that the Englishman loves a lord is true also of the average Austrian. In theory, the days are past when it could be said that, in Austria, mankind begins with barons ; but though the title of baron is now, as often as not, an indication of Jewish descent, the social value of titles is still immense. The cabdriver or waiter well knows that there is no surer means of extracting a good tip from the ordinary citizen than to address him as " Count," and the shopkeeper never forgets to prefix the particle " *von* "—the indication of noble rank— to the names of his humblest customers. Servants constantly address very middle-class masters and mistresses as " Your Grace," and kiss their hands, in word and act, morning and evening. Snobbishness sometimes amounting to servility runs through the middle classes, whose chief ambition seems to be to resemble the nobility if not the aristocracy. In the old days, before the advent of motor-cars had detracted from the glory of the drive to the race-course, it was customary to have the chief avenue through the Prater heavily watered, with the result that carriages, *Fiakers*,[1] and their occupants were usually bespattered with mud on reaching their destina- tion. The faster the horses the thicker the mud and the greater the "smartness" of the bespattered. Cynics used to pretend that those who had ingloriously gone to the races in that tabooed conveyance, a one-horse cab, nicknamed " *Confortabel*," were wont carefully to besmirch themselves with mud before joining the crowd on the race-course—an alleged practice that caused a former French ambassador to exclaim, " Ici, on a tous les snobismes, même le snobisme de la boue ! "

A new and, in some respects, a healthier element has been introduced into Austrian public life by the rise of the working class under the guidance of the Social Democratic party. The movement itself is a generation old but it has only displayed its force—and some of its weaknesses—since the introduction of universal suffrage in 1906–1907. Whereas the Christian Social party recruits its electors chiefly among the lower middle class, the clergy and, in some districts, the peasants, the Social Democratic or Labour movement is, as in Germany, mainly a movement of the industrial working class led by middle-class politicians, several of whom are Jews. The Austrian Socialist leader, Dr. Victor Adler, is, as were Marx, Lassalle, and other prominent German Socialists, a Jew, but

---

[1] Two-horse broughams or victorias, now fast disappearing.

a Jew of the prophetic, self-sacrificing, zealous type that has so often saved the people of Israel from the reproach of worshipping solely the golden calf. His personal fortune, which was considerable, has been devoted largely to the needs of the party and especially to the maintenance of its central organ, the *Arbeiter Zeitung*. While maintaining, on party questions, the somewhat narrow standpoint of Marxist orthodoxy, the *Arbeiter Zeitung* frequently treats the larger political, social, and even diplomatic issues with a breadth of view and statesmanlike grasp that would honour any independent journal in Europe. At times, though not invariably, its columns are the only refuge of common sense and the only protection against the tide of semi-officialism and financial interestedness that pollutes the German press of Austria. Though its methods of party propaganda and of controversy are open to criticism and scarcely seem calculated to raise the moral and political standards of the working-class readers to whom they are supposed to appeal, the *Arbeiter Zeitung* is, on the whole and in comparison with the Socialist press of some other countries, an educative force, just as the Austrian Socialist movement has hitherto had an educative effect in view of the soullessness of the Church and of the absorption of the middle-class parties in petty racial or local interests. The broader questions of the ultimate effects of Socialism upon the populace of large cities like Vienna and Prague ; of its insistence upon the rights of the proletariate without any corresponding inculcation of a sense of duty, save the duty of loyalty to class and party ; and of its dogmatic attribution of all social evils to " Capitalism " and to the " Moloch of Militarism," have yet to be answered and will doubtless be answered in many a scene of turmoil and violence before Socialism and Capitalism are themselves merged in a higher synthesis by the irresistible march of economic and political development. The only standard by which detached observers can judge the ethical value of social and political movements is by the degree of sincerity that inspires them, the devotion

which they can command, and their power to place some
ideal higher than immediate self-interest before the eyes of
their adherents.   Every movement that can stand these
tests is respectable and deserving of sympathetic attention,
however much partisans of things as they are and advocates
of "vested interests" may feel bound to combat their professed objects and outward aspects.   The Austrian Socialist
movement has undoubtedly tended to raise the intellectual
level of the masses, to give the working-classes a keener
interest in public affairs, to overcome, though not with entire
success, the effects of racial rivalry, and to compel the
government to pay more heed to the welfare of wage-earners.
If it be objected that it has at the same time tended to
destroy the spirit of servility and even to undermine religious
and political reverence, the rejoinder must be that in a
country like Austria where the final abolition of serfdom
took place within the memory of living men and where
State and Church combine to prevent sturdy public life, the
development of capitalistic industry was bound to loosen the
hold of "the authorities" upon the masses of the people and
to be attended by consequences unwelcome to the partisans
of the moral and social *status quo ante libertatem.*

Ante libertatem?   The question how far the peoples
of Austria-Hungary are or can be "free," in the Anglo-
Saxon sense of the word, is one of the most interesting
issues in the Monarchy.   "Freedom" is, in Austria, con-
ditioned by the prerogatives of the all-encompassing State,
and resembles, in more than one respect, the freedom recognized by Scholastic doctrine to be the prerogative of
Christians.   The dictum of the American Constitution, that
man has "a natural right to life, liberty and the pursuit of
happiness," is as contradictory to the underlying principle of
the Austrian State as to the conceptions of the disciples
of Thomas Aquinas.   Just as Christians are presupposed
to be born in sin and their freedom to be strictly contingent
upon the performance of the primary duty of saving their
souls and of being, to this end, obedient children of the

Church whose Head holds the Keys of Death and Hell, so
Austrian liberty is contingent upon subservience to the
Supreme State conceived as an expression of the dynasty.
The Monarch is the fountain-head of all rights, and the rights
conceded from time to time by him to his subjects are, in
practice, circumscribed by the operation of laws, decrees
and ordinances in the framing of which the governed have
rarely a determining voice. But the feeling of liberty is
" subjective " ; and as long as restrictions imposed from above
are borne without discomfort, the degree of " objective " freedom is a matter of small concern to others. Birds hatched
in an aviary scarcely suffer from a sense of restriction ; and
the wire-netting may serve to keep marauders at a distance.
In the Hapsburg Monarchy the State has, in certain respects,
made good its claim to be the protector as well as the
warder of the public ; and though, in other respects, it
appears at times to be subservient to strong combinations
of private " interests," the balance of its action is perhaps
favourable to the general welfare of citizens. While it tacitly
and expressly allows " trusts " and " rings " to levy contributions upon the purchasing public in the form of higher
tariffs and higher prices than could be commanded in an
open market, it limits on the other hand the activity of
trusts and of all employers of labour, nay, even of individual
artisans, by a complicated Industrial Code that smacks at
once of the Middle Ages and of the Twenty-first Century.

The issues raised by State regulation of industrial and
commercial activity have been too often and too widely
discussed to need analysis here. In most civilized countries
the principle is now practically admitted that no form of
private activity is tolerable which exposes the community
at large to loss and detriment for the sake of assuring
advantages to small minorities. In Austria-Hungary this
principle has been applied not only to private trade and
industry but also to private finance, and its application has
been—from the Anglo-Saxon standpoint—all the healthier
and less dangerous, because it proceeded not from any pre-

conceived theory but from the practical necessity of remedying an actual and precluding a future evil.   Had the Austro-Hungarian Currency reformers who, in 1892, undertook the task of evolving order out of the monetary chaos of the Monarchy, been warned that the consequence of their efforts would be the establishment of the principle that private speculation in gold is inadmissible, and that, in a modern State, the trading public cannot be exposed to loss by the "arbitrage" operations of private bankers, they would have laughed the prediction to scorn.   They set themselves to establish an orthodox gold standard with free circulation of gold coin and perfect interchangeability between gold and notes.   They dethroned the old silver florin, so dear to "arbitrage" speculators,[1] and installed in its stead on a pedestal of gold a coin of half its value, the *Krone*, or Crown, worth 10d.   But they overlooked the fact that long familiarity with State notes under forced currency had accustomed the people to the use of paper money and had created so strong a prejudice against the use of gold coin that, whenever the Austro-Hungarian State Bank put gold into circulation, the coin was returned to it with unfailing regularity.   During the first ten years of this century, the State Bank issued nearly £84,000,000 of gold coin to the public.   Of this amount more than £74,000,000 speedily found its way back to the Bank.   A sum of less than £10,000,000 therefore represented the total gold hoarding of the 50,000,000 inhabitants of the Monarchy, and from this sum must be subtracted the amounts of Austro-Hungarian gold held by Austro-Hungarian and foreign bankers and money-changers, or melted down by goldsmiths and jewellers.   Probably not one in every thousand inhabitants of the Monarchy

---

[1] The constant fluctuations in the exchange rate of the silver florin (*Gulden*), formerly the standard coin of the Monarchy, was a source of immense profit to Jewish speculators in rates of exchange or "arbitrage" operators.   Many of the fluctuations were artificially provoked by these speculators who gambled with the currency of the country as with a private possession and exercised a disturbing influence upon the business and monetary relations of Austria-Hungary with other countries.

has a gold coin in his possession. Waiters, cashiers and shopkeepers are wont to apologize if shortness of paper money compels them to give gold as change for the larger denominations of notes. One effect of this preference for paper money has been to concentrate in the vaults of the State Bank almost the entire gold supply of the Monarchy. The Bank thus holds, as a rule, a gold reserve more than double that of the Issue Department of the Bank of England. Its paper circulation, which, by the terms of its charter, is only optionally convertible into gold, fluctuates between £90,000,000 and £100,000,000, and can be largely increased at the discretion of the Governors, subject to certain fiscal checks. Nevertheless its notes stand constantly within negligible distance of the mint par of exchange and, at times, even command a premium, while the Bank rate of discount shows an evenness inferior only to that of the Bank of France.

These results have been attained chiefly by what is known as the *Devisenpolitik* or Gold policy of the Bank, a policy based upon the immunity from gold drafts for the interior which the Bank enjoys by reason of its right to refuse specie payments in return for notes. As long as Austro-Hungarian Currency reformers believed their goal to be the establishment of an orthodox gold standard with complete interchangeability of gold and notes at home as well as abroad, they seemed blind to the positive advantages conferred upon the Bank by the public preference for paper money. Gradually, however, the Managers of the Bank came to perceive that they had a practical monopoly of the functions discharged in other countries by gold brokers and bill brokers. They understood that by opportune purchases and sales of foreign cheques and gold bills they could steady the market, and could, within the limits set by the balances of foreign payment, control both the movements of gold and the rates of exchange. They then took over the gold receipts of the Custom Houses and State Railways, and were commissioned to pay abroad the coupons of foreign investors in Austrian and Hungarian Stocks. They opened accounts with foreign

banks, and by drawing directly upon them, deprived
speculators of all chance of turning rates of exchange against
the Monarchy.   Emboldened by this success, the Bank
passed from what may be called a curative to a preventive
gold policy.   Having become the largest holder and broker
of gold bills, it began to dictate prices in such manner that
fluctuations of the foreign exchange rates round the mint-
par level became almost imperceptible.   Vienna, formerly
the home and high school of "arbitrage" speculation, gradually
lost her dubious pre-eminence.   Private bankers soon found
that their foreign speculative requirements were not complied
with and that this lucrative branch of their business was being
deliberately killed.   Not only did the Bank maintain the parity
of the exchanges by supplying legitimate demands for gold bills
at prices below the " outgoing specie point " but by refusing, in
certain cases, to supply gold, short bills or cash transfers at all,
even when the exchanges had reached or risen above the " outgoing specie point."   Intimate acquaintance with the market
enabled the Bank to distinguish between legitimate and speculative demands.   If doubt existed, applicants were called upon
to prove the legitimacy of their requirements.   Attempts to
circumvent the Bank's control were more than once punished
by the Bank which taught a severe lesson to speculators by
putting down the price of gold bills suddenly without apparent
cause.   Its object was naturally to prevent private financiers
from lending abroad more money than could well be spared.
The Bank thus laid down the important and almost revolutionary principle that it is not legitimate to lay upon the
whole trade and industry of a country the burden of a high
Bank rate of discount merely in order that private speculators
may profit.   In other words, it vindicated the truth which is
as yet ignored in England and only dimly perceived in
France, that the pecuniary resources of a country are a national
asset not to be left with impunity at the mercy of private
international financiers.   Though the peculiar circumstances
which enable the Austro-Hungarian Bank to maintain an
orthodox gold standard in dealing with foreign countries,

and an optionally convertible paper standard in its operations at home, may prevent the practice of the Bank from being readily imitated elsewhere, the principle on which the practice is based is so sound that it can hardly fail ultimately to affect the whole fabric of international finance.

It is strange that Austria-Hungary, geographically and, in a sense, psychologically the nearest European State to what has been called the "pre-economic" East, should have been the first to extend State control to a branch of private activity previously unregulated ; and should thus have taken a step towards the "post-economic" era which many students believe to be the unconscious goal of modern economic development. The era of individualism in trade and industry is fast passing away. There appears to be no reason why private finance and banking should escape the operation of a general economic law, though the fluidity of capital and the comparative intangibility of "irresponsible" liquid wealth may render those branches of business difficult to locate and to place under discipline. But the strong tendency of Capital towards agglomeration, as of trade and industry towards monopolistic organization, will assuredly facilitate in the long run the task of governments or communities that may deem it expedient to make financiers run in harness. The question as to the abstract desirability of progressive State regulation, or even of direct State management of enterprises hitherto individualized, has little positive importance. By the time an issue of this kind becomes ripe for practical treatment, a government, or the community it represents, has usually no choice save between two evils—the evil of the open or surreptitious control of the State by powerful economic corporations or the evil of restricting the economic activity of individuals. This subject has rarely been more luminously treated than by an English economist,[1] who, some twenty years since, drew an interesting parallel between the development of military organization and the probable development of capitalistic enterprise, and sustained the thesis that just

[1] J. A. Hobson, *The Evolution of Modern Capitalism.*

as national armies had succeeded to the old professional standing armies which had become at once insufficient for national defence and a political danger to the community, so national industries would probably succeed to private capitalistic undertakings. Such undertakings, he argued, would lose some degree of efficiency through bureaucratization, just as the modern soldier with his two or three years' training is less efficient than the professional mercenary of yore ; but he claimed that this loss of individual efficiency would be counterbalanced by greater political security and by setting free individual energies for activity in other and possibly higher spheres than those offered either by military or by industrial occupations. Whether this thesis be sound or the reverse, it is an unquestionable fact that in Austria-Hungary, quite apart from State control, the bureaucratization of financial and industrial undertakings is proceeding apace and that the large banks and the great manufacturing and commercial enterprises offer to-day fewer openings for individual talent than they offered twenty or even ten years since. Smaller firms tend, moreover, to seek the support of the larger Banks, and some industrial enterprises of respectable dimensions have of late been converted into mere dividend-earning departments of what were originally purely financial institutes. A few men of administrative talent find remunerative positions as business or technical managers of these amalgamated undertakings but the rank and file of business men are gradually drifting into the position of salaried officials in the employ of vast soulless machines over whose working they have no control. The restriction of average individual activity is thus already an incontestable fact without State interference. But the question of the relationship between the heads of such undertakings and the State remains open and requires careful consideration. This problem exists in its acutest form in the United States, where, however, the difficulty of defending the government and the public against the power of financial and industrial corporations under the control of wealthy individuals is aggravated by the loose-jointedness of American political institutions. In Austria-Hungary the difficulty lies rather in maintaining a line of demarcation between the industrial and financial bureaucracy and the bureaucracy of the State. A striking illustration of the nature of this difficulty is afforded by the tendency of high officials of the State to pass into the service of private and semi-private undertakings. Such officials inevitably retain their friendships and other connexions with their former colleagues, nay, it is possible that the very possession of such friendships and connexions may be regarded as increasing their potential value to private enterprises which have constant and confidential dealings with the State. The career of such an official is typical of what is possible in Austria, and indeed in Hungary. The son of an obscure provincial Rabbi obtains, by luck or protection, some subordinate appointment in a Department of State. By dint of quick-wittedness and pliancy coupled with a capacity for making himself useful, he gradually rises in the bureaucratic scale and enters the bureau which, in several State Departments, is entrusted with the work of "informing" the press. Hand in hand with the giving of "information," goes the giving of subsidies from the secret funds to "well-disposed" and "patriotic" journalists. The journalists —most of whom are Jews by birth—thus fed in money and kind, may be trusted never to bite the hand that feeds or has fed them ; otherwise, awkward facts in regard to them might come to light. With their help, the active and hard-working official is able to establish his control over a great part of the press and to render inestimable services to his chief, particularly if the chief be Prime Minister. Careful to keep all the wires in his own hands and to cow opponents by inspiring opportune attacks upon them in the journals at his disposal ; careful, moreover, to obtain, through his growing influence, the appointment or the promotion of trustworthy protégés to other Departments of State than that to which he belongs, the official is always in a position to know what is going on in those Departments, and, by judicious use of his knowledge in the press and otherwise, to defeat intrigues and ambitions of which he may disapprove, or to further aims and schemes that may appear to him worthy of encouragement. In a word, he becomes indispensable and, within certain limits, omnipotent. With his help and support, a Cabinet, or at least a Premier, can hold office long after its, or his, public usefulness has ceased ; and when the end appears nevertheless to be in sight, the omnipotent wirepuller is able, by withdrawing his support from his " chief" and transferring it to some other candidate for the premiership, to hasten the disappearance of the one and the appearance of the other. With skill, this process may be repeated until the wirepuller has exhausted the possibilities of bureaucratic advancement and has tasted to satiety all the joys of semi-clandestine power. He has long since changed his Jewish for a German or a Magyar name. A timely conversion, preferably to Roman Catholicism ; baptism with the support of authentic Catholic and, if possible, titled sponsors to whom he may have rendered in his official capacity some signal service ; a marriage with a well-endowed daughter of some influential but not too prominent family ; a recompense for his devotion to the State in the form of a Privy Councillorship that gives him the style of " Excellency " and entitles him to be addressed in the third person plural—these and other minor developments create for him a pedestal from which he is able to command an appointment to the House of Peers and to step into a lucrative position at the head of some economico-financial institute when occasion offers. In his new position he can at once acquire wealth and extend his influence over the financial while retaining his connexions with the official world. Such careers have been and are still possible in the Hapsburg Monarchy which, despite its reputation for conservatism, might with justice claim that it offers even to its humblest citizens a career open to talent especially when the talent is that of the Jew.

THE JEWS

Among the peoples of Austria-Hungary the Jewish people stands first in importance. It is not usually enumerated among the Hapsburg "nationalities," though the Zionist movement has brought into being a Jewish National Organization which was represented in the Parliament of 1907 by two Zionist deputies and by a politician who was described as a " Moderate Israelite." In Statistical Year Books the Jews figure only as a " denomination." Numerically they appear to be less considerable than the Germans, the Magyars, the Czechs, the Poles, the Ruthenes, the Serbo-Croatians, the Rumanes, and only surpass, with their official religious total of 2,300,000, the Slovenes and the Italians. Economically, politically and in point of general influence they are, however, the most significant element in the Monarchy. No foreign observer of Austro-Hungarian affairs can close his eyes to the Jewish question, however much he may seek to ignore it or to " beg " it by adopting an unreasoning philo-semitic or anti-semitic attitude. The greatest obstacle to a comprehension of the terms of the problem is the difficulty of obtaining precise and reliable information. It is far easier to get at the truth of the Czech-German question in Bohemia, of the Slav-Italian question in Dalmatia and Istria, and even of the complicated struggle between Magyars and non-Magyars in Hungary, than to ascertain the merits of the Jewish question. Other ethnico-religious issues are local and special. They can usually be expressed in terms of language, creed, or of avowed political aspiration. The Jewish question is universal and elusive. It cannot be truly expressed either in terms of religion, nationality, or race. The Jews themselves seem destined so to arouse the passions of those with whom they come into contact that impartiality in regard to them is rare. Some Jews, indeed, regard the very recognition of the existence of a Jewish question as a confession of anti-

semitism.   These are the " Assimilationists."   Others devote
their lives and energies to a solution of the question in the
Zionist sense and denounce as renegades all fellow-Jews
who seek to hide their race and religion.   Between the
conflicting statements and standpoints of the Jews themselves, unbiased enquirers are often bewildered and relinquish
in despair the attempts to "get at the bottom of" the Jewish
question either in its general significance or in its bearing
upon individual States and countries.

Yet it may safely be said that no question deserves
more earnest study.   It assumes a hundred forms, reaches
into unsuspected regions of national and international life,
and influences, for good or evil, the march of civilization.
The main difficulty is to find a starting-point from which to
approach it, a coign of vantage high enough to command
a view of its innumerable ramifications.   Is it a question of
race or of religion?   It is both and more.   Is it a question
of economics, finance and of international trade?   It is
these and something besides.   Are the peculiar characteristics that form at once the strength and weakness of the
Jews a result of religious persecution, or have the Jews been
persecuted because these characteristics have rendered them
odious to the peoples that have harboured them?   This
is the old question whether the hen or the egg should
take genealogical precedence.   Approached from the his-
torico-religious standpoint the Jewish question is inextricably
complicated and, despite its thrilling interest, is apt to
prove insoluble.   It needs to be approached practically, in
the light of direct experience of Jews both as individuals
and in the mass.   When such experience has been acquired,
the Jewish and the Christian Scriptures are seen to glow
with new light; the language of the Prophets becomes
intelligible; the fiery denunciations of John the Baptist, the
delicate irony and revolutionary force of the parables of
Christ are appreciated as never before; the conception of
Jehovah is seen to be a faithful reflection of the Jewish
mind, and the High Priests, Scribes, Pharisees, and Sad-

ducees fall into their places when modern experience has proved them to exist potentially or actually in the Jewry of to-day. No country in the world save, perhaps, the United States, is better adapted than Austria-Hungary to a study of the Jewish question. Though there are fewer Jews in the Monarchy than in Russia and though it does not offer, on the one hand, spectacles like those to be seen within the Russian Jewish Zone nor, on the other, such possibilities of advancement to the very highest positions in the State as have been filled by Jews in England and Italy where the Jews are comparatively few in number, the Hapsburg Monarchy presents the student with unequalled opportunities of observing the Jews as they are, in various environments and in all save the extremest stages of degradation and emancipation. In the Spanish Jews, or Sephardim, of Bosnia-Herzegovina and of Trieste, and in the German-Polish, or Ashkenazim Jews of Galicia, Hungary and Bohemia the two main branches of the Jewish faith, if not of the Jewish race, are to be met with. The question whether the Sephardim belong to a different and more aristocratic branch of the Semitic family than the Ashkenazim is still undecided by ethnologists, though experience suggests that the superiority claimed by the Sephardim over the Ashkenazim may well have a historico-social if not an ethnical basis. Physically, there is no doubt as to the superiority of the Sephardim type; and if it be objected that the degraded, bow-legged, repulsive type often to be found among the Ashkenazim is to be regarded as a product of persecution during the Christian era, it may be answered that the same type is to be found on Egyptian and Babylonian monuments, and that the Etruscan Museum of the Vatican contains vases and other *terre cotte* bearing caricatures of the identical type which anti-semitic caricaturists are wont to portray as that of the old-clothes dealer or of the German Jewish stock-jobber. Such evidence as is available goes to show that the various Jewish types are pre-historical if not aboriginal, and to furnish further proof, if proof were needed, of the strength of the Jewish stock and of the concentrated intensity of its race-character.

This intensity which the Law of Moses, in its Talmudic wrappings, has helped to maintain, is the main feature and foundation of the Jewish question — a question at once qualitative and quantitative. Whoever said, "The Jews are the salt of the earth—but you can't dine off salt," put the problem in a nutshell, in so far, at least, as it regards non-Jewish peoples. Anti-Jewish feeling can almost invariably be expressed in terms of the percentage of Jews to non-Jews intermingled with the other elements of a community. When the percentage rises above a certain point—a point determined in each case by the character of the non-Jewish population—anti-semitism makes its appearance and finds expression in ways varying from social ostracism to massacre. In Austria-Hungary, anti-semitism is both political and endemic. In the Slovak villages of Moravia and North-Western Hungary, it rises and falls with the number of Jewish usurers, pedlars, and liquor dealers in the region. During a recent electoral campaign in Hungary, a candidate of Jewish origin but no longer of Jewish faith, who was standing for Parliament in a Slovak constituency, enquired of his fellow-Jews how they fared and whether life were easy. "When we are two or three in a village," was the answer, "things go well and there is a living for everybody. But when others come, things go badly. Then there is competition and the peasants hate us." The same, *mutatis mutandis*, may be said of large cities. The Jews of Vienna would long since have ceased to be exposed to anti-semitic agitation were their ranks not swelled every year by thousands of new-comers from Galicia and Hungary who invade the field of exploitation conquered by their predecessors and make economic war upon Jew and non-Jew alike. The desirability of creating in Vienna, Lower Austria, and the German provinces of Bohemia a "preserve" against the influx from Galicia has often been discussed by well-to-do Viennese Jews, and as often abandoned as impracticable.   The existence of the idea tends, however, to show that the Jews themselves recognize the nature of the problem with which their race confronts the rest of civilized mankind.   Apart from the freedom of movement constitutionally guaranteed in Austria, the overcrowding of the great Jewish reservoir in Galicia would make the imposition of restrictions a matter of difficulty even were such restrictions otherwise justifiable.   The Jew may be an exploiter of others' labour but it is false to suppose that he exploits only non - Jews.   The sweating dens of East London prove the contrary.   In Galicia, as in several parts of Hungary, Jew exploits Jew with a remorselessness not surpassed by any Jewish exploitation of Christians.   The exploited are gradually reduced to a "standard of life" pitifully near starvation - point ; and when even such a standard is not obtainable, the reservoir overflows in the form of migration and emigration.   Without incurring odium, a modern State cannot check the overflow within its own borders ; but one of the grave, if not the gravest, aspects of the Jewish problem to-day is the manner in which the overflow by emigration is being checked, and necessarily being checked, by countries like the United States and England that formerly allowed pauper aliens to enter free.

It is estimated that between 1881 and 1908 some 2,000,000 Jews emigrated from Russia, Austria-Hungary, and Rumania to the United States and England.   Of this total Austria - Hungary furnished more than 300,000. America received 1,750,000, and England most of the remainder.   The American immigration statistics show that the poorest of the emigrants entering the United States are Jews.   The regulation that immigrants must prove themselves to possess on arrival a minimum sum of 25 dollars excludes thousands of Jews annually—in 1911, 14,500 were sent back to Europe from New York alone.   In 1901, when the regulations were less severe, the average amount possessed by Jewish immigrants was only 8.7 dollars as compared with 41.5 dollars possessed by Scottish, 38.7

dollars by English, and 37.6 by Japanese immigrants. The British Immigration Laws also prevent the emigration of large numbers of Jewish paupers who would otherwise leave the Ghettos of Russia and the Jewish districts of Austria-Hungary. The poverty of the mass of Russian Jews is often attributed to political persecution and to the confinement of the Russian Jews within a Jewish zone. In Galicia there is no such confinement, yet the mass of the Jews remains poverty-stricken. Whereas in Galicia they form only 11 per cent of the population, they make up more than one-half of the inhabitants without regular employment. Jewish workmen who earn as much as 14s. a week are considered fortunate ; the more wealthy Jews are dealers in spirits, pedlars, usurers, and horse-brokers. Their life is still in most respects the life of the Ghetto.

The tendency of the Jews to congregate in and overcrowd one quarter of a city or town—they seem to feel invincible repugnance to life in the open country—is the most striking characteristic of the race taken in the mass. This explanation of the tendency currently given by Jewish and pro-Jewish writers is that it is a consequence of Ghetto life, the Ghetto having been invented by oppressors in order to facilitate control over an alien and too active race. The view that the Ghetto is a necessary and inevitable consequence of the Mosaic Law as developed, or perverted, by the Mishna and the Talmud is, however, more logical and historically sounder. It was recognized by implication in a memorandum presented some years ago to the Ottoman Government by a German-Jewish Society for Jewish Colonization in which it was pointed out that "the sending of immigrants to various points (in Turkey) must not entail the entire separation of individuals and families from each other ; for, in order to be able to fulfil his religious duties, a Jew is forced to live among his co-religionists." If it be true that, in one form or another, the Ghetto is an internal Jewish necessity in so far as the Jews remain faithful to their creed—a necessity proceeding from the

command that the Jewish people keep itself pure and un-
defiled by contact with the Gentiles—it would follow that
the tendency to congregate in Ghettos must have facilitated
the control and segregation of the Jews by police arrangements imposed from outside. There are no external police
arrangements of the kind in London, Vienna, or New York,
yet in each of those cities there are Jewish quarters where
overcrowding is almost as noticeable as in the Ghettos of
Odessa or Lodz. Among the more recent and sincere
literature on the Jewish question that has grown up under
the influence of the Zionist movement, striking admissions
are to be found of the truth of the view that the Ghetto is
a Talmudic necessity. Dr. Jacob Fromer, a native of the
Ghetto of Lodz in Russian Poland and sometime librarian
of the Jewish community at Berlin, has, as an authority
on the Talmud and as a critic of Professor Werner
Sombart's important work *Die Juden und das Wirtschaftsleben*, helped to define the question in its veritable terms.
In endeavouring to reconstruct his well-known work on
Modern Capitalism, Werner Sombart was led to investigate
the origin of the "Capitalist Spirit," and in course of
analysing Max Weber's theory of the relationship between
Puritanism and the development of Capitalism, came to the
conclusion that all the elements of Puritanism which really
contributed to the growth of the capitalist spirit were drawn
from the Jewish religion. Going a step further in his investigation, Sombart, after patient study of Judaism and
Jewish history, established a causal connexion between the
Jews and the development of economic life in its capitalistic
form ; that is to say, he ascribes to the Jews the chief influence in the passage of the civilized world from the "pre-
economic" into the economic stage. Those whom the
question interests as a problem in economics must be referred to the original work ;[1] but for present purposes a
brief summary of his thesis may be given.

[1] *Die Juden und das Wirtschaftsleben*, Leipzig, Duncker und Humblot,
1911.

With the realism of the modern German savant, Sombart lays down the principle that the man of business can have no other object than the making of profit. System, expediency, and calculation are his three guides. These fundamental postulates of Capitalism are to be found in the Jewish religion. The relationship of the Jew to Jehovah is not a filial nor a loving relationship. Judaism, in its essence, contains no trace of belief in Divine grace and no mysticism properly so called. The intercourse of Jews with their Deity is sober, mechanical, and businesslike ; all their acts are believed to be registered in a celestial ledger, the good deeds on the credit, the bad deeds on the debit side. Even interest is reckoned. The Old Testament scarcely mentions other reward for righteousness or punishment for unrighteousness than the gain or loss of temporal goods. Post-Biblical Judaism transferred the profit and loss into the other world but retained the acquisition of wealth as the most laudable object in life alongside of the observance of Divine commands. The Talmud, which is a codification of commentaries upon the Mishna which was in its turn a codification of commentaries upon the Torah, or Mosaic Law, is filled with acute business precepts. The application of these precepts has been facilitated by the distinction between Jews and Gentiles, a distinction that made non-Jews a legitimate object of exploitation by Jewish usurers and money-lenders. Sombart, who claims that there is hardly a people in the world so closely bound up with its religion as the Jews, finds, therefore, a *prima facie* case for the belief that Capitalism is essentially a product of the Jewish mind.

Nevertheless religion is not the only nor, perhaps, even the primary element in the life of a people. It is subject to development and change. If, in all phases of the evolution of a race, permanent features can be detected, they must be attributed to some deeper cause, and religious precepts themselves must be assumed to have found acceptance because they corresponded on the whole to the aboriginal temperament of the race. Following some modern Jewish writers and, indirectly, Spanish writers of the seventeenth century, Sombart finds the explanation of these permanent Jewish qualities in the nomadic character of the tribes that formed the Jewish people. During the period of their wanderings in the desert—a period estimated to have lasted many thousands of years—the Jews acquired an ineradicably nomadic character. On the hot sandy wastes, wandering from oasis to oasis, the race characteristics of the Jews became fixed, their blood acquired its peculiar quality. Without a present, ever looking forward to a brilliant future, carrying with them their treasures, they passed from region to region, from country to country, from people to people, nowhere taking firm root, not even in Canaan, the Promised Land. Sombart believes that if the Jews had remained in the East or among quick-witted, " hot-blooded " peoples, modern capitalism would never have been created. But the migration of the Jews from Spain and Portugal to the North of Europe and their settlement among "cold-blooded," slow-minded Northern peoples, led, after the discovery of America, to the development of capitalized trade and industry in its modern form, a development facilitated by the dispersion of the nomadically constituted Jews throughout the Old and New Worlds.

Like many a German scientific system, Sombart's thesis would have gained in plausibility had it been less completely worked out. In some respects it is probable that Oriental quick-wittedness, long familiarity with financial transactions in theory and practice, dispersion in various countries and an exceptional position among the peoples of the earth, enabled the Jews to take the greatest advantage of " epoch-making " events like the invention of the compass, of printing, and of the steam engine, just as they subsequently exploited the electric telegraph and other forms of scientific enterprise. The Medieval guild system, the limitation of commercial and industrial activity, the principle that an honest merchant must give good value for money and should disdain to seduce his neighbour's customers, were bound to give way before Jewish impatience of artificial restrictions and the

Jewish practice of hawking wares, cutting prices, advertising
and selling on credit.   Bills of exchange, stocks, shares,
bank-notes and debentures, the creation of Stock and
Produce Exchanges, the financing of Princes, Governments,
and commercial undertakings are doubtless in large measure
Jewish inventions, all or most of which appear to be contained
in germ in the Talmud and its doctrines.   But it seems as
serious an error to attribute to the Jews the creation of the
capitalist system as it would be to make them responsible
for the present bureaucratization of finance and industry, a
process which, as Sombart himself observes, is tending to
decrease the number and possibly even the influence of
Jews in the management of big financial concerns in Germany
and other countries.   Sombart writes, "To all appearances
the influence of the Jewish people (in economic life) has
begun quite recently to diminish.   It is indubitable and can
be ascertained by simple enumeration, that among the
managers and directors of the big banks, Jewish names are
becoming rarer.   The Jewish element seems really to be
losing ground.   It is interesting to inquire into the causes
of this significant phenomenon.   They may be of several
kinds.   On the one hand, non-Jews have adapted themselves
more completely to the requirements of the capitalist system,
they have become 'skilled' whereas the Jews have partly
lost their former special aptitude for capitalism in consequence
of the improvement of their social position and of a decrease
in the intensity of their religious feeling.   On the other hand,
we must probably look for the causes of the diminution of
Jewish economic influence in the change that has taken
place in the conditions of economic life itself.   Capitalist
undertakings are transforming themselves more and more
into bureaucratic administrations that do not require special
trading capacity in the same degree as formerly.   Bureaucratism is taking the place of commercialism." [1]

There are other reasons than those mentioned by Sombart for a diminution of Jewish influence in and over big

_____
[1] Sombart, *op. cit.* Vorwort, pp. viii-ix.

capitalist undertakings. Though the gregarious instinct is strong in the Jew, he remains psychologically an individualist, refractory to external discipline, and a speculator in the widest sense of the term. A circumscribed, bureaucratic career has few attractions for him. His mental sensitiveness leads him to prefer other walks of life and to transfer to them his trading proclivities in proportion as finance and industry become bureaucratized. Art, the stage, the law, music, journalism, and politics appeal to him as offering a freer field for his activities. Confidence in his own superior mental agility has always made him an advocate of " liberty " and rendered him impatient of restrictions. Hence his political Radicalism. The body of economico - political doctrine known as " Liberalism " was largely built up by Jewish, crypto-Jewish or pro-Jewish writers ; and, in German-speaking countries especially, the " Progressive " parties have been recruited largely from Jewish politicians and supported by Jewish organs. The German advocates of the "Manchester School " in economics were principally Jews, whose object seemed to be the establishment of freedom of the kind defined by Kürnberger, in another connexion, as " the free fox in the free hen-roost." The State Socialism, opposed by Bismarck to German Radical and Social Democratic tendencies, bore a strongly anti-Jewish character, just as the Christian Socialism of Lueger was anti-semitic and aimed at protecting the economically unfit against the most glaring evils of unrestricted capitalistic enterprise. In Germany and Austria-Hungary at least, " Revolutionary " Socialism and Social Democracy have been guided by Jewish leaders and inspired by Jewish doctrine. Karl Marx, a Jew, wrote *Das Kapital,* the socialist economic bible ; Lassalle, his rival and co-founder of the German Social Democratic Party, was also a Jew ; Jewish names like Singer, Bernstein, Arons, Fischer and Stadthagen are prominent in the more recent history of German Socialism ; and, to-day, half the Socialist party in the German Reichstag is composed of Jews. In Austria-Hungary the spread of Socialism has been largely the result of Jewish propaganda. Dr. Victor Adler, the founder and leader of the Austrian party, is a Jew, as are many of his followers. In Hungary the party was also founded and inspired by Jews. These phenomena are doubtless attributable in part to the quickness of Jewish intelligence and to the ingrained Jewish proclivity to discount the future or, so to speak, to deal in "futures," political as well as commercial. Recognition of the fact that the capital-istic system tends to develop in the direction foreseen by Marx, and that the casting vote in the great struggle between the State and wealthy capitalistic corporations is likely to be given by the organized masses of the people, has undoubtedly influenced the more wide-awake of the Jews and induced them to strive in time to control the masses through Socialist organizations, in the hope of securing a potent influence upon legislation and upon the future construction of society. Socialism possesses to boot the virtue of being an antidote to economic anti-semitism. The stock reply of German Socialist leaders to the attacks of anti-semites and to the grumblings of their own followers against the deleterious effects of Jewish economic activity, is that the evils complained of are inherent in the capitalist system of which the Jews are, it is true, the most prominent representatives but which are not specifically Jewish ; and that the only means of removing these evils is to be found in the struggle of classes, the organization of a class-conscious proletariate, and in the conquest and reformation of society by International Revolutionary Social Democracy.

Whatever its cause or causes, the prominence of Jews in contemporary Socialist movements, as in the Liberal and Radical movements of older generations, is a fact too well established to need demonstration. The sayings that the Jews are as yeast working in the lump of human society, or that they are as foreign matter in the blood-social, causing fever by their presence, go but a little way to explain the phenomenon. Neither is the euphemistic thesis which attri-butes the revolutionary activity of Jews to a strong sense of abstract Justice that impels them to revolt against social and political inequalities, much more adequate an explanation than the more cynical argument that the Jews invariably favour the removal of disabilities and external restrictions, because they are conscious of their ability to outwit competitors in an open field.   If any explanation is to be found, it must probably be sought in the mental characteristic which most distinguishes the Jew from the Indo-German or "Aryan."   This characteristic is superabundant intellectualism or power of abstract ratiocination.   Were the world governed by logic and organized on rational principles deduced from established premises, the Jew might excel in constructive statecraft.   His faculty of concentration, his intense inner life, his freedom from the trammels of place and country, his practical rationalism and workaday purposefulness would fit him in a peculiar degree to rule a world organized on some symmetrical, intellectual plan.   In such a world every act would have its reasonable object, every political privilege its well-defined constitutional sanction.   Socialist movements, particularly those of the Marxist type, are directed towards the rationalization of the social structure and the substitution of " wits " for force in national and international life.   Sombart maintains, in the course of an acute analysis of Jewish psychology,[1] that "the whole Jewish question is contained in the words "Mojech *versus* Kojech" (brain against force) ; and cites the characteristic Yiddish proverb, " Gott soll behüten var jüdischen Mojech und var gojischen Kojech" (May God preserve from Jewish wits and Gentile force). The belief that " Force rules the world still, has ruled it, shall rule it " is antithetical to the Jewish ideal which is expressed in the modern Jewish-Radical thesis that the internationalization of business and financial interests must in the long run prevent the outbreak of wars, because wars will not be " worth while."   " Worth while " and " not worth while " are essentially Jewish conceptions, just as the feeling defined by an Irish-American wag in the phrase " Not all

[1] *Die Juden und das Wirtschaftsleben*, pp. 312-328.

the 'worth whiles' of life can be expressed in terms of the United States currency" is fundamentally non-Jewish. Jewish activity has always some rational purpose in view—usually an immediate purpose. If there be a chance of ulterior advantage, religious, intellectual, financial, or political, so much the better. But acquiescence in an apparently purposeless universe, joy in valueless things, a sense of forming part of a world that is rolling on throughout the ages with no discoverable aim or object, a desire for mystic communion with the Spirit of the Cosmos, are rarely to be found in Jewish minds. As Sombart truly observes, the semi-sentimental pessimism of modern Jewish writers like Schnitzler and George Hirschfeld proceeds from a conviction of the purposelessness and, therefore, of the sadness of the world. Childlike delight in the mere fact of existence, and the old Greek joy in effort without care for result, are profoundly non-Jewish. Goethe's enquiry in " Gott und Welt,"

"Was wär' ein Gott, der nur von Aussen stiesse ?
Im Kreis das All am Finger laufen liesse ? "

seems to be directed against the conception of a Jehovah-like deity who, standing outside the universe, controls everything according to his own pleasure. The true Jewish thinker has "no use" for an illogical universe and little admiration for irrational Genius. One such, in dealing with the problem of races and the purpose of civilization, says,[1] " In civilized man, the consciously creative intellect replaces blind instinct. The task of the intellect is to extinguish instinct, to replace impulses by purposeful will, to reflect instead of merely perceiving. The individual only becomes a complete man when the activity of his reason dissolves and replaces all existing predispositions and quenches his instincts. When the detachment from instinct is complete, we have before us absolute Genius with its entire inner freedom from natural law. It is the task of civilized life to

---

[1] J. Zollschau, *Das Rassenproblem unter besonderer Berücksichtigung der theoretischen Grundlagen der jüdischen Rassenfrage* (1910), p. 298.

emancipate itself from all mysticism, from everything obscure and impulsive in the life of instinct, and to develop the purely rational form of the intellect." Judged by this standard, Leonardo da Vinci, Shakespeare, and Goethe, who have some claim to rank as geniuses, would cut a poor figure, even if they were admitted to be embryonically civilized! Such a civilization would leave little place for unreasoned perception, for spontaneous delight in beauty,—natural, artistic, or moral. Yet this delight has usually been considered an index of civilization, nay, the level of a civilization has been judged by the fineness of the taste that characterized it. Were it practicable, this Jewish conception of civilization would produce a world of intolerable rational beings similar to those abstract individuals conceived by orthodox political economists ; a brainy, brainglorious, uninhabitable world, a universe of pharisaical, hairsplitting ergotists from whom the breath of life would have departed.

It is nevertheless clear that the penetrating intelligence of Jewish minds and their power of rapid reasoning and combination, have rendered and are likely to render valuable service to civilization within certain limits, especially in those branches of human activity that are susceptible of logical treatment. The danger to civilization involved in the Jewish Question is that failure, on the part of Jews and non-Jews alike, to perceive the profound differences between the Jewish and the non-Jewish mentality, together with the concentration of financial and political power in Jewish hands, may lead once again to those instinctive revolts of non-Jewish majorities against Jewish minorities that figure so largely in the troubled history of the Jewish people. Jewish immoderation and non-Jewish resentment have, again and again, impeded what might have been fruitful co-operation for the common good. The Jews themselves scarcely seem to know how strongly the tide of anti-Jewish feeling is already running in many highly civilized countries. Even in Germany, the country for which Ashkenazim Jews feel, or profess to feel, special devotion, recent publications of a pronouncedly anti-Jewish character have met with singular success.   One such[1] roundly proposes the expulsion from Germany of all Jews not possessing German citizenship ; the degradation to the position of tolerated aliens of all Jews and descendants of Jews, whether of pure or mixed blood, who possessed citizenship and were registered as Jews in 1871 ; the exclusion of Jews, baptized and unbaptized, from all public offices, from service in the army and navy, from the bar, from the franchise and from eligibility to Parliament, from the directorships of banking companies and theatres, from the proprietorship and editorship of newspapers and from journalism in general. The Jews should also, urges this writer, be deprived of the right to own land or to lend money on landed mortgages, and should be required, as aliens, to pay double taxation.   It is a question, he adds, of "saving the German soul." That a book, not a mere pamphlet, containing such proposals should run through a dozen editions in a few weeks is assuredly a sign of the times.   Its success brings into stronger relief the importance of the service rendered by Sombart to students of the Jewish question, and indeed to the Jews themselves.   This service has been recognized by competent Jewish writers and by none more warmly than by Dr. Jacob Fromer, the Talmudist above referred to, whose striking review of Sombart's work in the *Zukunft* of October 28, 1911, is in itself an illuminating contribution to the literature of the Jewish question.   Despite over-systematization of its thesis and the questionable value of some of the evidence adduced, Sombart's book, writes Dr. Fromer, is of extraordinary significance for the study of Jewry.   In virtue of its intuitive recognition of historical connexions, its author's deep knowledge of the well-nigh inaccessible literature of his subject, his honest effort to avoid special pleading and to view questions impartially, the book surpasses anything of the kind hitherto written.   It is the first serious attempt to approach the Jewish problem in a scientific spirit,

[1] *Wenn Ich der Kaiser wär*, by Daniel Frymann, Leipzig, 1913, pp. 71, 78.

and to employ methods that ought to have been adopted from the beginning—the method of seeking for knowledge. "If any kind of solution for the Jewish problem is to be found, three points must be settled ; first, whether the forces working in Jewry are not so valuable as to merit preservation, despite the disturbances they cause in the life of the peoples among whom the Jews live ; secondly, whether, in any case, these forces are not indestructible, and therefore to be made the best of; and thirdly, by what means these forces can successfully be combated if they prove to be destructible and of inferior quality. If the need for knowledge is once recognized, it will easily be understood how much damage has been done by modern Jewish historians. Nobody who has accustomed himself to regard things from their standpoint can acquire, without difficulty, a clear and accurate idea of Jewry." The modern Jews, whose prototype was Moses Mendelssohn, continues Dr. Fromer, have broken with the tradition of their fathers and have plainly declared that they wish to remain permanently among the Gentiles and to be absorbed by Gentile civilization. On the strength of this declaration they have demanded and received equality of rights. But instead of stating plainly that certain ancient characteristics, usages and views were bound to stick to the Jews for generations, modern Jewish writers have systematically striven to obscure the truth and to render yet darker and more difficult the arduous approaches to knowledge of Jewry. They have declared Talmudism—the central organ into which the sap of Jewry has flowed since Biblical times, the organ that has nourished all Jewry, the Modern not less than the Orthodox, and has worked the unprecedented miracle of keeping a landless people mentally and physically healthy throughout the centuries—to be an excrescence raised on the body of Jewry by stress of untoward circumstances. They have minutely demonstrated that the Jews who have remained true to Tradition—the overwhelming majority of the nation—are degenerates from type, and that the Ghetto, the segregation necessary for the preservation of the type,

the Ghetto in which the Jews have always lived since their
entrance into History, in the Land of Goshen and in Canaan,
in Alexandria, Rome, Spain, Portugal, and elsewhere, is an
invention of the peoples in whose midst they have dwelt;
and that the Jewish martyrdom, the inevitable consequence
of voluntary segregation, has in all times and places been
due to Gentile brutality.   Finally, these modern Jewish
historians have removed the name of Jewry from the list
of nations and have represented it to be a group of human
beings bound together merely by the bond of a religious
denomination.   This has been proclaimed in the name of
Science, Truth, and strict " objectivity " !

Professor Sombart, claims Dr. Fromer, deserves recognition as the first non-Jewish student to fight his way
through the insulating Talmudic crust into clear comprehension of Jewry and to take the first step towards agreement between two worlds hitherto strangers to each other.
But the question arises, What is Talmudic Jewry, and
whence the power of the Talmud?   The Talmud, answers
Fromer, is largely a product of the Pharisee reaction against
Hellenism with which Jewry came into contact after the
conquest of the East by Alexander the Great.   The Jews
have ever been influenced by two tendencies—on the one
hand the nomadic, Mosaic, Pharisee, Talmudic tendency,
and, on the other, the tendency to adapt themselves to their
environment, to become assimilated by the Gentiles and to
forget the Law.   Their yearnings for the flesh-pots of
Egypt, their worship of the golden calf, their propensity to
intermarry with the heathen despite the warnings of the Law
and the Prophets, show how strong was the assimilationist
tendency from the beginning of their recorded or symbolic
history.   The formidable list of names given by Ezra [1]
proves how many even among the sons of the priests had
married strange women; just as the defiant reply of the
Jewish women to Jeremiah in Egypt [2] showed the extreme
reluctance of the Jews to cease " to burn incense unto the

[1] Ezra x.   [2] Jeremiah xliv. 16-18 (Revised Version).

Queen of Heaven, and to pour out drink offerings unto her, as we have done, we, and our fathers, our kings, and our princes, in the cities of Judah, and in the streets of Jerusalem." The reason for this reluctance was characteristic of the profit and loss relationship of the Jews to Jehovah, as indeed to the " Queen of Heaven." " But since we left off to burn incense to the Queen of Heaven, and to pour out drink offerings unto her, we have wanted all things, and have been consumed by the sword and indeed by the famine." The history of the Jews in Canaan is largely the history of a struggle between the nomadic, Mosaic tendency, and the assimilationist agricultural instinct. But, in the long run, the nomadic, Mosaic tendency always proved the stronger ; and the popularity of the Pharisees who, with their strict literal observance of the Law, incorporated it, is a sign that it lay deep in the temperament of the people. Whether it would have succeeded in preserving the Jews from absorption by other peoples and races had not the impact of Greek culture driven Judaism back upon itself is an interesting but now largely academic question. Against the Greek teachings and reasonings that threatened to seduce the Jewish intelligence, and did, in fact, make headway among the more cultured classes, the Assidean party waged desperate war, and the Pharisees, the spiritual children of the Assideans, completed their work. " The preservation of Judaism in its ancient exclusiveness was their programme," writes Mr. G. E. Abbot (*Israel in Europe; Hebraism and Hellenism*, p. 6). " All public undertakings, all national acts as well as all private transactions, were to be measured by the rigid standard of religion. The Law in the hands of the Pharisees became a procrustean bed upon which the mind of the nation was to be stretched or maimed according to the requirements of nationalism and the interpretations of the Scribes. This inflexible orthodoxy, with its concomitants of discipline and sacrifice of individuality, was in perfect accord with the Hebrew temperament, and the Pharisees must be regarded as the interpreters of the views dear to the great mass of their compatriots." To the *Sophia* of the Greeks the Pharisee opposed the "Law," the Torah, which he meditated and commented upon with the subtlety of a casuist and the gratitude of a shipwrecked mariner who has found a plank of safety. The study of the Torah day and night and the observance of its innumerable ceremonial precepts, became the ideal of Jewish piety. "Blessed is the man that walketh not in the counsel of the ungodly . . . nor sitteth in the seat of the scornful. But his delight is in the law of the Lord, and in His law doth he meditate day and night. . . . *Whatsoever he doeth shall prosper.*"[1] Here again the profit and loss relationship to the Deity is clearly indicated. As Dr. Fromer observes, nothing in the Jewish religion is done for nothing, everything has its reason and object. "This original trait of cool-headed piety runs from the Patriarchs by way of Mosaism and Talmudism uninterruptedly down to the present day. There are no essential differences between the service of Abraham to Jehovah and the religiosity of the pious men who predominate in the Ghetto. Both are based on a *do ut des* system and are diametrically opposed to the Christian doctrine of unearned grace."[2]

The Sadducees struggled for centuries against the Pharisee tendency to wrap Judaism in an insulating mantle of precepts and commentaries, but the fall of Jerusalem decided the struggle definitely in favour of the Pharisees, who so multiplied commentaries upon the Law that codification became indispensable. A code named Mishna (Doctrine) was elaborated. It consisted of six parts dealing with agriculture, feasts, marriage law, the civil and penal law, the law of the Temple and cleanliness. The Mishna became in its turn an object of veneration, study, comment, and casuistical interpretation. Every letter and syllable was examined and stretched to its utmost capacity. From generation to generation the Mishna commentaries grew until their volume became unmanageable. Once more codification proved

[1] Ps. i.   [2] *Die Zukunft*, Oct. 28, 1911, p. 113.

necessary. Towards the middle of the fifth century A.D. a Mishna Code was formed in Palestine and, at the end of the same century, a second code at Babylon. Both codes were called " Talmud " (Research or Investigation). While the Palestine Talmud played an insignificant part in the subsequent life of Jewry, the Babylonian Talmud was regarded as a national possession. It has remained " The Book " for Orthodox Jewry. It replaced the Torah as the fountain of all wisdom and as the guide in every detail of daily life. The Talmud, despite its character as a commentary upon a commentary upon a Law of uncertain origin, has not only preserved the Jewish Nation but has imbued it with a Pharisee spirit and separated it, perhaps for ever, from the main stream of human culture. The teachings of Christ were a running protest against the mummifying influence of Phariseeism, but a protest addressed, in the first place, to Jews and based on the approaching fulfilment of Messianic prophecy. Pauline Christianity went further, took the offensive against Hellenism and vanquished it, but its victory was bought at the expense of Jewry and of the distinction between Jew and Gentile. Pharisee Jewry, on the other hand, continued to " kill the prophets," remained on the defensive behind its phylacteries and commentaries, and ultimately took refuge in the Ark of the Talmud, in which it has lived to this day.

An enlightening picture of the bearing of the Talmud upon the Jewish question is given in Dr. Jakob Fromer's autobiographical book, *Ghetto-Dämmerung*.[1] The intensity of the respect that surrounds the learned Talmudist in the Ghetto even though he be poverty-stricken and accustomed to rely for his sustenance upon the meagre earnings of his wife ; the economic value of children versed in the Talmud and in commentaries like the Schulchan Aruch Code can hardly be conceived by the Gentile who finds no counterpart for such phenomena in the range of his experience. Boys able smartly to solve questions on the interpretation

[1] Schuster & Loeffler, Berlin, 1911.

of the Law are much sought after as husbands for marriage-
able " heiresses." Such questions are often of the most
pettifogging kind. Dr. Fromer gives an example of the
" problems " that formed part of his " discursive training " in
the study of the Talmud. Discursive study, he writes,[1]
consists of collecting, examining, and comparing everything
that the Talmud and its commentators say on a given
subject. Some questions are juridical as, for instance, " May
a judge be called as a witness ? " Others are psychological,
e.g. " A man has admitted half of a total liability that is not
susceptible of proof. Some Talmudists consider him credible
since he might have denied the whole liability. Others
think that to deny the whole liability would require more
impudence than everybody possesses, and conclude that he
only admitted half of his liability out of weakness." On
this point the youthful Talmudist is expected to give a
reasoned opinion. Further, " An egg laid on the Sabbath
day may not be eaten. But what if half of it be laid before
sundown on Friday and half after sundown, that is to say
on the Sabbath ? " The legendary curate would reply, " Parts
of it are excellent," but the Talmudist cannot escape from
his problems by joking. He must conscientiously work
through the countless ritual, business, social and legal
problems, and the smarter or the more casuistical his
answers the greater his renown. Dr. Fromer gives a striking
account of his experience when on his way to visit his uncle,
the miracle-working Rabbi of Szochlin. Among the pilgrims
to the Rabbi were a number of Jews on the look-out for
profitable husbands for their daughters. One such met an
acquaintance who was accompanied by his son, a weedy
youth of fifteen years, whom the acquaintance sought to
embarrass by questions on Talmudic problems. The boy
" lay low," answered warily, and presently turned the tables
on his questioner, who, struck by the boy's knowledge, asked
the father whether a wife had already been found for him.
The father replied scornfully that the *Schadchonim* (marriage-

[1] *Ghetto-Dämmerung*, p. 20.

brokers) were always bidding for the boy, but that there was no hurry because his learning grew from day to day, and with it his value. Bargaining then began. It ended with the conclusion of a contract under which the boy was bound to marry the questioner's daughter, three years his senior, in return for a payment of £40 and ten years' keep for the boy-husband, including meat every day !

Similar scenes are often represented in the Jewish jargon plays—plays usually full of wit and pathos, full, especially, of the characteristic " Jewish jokes " which the Jews love to crack even at their own expense, though rarely without pride in the smartness of Jewish intelligence. Those who have never lived amongst or come into regular contact with Jews in the mass can hardly realize how completely the Jewish differs in its essence from the Gentile world, and how acute are the issues with which the Jewish problem confronts modern civilization. The Jews themselves are now divided into two main schools of thought upon the problem, the one more or less assimila-tionist, the other more or less Zionist. The standpoint of the assimilationists is roughly that the entire removal of restrictions and disabilities is all that is needed for the problem to be solved automatically by the gradual absorp-tion of the Jews. Where no disabilities exist, the Jewish question, they contend, rapidly assumes an inoffensive denominational character and ceases to have ethnical or political significance; even the religious practices that tend to preserve the children of Israel as a " peculiar people " lose intensity under the benign influence of Gentile culture and society. To some extent the assimilationists take up the old Sadducee standpoint ; and it would be easy to prove their claim that, when granted complete equality, numbers of Jews have become, to all outward appearances, good Englishmen, Germans, Frenchmen, Italians, or Americans. The debatable point is whether the thesis that appears to hold good in regard to some individuals would hold good for the mass, always supposing the mass to be anxious for assimilation. On this point it is impossible to speak with confidence, especially in the affirmative.   The intensity of the Jewish race character is such that the Jewish strain will persist for generations in non-Jewish families into which Jewish blood has once entered.   The strain may be productive of beauty or genius, or it may, on the other hand, bring the mental derangement so common in the better-class Jewish families.   In his pamphlet, *Die Zukunft der Juden*, Werner Sombart gives on the authority of Dr. Wieth-Knudsen some striking, though incomplete, statistical data tending to show marriages between Jews and non-Jews to be less fruitful than the average of purely Jewish or purely non-Jewish unions in analogous circumstances, and asserts that the children of mixed marriages are apt to lack mental unity and equilibrium.   It is indeed a question whether the children of mixed marriages escape, in the first generation at least, the dualism of character noticeable in half-breeds the world over.   When they escape it the characteristics of one race usually dominate those of the other.   The present writer has in his possession a remarkable letter from the son of an Austrian-Jewish father and non-Jewish mother, born and educated in Western Europe, and, to all intents and purposes, completely assimilated as regards taste, habits, and general views of life.   The letter was written in the autumn of 1905 from the Hungarian capital—a city commonly nick-named " Judapest."   It runs :—

" . . . I have for years past realized to a partial extent (for wholly to understand its endless bifurcations and ramifications must ever be beyond my grasp) the vital importance to nationalities and the political and economic significance of the Jewish question.   But I was not prepared, nor do I believe that one well-informed person in a hundred would have been prepared, for what I have met with here.   Having heard of the Budapest ' night life,' prepared therefore to hear the sound of revelry and to return exhausted from the customary *tour des Grands Ducs*, I found, to my amazement, that the streets were lifeless, the theatres, cafés, music halls, and even less reputable places deserted.

The Day of Atonement was at hand! In this populous centre of a nation, on the fast-day of an alien race, such life (miserable excuse as it may be for setting at nought the reality of Death) as involves the spending of money and its possession is, for the period of the fast, entirely suspended, and the city, famous throughout Europe as the Mecca of the *fêteur* and of those hungry for licence and debauch, is dead. How many reflections this brings in its train you can imagine better than I can describe even had I time!

"Is it indeed true that this race battens so upon the land it has fastened its tentacles on that, whether the race be comparable with orchid or spider, nothing remains but the dead trunk or the bloodless corpse? Is it true that all the banking, all the distributing trades, nearly all the retail trades and most of the land are in Jewish hands; that the Hungarian noble leaves his land to Jews who own the peasants, body and soul; that by usury they extract from the smaller freeholders what they possess, and that, having exploited the nation which harbours them from the sowing to the reaping, they then minister to their physical weaknesses and their moral by the ultimate exploitation of the tavern and the brothel?

"If this, or nearly this, be true, there is no Hungarian question in the true sense. There is a Jewish question, and this terrible race means not only to master one of the grandest warrior nations in the world, but it means, and is consciously striving, to enter the lists against the other great race of the north (the Russians), the only one that has hitherto stood between it and its goal of world-power.

"Am I wrong? Tell me. For already England and France are, if not actually dominated by Jews, very nearly so, while the United States, by the hands of those whose grip they are ignorant of, are slowly but surely yielding to that international and insidious hegemony. Remember that I am half a Jew by blood, but that in all that I have power to be I am not. I admire their strength, their constancy, their intelligence, but I hate the Jew because of his nature he is evil, while the Aryan of his nature is good."

No full-blooded "Aryan" could write more incisively, however meagre his sympathies for the Jews, and none could write so bitterly because none can have experienced the struggle between the two race-natures that goes on in the minds of half-breeds when they are conscious of their dual mentality. Some full-blooded Jews have, however, written with almost equal bitterness ; Heine, for instance, who wrote of his own people : " This race of Original Evil (*Urübelvolk*) has long been damned, and drags from Age to Age its tortures of the damned. Oh ! this Egypt ! Her products defy time ; her pyramids still stand unshaken ; her mummies are as imperishable as that mummy people which wanders across the Earth bound up in its old wrappings of the Letter, a case-hardened fragment of world-history, a ghost that sustains itself by trading in I.O.U.'s and old trousers." But rhapsody cannot elucidate the Jewish problem. Knowledge and the understanding born of knowledge are needful. Though the problem in itself may be found insoluble, know-ledge will at least permit outsiders to assume in regard to it some attitude less barren than one of mere antisemitism, and will, on the other hand, prevent them from being misled by " semi-official assimilationist " statements of the Jewish case. Such statements are usually based upon the unproved assump-tion that the Jews are perfectly assimilable. That Jews have a remarkable faculty for external adaptation to environment is incontestable, but it remains to be seen whether, with all their pliancy and pertinacious direction of will toward their immediate object, they are capable of adapting themselves internally. Experience and observation now extending over more than twenty-one years, in Germany, France, Italy, and Austria-Hungary, incline me to answer this question in the negative. Of the two main branches of Jewry in Europe— the Sephardim or Spanish-Portuguese, and the Ashkenazim or German-Polish-Russian Jews—the Sephardim are un-doubtedly the better stock. In their case adaptation and assimilation seem to be easier than in the case of the Ashkenazim, though, among the Sephardim also, the intensity of the race-type and of its mental characteristics seems almost invincible. Quantitively, the question is, in their case, less urgent than in that of the Ashkenazim, because they are fewer in number and less prone to congregate voluntarily in Ghettos. Even where they are most numerous, as at Salonica and other Balkan centres, the Sephardim do not present a " problem " in the same sense as do the Ashkenazim Jews of Galicia, Russian Poland, Posen, the East-End of London, and New York. It is besides an interesting historical fact that the Sephardim have repeatedly made a stand against or assumed the control of the Ashkenazim. In the seventeenth century at Hamburg, for instance, the Portuguese Jewish community made itself responsible towards the authorities for the *Tedescos*, or German Jews, and obliged these Tedescos to bind themselves not to trade in stolen goods nor to engage in other kinds of dishonest business. But within a few months the elders of the Tedescos were summoned before the presidency of the Sephardim and taxed with violation of their engagements. Similar and even more drastic instances could be cited from the history of the Sephardim in France. Though Sephardim and Ashkenazim often present a united front to the non - Jewish world, the distinction between them is well marked in Jewry itself, where the Sephardim enjoy the greater prestige. From the assimilationist standpoint, however, the only serious problem is that of the Ashkenazim. These may broadly be described as " German Jews," whether their country of immediate origin be Russia, Austria-Hungary, or Germany. As to the origin of their Jewish name, theories and legends differ even among their own learned men. Some claim descent from Ashkenaz, son of Gomer and grandson of Japheth ; others put forward a theory to the effect that, after the fall of Jerusalem, in which the flower of the nation in Palestine perished, a part of the plebs was carried into slavery by the Romans and settled in a district, corresponding to the present Bavarian Palatinate, called Ascania, after its first governor, Ascanius. The speech of these Ascanian or Ashkenazim Jews became corrupted by the German dialects of their neighbours, and acquired the semi-German basis noticeable in the Yiddish (*jüdisch*) jargon.   When   persecution   ultimately   drove the bulk of them to accept the protection offered by the Kings of Poland, they migrated in large numbers to Poland and settled in the present provinces of Galicia, Russian Poland, and Posen.   Here their jargon became further corrupted by the addition of Polish and Russian elements. Many Jewish families retained, however, their German names, a circumstance which, together with the subsequent imposition of German names by Maria Theresa, is held to explain the frequency of German patronymics among the Polish and Russian Jews.

This theory, in which fact and fancy seem to be inextricably mingled, was advanced to the writer by a learned Austrian Hebrew in explanation of the pro-German tendencies displayed by Ashkenazim Jews the world over.   " German," said this pundit, " is the basis of our jargon, and, next to Palestine, Germany is the country which we regard as our home.   Hence our sentimental leaning towards Germany." Though other and less sentimental explanations of the undoubted pro-German leanings of the Ashkenazim have been put forward—explanations often summarized in the assertion that, since 1870, the Jews have believed Germany to be the rising Power and have consequently striven to " back the winner "—no observer who has had dealings with the Jews of Austria will doubt that some impulse more subtle than the expectation of immediate advantage drives them to pose as Germans and to associate themselves with Germanism rather than with any non-German tendency.   The Jews who have deliberately associated themselves with and sought to become assimilated by Slav races like the Czechs, the Serbo-Croatians, the Slovenes, the Slovaks, or by the Rumanes of Hungary, are exceedingly few in number.   The case of the Hungarian Jews—who appear to have accepted Magyarization—is peculiar, and the sincerity of their attachment to Magyarism has yet to be proved. The bulk of the Galician and Hungarian Jews who migrate to Vienna and other parts of Austria claim German "nationality." When authentic Germans disown them, these Jews reply that they "feel like Germans," an assertion which authentic Germans passionately deny. Controversy upon the question whether a Jew can "feel like" a German has given rise to tautological designations such as that of "Germanic Germans," used not long since by Dr. Sylvester, the President of the Austrian Chamber—a designation comprehensible only as establishing a distinction between Germanic and Semitic Germans. So large a part does this distinction play in Austrian-German politics that a leading Jewish journalist has declared, bitterly but truthfully, that antisemitism forms the only bond between the various sections of the Austrian-German "National" party. Pan-Germanism, in Austria at least, has always had an anti-Jewish tendency. It is related of Herr Schoenerer, the founder and former leader of the Austrian Pan-German party, that after the original party programme had been drafted for endorsement by a congress at Linz, a clause was added to it excluding from membership all Germans of non-Aryan descent. The historian, Dr. Friedjung, who had drawn up the programme, and whose Pan-German leanings were strong, was thus, as a full-blooded Jew, excluded from the party he had helped to form. It is an irony of fate that while these exclusive tendencies prevail among the "Germanic" German "Liberals," the whole "Liberal," i.e. non-Clerical, press of Austria should be in Jewish hands ; and that the home policy of the German "National" parties in Austria should be largely determined by the influence of the Germans of Prague, most of whom are Jews. The political interests of the veritable Germans in other parts of Austria—those of Styria, Carinthia, Upper and Lower Austria, the Salzkammergut, Tyrol, and Vorarlberg—have long been subordinated to the exigencies of the struggle between Czechs and Germans of Bohemia, in which the Jewish-German press of Prague and its ally, the Jewish-German *Neue Freie Presse* of Vienna, have been important if not determining factors. It sounded therefore like black ingratitude when a Viennese Jewish review recently warned the Jews of Prague that the time had come to " neutralize " themselves in the view of the then prevailing tendency of Czechs and Germans in Bohemia to come to an understanding. " As long as the Czech-German quarrel lasted," wrote this review,[1] " the Jews were often protected by the circumstance that the decision lay in their hands. Therefore neither side ventured to do them much harm. But when the two Bohemian races have defined their spheres of influence, they will have no regard for the Jews and will pay them out for the way they have behaved in ' national ' questions (*i.e.* in the Czech-German race struggle). Hitherto the Jews of Bohemia have pursued a purely idealist policy corresponding to their German culture, and have followed the Germans unconditionally—the worst possible tactics, judging by results. The Czechs, originally tolerant, propagated antisemitism, while the conceited Germans did not give up their antisemitism although the Jews were often more Pan-German than Schoenerer and followed a flag that was often a battle-standard against the Jews themselves. Henceforth the Jews must pursue none but a Jewish policy, and must so determine their conduct as to inflict damage upon economic and moral antisemitism."

Whether ungrateful or not, this frank declaration must be regarded as a healthy sign. The Jewish " danger," if danger it be, does not lie in the proclamation and defence of a specifically Jewish standpoint but in the dissimulation of Jewish ideas and interests under a non-Jewish cloak. The Jews *qua* Jews are as entitled as any other people in the Austro-Hungarian Monarchy or in the world, to full consideration of their rights and interests, but they cannot

[1] *Österreichische Wochenschrift* (Central Organ for Jewish Interests), August 1912.

enjoy esteem as long as they attempt to out-German the
Germans in Pan-Germanism or to out-Magyar the Magyars
in oppression of the non-Magyar races of Hungary. There is
something peculiarly repugnant in Jewish chauvinism on behalf
of a dominant race. The writer will never forget the disagreeable impression made upon him some years ago by a Jewish
professor of Social Science in Hungary, who claimed that
the Slovaks of North-West Hungary ought to be oppressed,
and if necessary exterminated, because they were refractory
to Magyarization. Healthier ideas are beginning to prevail
among the younger generation of Jews in Austria-Hungary,
thanks largely to the influence of Zionist propaganda. Into
the question of territorial Zionism it is not necessary now
to enter,[1] though the overcrowding of Galicia, of the Jewish
zone in Russia and of parts of Rumania, render it, in view
of the restriction of emigration,[2] a question of no little
importance ; but moral Zionism, or, rather, the ethical and
psychological effect of the Zionist ideal, demand attention.
When Theodor Herzl, the literary editor of the *Neue Freie
Presse*, started the Zionist movement, the younger intellectual
Jews of Austria-Hungary were veritably at the parting of
the ways. Contact with the outer world had deprived many
of them of the faith of their fathers, and had divested
their minds of the grosser Talmudic wrappings without
providing other substitute than a scepticism which tended
constantly to become more cynical. Many cultured Jewish
youths sought to discard their very nature and to identify
themselves completely with Germanism, accepting German
political and ethical ideals and trying honestly to " feel like "
Germans. One such committed suicide on discovering, after
years of endeavour, that a Jew can no more become a
Teuton than an Ethiopian can change his skin or a leopard
its spots. To minds like these Zionism came with the
force of an evangel. To be a Jew and to be proud of

---

[1] Zionism in its territorial aspects is now an integral, if not indeed the most
significant part of the Near Eastern Question, at least as regards the future of
the Ottoman Empire. [2] Cf. p 149.

it ; to glory in the power and pertinacity of the race, its
traditions, its triumphs, its sufferings, its resistance to persecution ; to look the world frankly in the face, and to enjoy
the luxury of moral and intellectual honesty ; to feel pride
in belonging to the people that gave Christendom its
Divinities, that taught half the world monotheism, whose
ideas have permeated civilization as never the ideas of a
race before it, whose genius fashioned the whole mechanism
of modern commerce and whose artists, actors, singers, and
writers have filled a larger place in the cultured universe
than those of any other people : this, or something like this,
was the train of thought fired in youthful Jewish minds by
the Zionist spark.   Its effect upon the Jewish students of
Austrian Universities was immediate and striking.   Until
then they had been despised and often ill-treated.   They
had wormed their way into appointments and into the free
professions by dint of pliancy, mock humility, mental acute-
ness and clandestine protection.   If struck or spat upon
by "Aryan" students, they rarely ventured to return the
blow or the insult.   But Zionism gave them courage.   They
formed associations and learned athletic drill and fencing.
Insult was requited with insult, and presently the best fencers
of the fighting German corps found that Zionist students
could gash cheeks quite as effectually as any Teuton and that
the Jews were in a fair way to become the best swordsmen
of the University.   To-day the purple cap of the Zionist is
as respected as that of any academical association.

This moral influence of Zionism is not confined to
University students.   It is quite as noticeable among the
mass of the younger Jews outside, who also find in it a
reason to raise their heads and, taking their stand upon
their past, to gaze straightforwardly into the future.   To
attend a Zionist gathering in the Leopoldstadt, the Jewish
quarter of Vienna, is an enlightening experience to those
who have seen the filth and misery of the Ghettos where
Jew exploits Jew and where contempt for the Gentile does
duty for self-respect.   Hundreds, sometimes thousands of

well-washed youths and trim maidens, with a large sprinkling of Jewish working-men, may be seen listening enraptured to readings from the Scriptures. The territorial ideal, that is to say, the foundation of a Jewish state in Palestine or elsewhere, doubtless appeals to the bulk of the Zionists, but the main effect of the ideal is to give them self-confidence and the courage of their convictions. It is too much to expect that Zionism will suddenly endow all Jews with courage, tact and uprightness ; but it is much that it should already have provided an intellectual and moral *élite* among them with an ideal capable of arousing faith and enthusiasm.

Many orthodox and semi-orthodox Jews nevertheless regard Zionism with grave misgivings and scarcely disguised hostility. They seem to fear that, by coming out into the open, the Zionists may be playing into the enemy's hands. Quite recently (March 29, 1913) an influential German Jewish association, the " Central Society of German Citizens of Jewish Faith," adopted a strongly anti-Zionist resolution. " The Society," it ran, " demands of its members not only the fulfilment of their duties as citizens but German feelings and the exercise of those feelings in civil life " ; and continued : " On the soil of the German Fatherland we wish, as Germans, to co-operate in German civilization and to remain true to a partnership that has been hallowed by religion and history. In so far as the Zionist endeavours to provide an assured home for the Jews of the East who are deprived of their rights, or to increase the pride of Jews in their history and religion, he is welcome to us as a member ; but we must sever ourselves from the Zionist who denies German National (racial) sentiments, feels himself to be a guest among a strange people, and only feels nationally (racially) as a Jew." [1]

This resolution is a precise definition of the semi-assimilationist standpoint. It is directed principally against the " Young Jewish " movement in Germany, whose literary leaders have adopted the device " Truth for Truth's sake "

[1] Cf. *Neue Freie Presse*, March 31, 1913.

and have, like Dr. Fromer, frankly proclaimed facts which the Assimilationists and semi-Assimilationists have for generations striven to hide. It admits the potential uses of Zionism but condemns its guiding idea. Doubtless Zionism, like every great movement, has its questionable sides. Many German Jews, filled with the assimilationist spirit, perceive that if cunningly exploited, the movement can be turned to account both politically and financially. An account of the numerous schemes and memoranda presented to the Porte during the Young Turkish era and of the machinations carried on in the name of "Zionism" with the support of Jewish financial and pseudo-philanthropical organizations, would form an interesting chapter in any veracious history of modern Jewry. One such memorandum, emanating from a Society of German Jews, pointed out that, "if Turkey opens her doors to Jewish immigration, our co-religionists, who occupy high positions (in other countries) will, without running counter to the duties they owe to their own countries, use all their influence for the political and economic advancement of the Constitutional Ottoman Government. Important advantages will thus accrue to Turkey as she makes her way straight towards Progress and Advancement, and the way of sure and influential alliances will be opened to her. The Ottoman Statesmen who undertake the foundation of this lasting alliance (between the Jews and Turkey) may be certain of obtaining the thanks and gratitude of the nation. We can promise and assure the attachment and friendship of the Jews towards the new Jewish emigration centres (Palestine, Syria, Mesopotamia, and Anatolia), and towards the Government which protects them, *for we have the means of bringing about these feelings.* As we are a Society composed of representatives of the largest Jewish Societies, we are sure that our recommendations and requests will be well received by the persons and circles that direct the Jews."

The idea on which this memorandum was based is diametrically opposed to the fundamental idea of Zionism.

It aimed not at the Constitution of a Jewish State—an aim with which every impartial student of the Jewish question must sympathize—but at the Judaization of Turkey in return for political and financial advantages that would ostensibly accrue to the Ottoman Empire through the favour of Jews holding influential positions in all countries. Of all forms of "Zionism" this would be surely the least desirable, the least sincere, and the most productive of confusion. It would tend to perpetuate the equivocation characteristic of assimilationist apologetics. The only hope of reaching a tolerable solution of the Jewish question is in openness and honesty. It is because the true Zionist ideal tends in this direction that it is the most hopeful sign noticeable in Jewry for centuries. Against it the Assimilationists urge that, were a Jewish State ever to be constituted and recognized, Anti-Semites, the world over, would arise and say to the Jews, " Now you have a land of your own ; go to it ! " This argument is disingenuous, and reveals the ambiguity of the position hitherto taken up by assimilationist Jewry. While explaining and justifying their dispersion by their lack of any country of their own and while maintaining belief in the Messiah who shall restore the Kingdom of Israel, nothing is farther from their hearts than the fulfilment of the prayer " Next year in Jerusalem ! " Hence the bitter dislike of genuine Zionism noticeable among prosperous Assimilationists and " Dispersionists," whose ideal seems to be the maintenance of Jewish international influence as a veritable *imperium in imperiis*. Dissimulation of their real objects has become to them a second nature, and they deplore and tenaciously combat every tendency to place the Jewish question frankly on its merits before the world. In reality there is no danger whatever that the eventual establishment of a Jewish State would lead to the expulsion of Jews from other countries, least of all to the expulsion of the well-to-do Jewish communities in Western Europe and America. The establishment of the Hellenic Kingdom has not led to the expulsion of Greek communities from France,

England, and the United States.   It is nevertheless probable that the creation of a Jewish State would, sooner or later, affect the position of the Jews throughout the world.   They would be obliged eventually to choose between acceptance of Jewish citizenship and absolute identification with the countries of their adoption.   The bond between German, English, French, and American Jews would tend to be reduced to a bond merely religious or denominational.   The issues would be clarified and simplified.   Whether the establishment of a Jewish State in Palestine or elsewhere will ever be feasible is a question of the future.   But in the meantime, Zionists are working to create conditions that shall facilitate its realization ; Zionist colonies have been and are being established in Palestine, Hebrew is again being taught and spoken in place of the Yiddish jargon, and the Agrarian law of Moses with its healthy provision that a family has no right permanently to possess what it cannot use or cultivate, is being brought into application.   The proud boast made some time ago by the German Zionist, Dr. Franz Oppenheimer, to a Zionist assembly in Vienna—that " after having taught the world monotheism, the Jews will, by the Light of the Mosaic Law, presently teach it a solution for the problems of property and misery "—may be a long way from realization ; but it goes in a sense to the root of the Jewish question in its capitalistic and propertied form.   The Jewish question can only be solved by Jews, and it may well be that Moses, who knew them and their tendencies, laid down the principles that will save them from themselves.   Non-Jews can only watch the process with sympathy proportionate to their acquaintance with the conditions of the problem— active sympathy in welcoming healthy symptoms, negative sympathy in striving to resist tendencies that are unwholesome ; but, above all, by seeking to acquire knowledge of Jewry, by having the courage to call things by their names, by refusing to be deluded into a sentimentally uncritical " philosemitic " attitude, and by rejecting mere uncritical antisemitic clamour.   The Jewish problem is one of the

great problems of the world, and no man, be he a writer,
politician or diplomatist, can be considered mature until he
has striven to face it squarely on its merits.

THE PRESS AND THE PUBLIC

"Every country has the Jews it deserves," runs a
hackneyed saying ; and every country, it is often added,
has the press it deserves.   Such sayings are, in reality,
question-begging truisms that go but a little way to elucidate
the problems they airily dispose of.   A "country" or, rather,
the public of a country is not an undifferentiated medium
of constant quality that invariably gives, as in a testing
tube, the same "reactions" when exposed to the influence
of specified "agents."   Race-character, conditions of development, traditions, and the strength of constituted authorities
all play a part in determining the "reaction" of the public
under the influence of "agents" like the Jews and the press.
When, as in the Hapsburg Monarchy, the press is almost
entirely Jewish, the problem is at once simplified and complicated, for the press which, in other hands, might assist
the public to "have the Jews it deserves," deprives the Jews
themselves of the educational influence of fair criticism and
removes from their path those minor checks and warnings
that might otherwise induce them to be wise in time and
to practise the, for them, supremely difficult virtue of self-
restraint and moderation.   Centuries of segregation and—
as regards the mass—of pauperism, working upon non-
European temperaments, have prevented the Jews from
knowing instinctively how much Jewish influence a non-
Jewish public will tolerate.   They unconsciously violate
the unexpressed canons of non-Jewish taste, and are filled
with amazement and a sense of injustice when an outburst
of violent antisemitism in word or deed reminds them too
pertinently that the days of persecution may not be past.
They then tend to confound effect with cause and to
attribute to antisemitic agitation the outburst which could

not have occurred had not the agitators found a mass of explosive material ready to hand. Most Austrian Jews still attribute the Christian Social antisemitic movement to the agitation of Lueger and his associates, ignoring the fact that Lueger only gave shape and political consistency to a powerful current of feeling due partly to public resentment of Jewish display of newly-gotten wealth and partly to a comprehensible though not wholly justifiable tendency to make of the Jews scapegoats for the losses of the community in the financial disasters of 1873. Some clearer-sighted Jews attribute, albeit with conscious exaggeration, the growth of political antisemitism in Austria to detestation of the *Neue Freie Presse*, a journal that embodies in concentrated form and, at times, with demonic force, the least laudable characteristics of Austro-German Jewry. The simple truth is that in the Hapsburg Monarchy, as in most non-Oriental countries, the Jews are only half-acclimatized and less than half-assimilated ; and that, in these circumstances, it should be their first care to reduce to a minimum the friction and jarring that are inevitable when elements ethnically diverse inhabit one politico-social body. But the more circumspect and enlightened Jews are deterred, by fear of playing into the enemy's hands, from public criticism or rebuke of their co-religionists' indiscretions. Consequently such restraining influence as is publicly exercised remains a monopoly of professional Anti-Semites and of Clerical demagogues.

Moreover, in the Hapsburg Monarchy and particularly in Vienna, the press consists less of "organs of public opinion" than of instruments working to manufacture public opinion, primarily in accordance with the wishes of the State authorities and, secondarily, in the interests of financial and economic corporations. As has been said, the Jews control practically the whole press. They control also the financial and economic corporations. They have, too, a footing in those minor offices of State from which the press is inspired and they frequently hold influential posts among the police and semi-judicial functionaries by whom the press is exter-

nally " kept in order." Thus the dual supervision exercised
on the one hand by the Press-Bureaux of the various State
Departments, and, on the other, by the State Attorneys or
public prosecutors who are entitled to confiscate offending
journals, is sometimes strangely circumscribed. It is true that
the history of the Austrian press is largely the history of a
struggle to widen the field of activity that lies between the
extremes of official inspiration and official confiscation. But,
in practice, the struggle has resulted in a compromise that
allows the press great liberty, and even licence, in certain
directions and, in others, permits the State to retain, directly
and indirectly, the control ostensibly removed when preventive
censorship was abolished. A symbol of the status of Austrian
newspapers may perhaps be descried in the fact that, save to
subscribers, they are still retailed to the public, like cigars,
matches, postage stamps and lottery tickets, in the State
tobacco shops and are not allowed to be sold by news-
vendors or by newsboys in the streets. Confiscation of the
whole issue of any journal is thus a comparatively easy
matter, inasmuch as the police authorities are able within a
few minutes to put their hands upon nearly every copy
printed. In extreme cases the Government can forbid the
sale of an opposition journal in the tobacco shops—a punitive
measure that nearly killed one flourishing gazette some years
ago. State inspiration and control naturally apply chiefly to
expressions of opinion and items of information politically
interesting to the authorities. It matters little to the State
if the letterpress and advertisement columns of a journal or
periodical tend to encourage vice and immorality. The old
principle that, when the public is " amusing itself," it is likely
to refrain from meddling in the public affairs which are the
concern of the Government, is still held in honour. The
Austrian press, to do it justice, wears its fetters with a good
grace and might even, in the American phrase, " feel lonely
without them." It knows that there are paths that lead
under, through and round the most formidable obstacles,
and that, in an easy-going country, no tree ever grows into

the sky and no food is eaten at cooking temperature. In the relations, open and surreptitious, between the press and the authorities, the Jews naturally find scope for their peculiar adaptability and power of combination—the more so in that some important groups of newspapers are affiliated to industrial and financial concerns which the State has every interest not to estrange. There are exceptions, apparent or real, to this as to every rule but, as will appear from a brief analysis of the position and characteristics of the leading Viennese journals, the principle holds good that the Austrian press is a semi-private, semi-public institution, worked chiefly by Jews under a dual control exercised through official press bureaux and the public prosecutor.

No aspect of the Jewish question, not even the Jewish control of money-power, has so immediate an interest for the Gentile world as that of Jewish influence over the public press. In all countries, except perhaps in Russia, this influence is strong, but in no country is it stronger than in Austria-Hungary. Precise figures are hard to obtain, but estimates by competent judges place the proportion of Jewish journalists on the Magyar press of Budapest at 90 per cent, and on the press of Vienna at 75 per cent. The relatively high percentage of Jews in the population of Lower Austria and Vienna (5.23 per cent) is insufficient to account for this predominance, nor can the higher percentage of Jews in Hungary adequately explain what is practically a Jewish monopoly of journalism. The "intellectualism" and quick-wittedness of the Jew, his versatility and power of adaptation to circumstances, evidently fit him in especial degree to discharge functions which are practically those of a middleman between the public and matters of public interest. Newspaper enterprise is, moreover, a business, albeit a business *sui generis*, and is governed largely by the considerations that apply to all commercial undertakings. If a newspaper be regarded as a mere commodity, it is comprehensible that the Jews should possess the same advantages in manufacturing and selling it as in the manufacture and sale of other wares. Besides, the Jews have had for centuries unrivalled experience in the collection and dissemination of news. Their very dispersion has given them an advantage by which they have been quick to profit. They were the first to understand the value of constant intercommunication, just as, so far as records go, they were the first systematically to use the press for commercial advertising. The development of the electric telegraph was furthered and exploited by them. Jews founded the chief European telegraph agencies both for the purpose of organizing and of controlling the main supply of international information. For legitimate business and for speculation such control is alike essential. Similarly the Jews, after their emancipation, understood the importance of using the press to propagate the liberal views to which they owed the removal of disabilities, and to combat reactionary or anti-Jewish tendencies. These aspects of Jewish influence in the press are unexceptionable in so far as they are frankly recognized. But when the influence is clandestine or disguised it becomes questionable. Save from the newsvendor's standpoint, a newspaper cannot be regarded as a mere commodity, even though it confine itself to matter-of-fact statements or to the publication of telegrams. The formulation of the statement and the choice of the telegram may go far to produce the impression desired. When comment is added the influence of the newspaper is more patent and the issue more clearly raised. Freedom of the press and the right to publish fair comment are justly considered indispensable to political liberty, but they should evidently connote a sense of journalistic responsibility equal, at lowest, to the responsibility felt by conscientious tradesmen towards their customers. There is such a thing as the freedom of the public and its right not to be exposed to misleading statements of fact or insidious comment. The objection that the public is not obliged to read newspapers is not valid. Nowadays the reading of newspapers is as inevitable as the use of railways or other mechanical means of locomotion. The newspaper press needs therefore to be controlled by a high sense of duty

towards the public, a sense which ought not to be inferior
to that of a university professor towards his students or of
a preacher towards his congregation.   Otherwise restrictive
measures and the application to journalism of the principle
that inspired the Merchandise Marks Act may become necessary in the public interest.   In England, as in some other
countries, the interest of individuals is protected, perhaps to
excess, by the law of libel, but the public in general has no
protection against the dissemination of false or tainted news
and the suppression of facts necessary for the formation of
healthy public opinion.   It may be maintained that, as the
field of journalistic competition is free, those who dislike
views and tendencies openly or surreptitiously represented
in the press are at liberty to set up rival journals and combat
the influences they deplore ; and that the public mind grows
more robust by learning to pick and choose for itself.   Such
contentions are specious.   The public mind is no more likely
to grow robust by picking and choosing between a variety
of journals representing clandestine tendencies or simply
peppering the public brain with items of disjointed " newsy "
intelligence, than schoolboys would be likely to develop a
taste for scholarship were they obliged to limit their choice
of reading to novels with a purpose and penny dreadfuls.   In
practice, the freedom of journalistic competition is limited
by the immense difficulty of establishing any new journal of
sufficient dimensions to make it a public force.   In modern
journalism, even more than in other spheres of enterprise,
possession is nine-tenths of the law.   Apart from the capital,
labour, energy and special talent required to create a newspaper and to give it a hold on the public, it is no easy
matter to loosen the grip of an established journal even
upon readers who do not entirely agree with its opinions.
In no European country is this fact more strikingly demonstrated than in Austria.   Detestation of the leading Austrian
journal, the *Neue Freie Presse*, is general, yet it has an
influence probably unsurpassed by that of any journal of
equal circulation in the world.   To be attacked by the *Neue*

Freie Presse is a certificate of political uprightness, but politicians and officials nevertheless fear it. It is owned, edited
and written by Jews and appeals in the first instance to a
distinctly Jewish community of readers, many of whom, like
the bulk of its non-Jewish readers, suspect it of aiming constantly at influencing the Stock Exchange and profess disgust
at its chronic unfairness, blatant self-sufficiency and per-
sistent advocacy of its peculiar conception of Jewish interests.
But one and all read it from day to day, or, rather, twice a
day, unconsciously adopt its standpoint and allow it to colour
their views of public affairs. The greater part of what does
duty for "Austrian opinion" is dictated or suggested to the
public by the editor-proprietor of the *Neue Freie Presse*, of
whom it has jokingly but, in a sense, not untruthfully been
said that "next to him the Emperor is the most important
man in the country."

It is a debatable point whether the influence of journals
like the *Neue Freie Presse* and of similar organs in Germany,
would be affected were they obliged to print as a sub-title,
"Organ for the propagation of German-Jewish ideas." The
public would gain by knowing what it was reading. The
journals themselves might lose no more than Austrian and
German manufacturers lost when the Merchandise Marks
Act introduced the designations "made in Germany" and
"made in Austria." The superior talent of the Jewish
journalist might triumph and obtain for itself frank and
open recognition. But it would no longer masquerade as
"German" or "Magyar." The editor-proprietor of the *Neue
Freie Presse* is a journalist of genius—a tyrannical, vindictive
genius, under whom his staff and many of his readers groan,
but a genius nevertheless. His journal would be read for its
own sake but would no longer be regarded by an uninstructed
world as the chief mouthpiece of Austrian-German opinion.
As it is, no suggestion is more fiercely resented by the *Neue
Freie Presse* and its editor than that they are not and cannot
be "German." They claim to "feel like Germans"—careless of the scholastic maxim, *Quidquid recipitur secundum*

modum recipientis recipitur, and of the psychological fact
that no Teutonic or " Germanic German " contents have ever
entered a Semitic-German mind without undergoing a subtle
change of quality and form.   But as long as the Germans
of Austria, who are antisemitic almost to a man, are content
to draw their notions of home and foreign affairs through a
Jewish medium, they have only themselves to blame if current
notions of public affairs bear a Semitic-German stamp.

Yet, despite defects, the *Neue Freie Presse* possesses one
quality that distinguishes it advantageously from the bulk
of its " Liberal" contemporaries.   It stands for an idea, and
is not a mere contrivance for the sale of printed paper.
Herein lies its force.   Whatever may be said against it and
the methods of its editor, no one has ever accused him of
not being fanatically devoted to the propagation of Jewish-
German " Liberal" assimilationist doctrine and of not being
ready to sacrifice journalistic and other advantages on the
altar of his peculiar politico-racial faith.   It is this that
makes his paper ring true when the cause which he has at
heart is engaged, and it is this that groups round him and
it all those commercial, financial, and politico-religious
elements which are directly or indirectly interested in the
cause.   The bulk of the " Liberal" contemporaries of the
Neue Freie Presse serve no idea save that of selling profitably as much as possible of the pressed-out wood pulp
manufactured by the various paper " Mills" to which they
belong.   Of these newspapers the *Neues Wiener Tagblatt* is
the highest type.   It and its satellites are controlled by the
" Styrian" Paper Mill.   It calls itself a " democratic organ,"
and is largely read by the lower middle class.   Its circulation is probably double, if not treble, that of the *Neue
Freie Presse* but its driving power is incomparably smaller.
Edited and mainly, though not exclusively, written by Jews
for a public chiefly Christian, it defends Jewish interests by
omission rather than by commission.   In most respects it is
a monument of easy-going, trimming profit-making.   Its
pages—there are some scores of them on week days and

sometimes more than two hundred of them on Sundays and holidays—consist of oases of inoffensive text in a wilderness of advertisements, not all of which *non olent.* It is a flourishing enterprise and, as an enterprise, incorruptible. Though constantly at the disposal of the authorities for the dissemination of semi-official views, it has never, under its present editorship, been suspected of receiving, as a journal, subsidies from official sources. It is a mild volunteer in the cause of semi-official and "German" patriotism and is maintained in unstable equilibrium by fear of giving offence in official quarters on the one hand and of losing subscribers and, consequently, advertising potentiality on the other. It gives no shocks to the Stock Exchange, leaves "bulls" and "bears" to their own devices, never terrorizes a government, is never "cranky," and ministers to the public taste for "topical" articles and sport. The more insignificant the paper from a journalistic standpoint, the more the Viennese appear to like it, buy it and advertise in it. If a newspaper be a mere commodity and its production simply a commercial enterprise governed by the all-sufficient object of making profit for wood-pulp magnates, the *Tagblatt* may claim to have realized approximately the ideal of what a newspaper should be.

Another important group of journals is owned by another paper-making syndicate, the "Elbe Mill," which, in its turn, is controlled by powerful industrial and financial interests. These journals do not exist only for the purpose of printing and selling and making revenue out of "Elbe Mill" paper. Their circulations are too small. They serve nevertheless other important purposes in various degrees. They are, one and all, at the disposal of the Government and particularly of the Foreign Office. The well-known *Fremdenblatt,* the official Foreign Office organ, the sensational but semi-official *Wiener Allgemeine Zeitung* and other obscurer news-sheets are among them. The *Fremden-blatt* which, when uninspired, is an effective soporific, has an insignificant circulation and is understood to be maintained

by the Government for official purposes. It has no physi-
ognomy of its own, represents no idea and is merely the
vessel into which the most authorized semi-official views are
poured. Like the majority of its contemporaries, it is edited
and written—except in the case of positively official announcements—by Jews.

Three Viennese journals deserve special mention as
tending to introduce an atmosphere of greater sincerity into
the Austrian press—the *Zeit*, the *Reichspost*, and the *Arbeiter
Zeitung*. The *Zeit* was established as a daily journal some
eleven years ago, and endowed with much capital for the
amiable purpose of killing or crippling the *Neue Freie Presse*.
In this purpose it has not yet succeeded ; indeed, the *Zeit* is
reported to have had from time to time some difficulty in
saving its own life. It may even have benefited its intended
victim by squandering what an eminent Jewish journalist
has called " the immense patrimony of Austrian hatred of
the *Neue Freie Presse*." The story of the *Zeit* is the story
of praiseworthy Jewish talent pitted against unscrupulous
Jewish genius—and the Jewish public is too shrewd not to
side with genius. Nevertheless the *Zeit* has rendered and
renders real service to the Austrian public. It is more
open-minded and less pusillanimous than its " Liberal " contemporaries of the " Mills." Save in its military information,
it has kept itself remarkably free from the semi-official taint.
Even if its criticism of Government action be sometimes
carping, it has the courage to call a spade a spade and
roundly to state facts which other journals are fain, for
" patriotic " reasons—that is to say, for fear of incurring
official odium—to cover up. During the annexation crisis
of 1908–9 it was the only non-Socialist organ to maintain
an independent standpoint in regard to Count Aehrenthal's
policy and to recommend a conciliatory attitude towards
the Southern Slavs ; and during the scandalous Agram High
Treason Trial of 1907–8, the Friedjung trial and its sequel,
it defended the cause of political honesty and fair play. Its
attitude during the more recent Balkan crisis has been frank

and fearless and has brought the journal its reward in a notable increase of prestige and circulation. Though sometimes
exposed to "influences," diplomatic and other, that ought to
play no part in self-respecting journalism, the fact stands
to its credit that it has let in more light upon the dark
places of Austro-Hungarian public affairs than any other
prominent middle-class newspaper and that it has approxi-
mated, at times, to what an independent organ of public
opinion might and should be.

The *Reichspost*, organ of the Christian Social Party and
of the *Piusverein*—a Clerical, mainly Jesuit, Society for the
development of a Roman Catholic, non-Jewish press—is the
only considerable daily organ of pronouncedly "Christian"
tendencies. It was founded with Catholic funds, is written
and edited by militant Catholics and is clerical, antisemitic,
military, chauvinistic and aggressive in tone. Just as critical
readers of the *Neue Freie Presse* are apt to exclaim, "A
plague on all scribbling Hebrews," so unprejudiced readers
of the *Reichspost* are often tempted to aver that Jewish
"Liberalism" is no worse than Clerical "Christianity." In
such Christianity, charity has little place. When Christianity
is claimed as a party monopoly, made subservient to party
ends and used as a flag to cover the merchandise manufactured by Jesuitism in the ostensible interests of Church
and dynasty, it becomes a stumbling-block to the simple-
minded and not to the simple-minded alone. At its best, the
propaganda of the *Reichspost* acts as a counterpoise to Jewish
"Liberal" and Social Democratic doctrines but it falls lament-
ably short of the Christian ideal which it professes to serve.

To the *Arbeiter Zeitung*, the chief Social Democratic organ,
reference has already been made.[1] Its influence extends far
beyond the limits of party and is, in the main, healthy. Whenever it can forget Marxist dogma and the inverted Clericalism
of its party creed, it speaks the language of good sense
touched by idealism. Though largely written by Jews and
sometimes curiously subject to clandestine Jewish influences,

[1] Cf. p. 135.

it keeps in reserve a whip for financial corruption and, unlike the middle-class Jewish organs, never attempts to whitewash the black sheep of the House of Israel.

No account of the Viennese press would, however, be even approximately complete without some mention of a biting, stinging, sometimes scurrilous periodical pamphlet called the *Fackel*, which keeps a vigilant eye upon the follies and failings of daily journalism and pillories them mercilessly. The editor, proprietor and staff of the *Fackel* consist of one and the same person, Karl Kraus, a Jewish writer of remarkable talent. The daily press maintains a conspiracy of silence in regard to his very existence but he has nevertheless a faithful public of readers who enjoy his mordant satire and find in his brilliant style relief from the pomposities and bathos of Austrian journalese. Occasionally he victimises the self-sufficient omniscience of the *Neue Freie Presse* by perpetrating at its expense some elaborate hoax. Kraus is a Viennese product, scarcely intelligible save in relationship to the Viennese press though his literary style finds recognition beyond the frontiers of the Monarchy. He is an Ishmael, courting and requiting the hostility of his contemporaries but rarely allowing their shortcomings to pass unpunished. In one respect his efforts deserve specially honourable mention. He has encouraged by precept and practice the tendency of modern writers of German to react against the artificial clumsiness of the language and to prove that German can be written harmoniously. Though Jewish writers of German abound, few of them write it purely and well. The work of men like the late Theodor Herzl, literary editor of the *Neue Freie Presse* and founder of Zionism, and the late Leo Veigelsberg, assistant-editor and chief leader-writer of the *Pester Lloyd*, was of a high order of literary merit. Herzl, a lovable, clean-hearted man, intensely proud of his race, brought to the service of his pen genuine human sympathy and a fine sense of humour. Veigelsberg, less widely known than Herzl, was justly regarded as the ablest political critic in the German press of any country. In style and point his work was incomparable. But, broadly speaking, the number of notable Jewish writers of German is singularly small in comparison with their numerical preponderance. Their easy knack of turning out readable "copy" on any subject seems a positive obstacle to the attainment of excellence; and their very facility of ratiocination appears to militate against the acquisition of literary power. Mere lucidity and flawlessness of logic are rarely convincing. Feeling, even imperfectly expressed, is far more effective. This is perhaps why non-Semitic writers of German, like Kürnberger, have made so deep a mark. Though possibly less gifted than their Jewish colleagues, they stand on firmer ground and speak with temperamental directness to the temperaments of their readers, whereas the Jewish writer speaks chiefly from the brain to the brain of an alien race. There is yet another reason for Jewish literary inferiority. The mother tongue of most Jewish journalists in Austria is or was Yiddish. The influence of the jargon is frequently discernible in their work. Their vocabulary, their turns of phrase reveal it. When they strive to escape it they are apt to fall into artificiality. The contorted " high-falutin' " style of " Maximilian Harden," editor-proprietor of the Berlin *Zukunft*, is a case in point. No pages of the *Fackel* are more amusing than those in which Kraus, under the heading " Desperanto," translates Harden into German. The Jewish jargon press and especially Yiddish plays show, on the other hand, how powerful and direct Jewish authors can be when expressing their own thoughts in their own way, and speaking without mummery to a public they know. Should the Zionist movement eventually lead to a revival of Hebrew as a living language, the literature of the world might yet be enriched by masterpieces not unworthy of the old Jewish Scriptures. In the meantime writers who, like Heine, produce masterpieces in a non-Jewish tongue are likely to be rare. The assimilated Jew, who knows neither Hebrew nor jargon, is usually too far removed from his native stock to possess the originality that springs from the instinctive expression of race-temperament. He may have the form but is likely to lack the substance of his adopted language, to be a master of the letter but incapable of expressing its spirit save in rationalized, artificial fashion. Unassimilated Jews, who retain their native temperament and directness of feeling, are wofully handicapped by having to use a foreign tongue. At its best their German work often exhales an exotic savour ; at its worst, it is current German journalese.

THE PRESS BUREAUX

The main defect of the Austrian press is, however, its semi-officialism. The term " semi-official " sounds strange to English ears but there is no other equivalent for the German expression *offiziös*—an expression intelligible only in relation to bureaucratic control over public life, and indicating that the opinions of the press are inspired by officials on behalf of " authorities." Semi-officialism is intended to influence the public without letting the public know that it is being influenced. In Austria-Hungary, several Departments of State maintain special bureaux for this purpose—notably the War Office, the Premier's Office, the Home Offices in Austria and Hungary, and especially the Vienna Foreign Office—and endow them liberally with secret funds for the " encouragement " of journals and journalists. Ostensibly the object is to supply the press with authentic and reliable information but, in reality, the work of a press bureau is to control, inspire, corrupt, spy upon and intimidate the press and its representatives. The insidious power of a well-organized press bureau needs to be experienced in order to be fully understood. In the case of the Press Bureau, or, as it styles itself, the " Literary Department " of the Foreign Office, the power is international and extends to Berlin, London, Paris, Rome, St. Petersburg, the Balkan Capitals, and even to the United States. Its methods vary according to circumstances and to the persons with whom it has to deal. The head of the Bureau is a Foreign Office official who has usually been, but is not invariably, of Jewish extraction. Attached to him is a large staff of journalistic officials conversant with the principal European languages and commissioned to report from day to day upon the foreign press. The "Literary Bureau" subscribes to the chief foreign newspapers and receives, besides, periodical reports from the Austro-Hungarian Embassies, Legations and Consulates abroad. An exact register is kept of the position, resources, proprietorship and connexions of each important foreign journal, while its representatives in Austria-Hungary are watched and their opinions and doings noted either by the secret police or by the Press Bureau itself. Alongside of the journalistic officials commissioned to report on the foreign press, a staff of regular official writers, recruited from the ranks of professional journalists, is employed to furnish semi-official articles to the home and foreign journals that are subsidized from the secret funds or otherwise controlled by the Bureau. Such articles are transmitted by telephone and telegraph or, if time allows, by mail, to the editors of the journals in question, who know that failure to publish would involve a withdrawal of the subsidies, the stoppage of official news and eventually a campaign of intimidation. Where editors or proprietors are unapproachable, recourse is had to their correspondents who are "shepherded" by "well-disposed" colleagues, plied with news and, in some cases, offered remuneration on a scale equal to that of the emoluments they receive from their journals. An under-paid and friendless correspondent in Vienna may thus be exposed to considerable temptation. Rejection of the advances made to him may earn him the hostility of the Bureau and its agents; acceptance may mean an increase of income, the advantage of being able to shine from time to time by supplying his journal or journals with tit-bits of "exclusive" information, and the certainty of official favour in his everyday work. To the honour of many foreign correspondents in Vienna be it said that they prefer the drawbacks of independence to the sweets of semi-officialism. The exceptions among them are well known ; but unfortunately it does not follow that the readers of journals supplied with tainted views and information are aware of the sources from which their "knowledge" is derived. The honest correspondent may even find himself circumvented by the action of the local agents of the "Literary Bureau" in the country where his journal is published. Cases are known of leading articles having been foisted, ready written, even upon reputable English newspapers whose editors had no notion of the veritable origin of the views to which they were giving currency and may even have felt flattered to find "their" leader subsequently reproduced in full as "an authoritative English opinion" in the Austro-Hungarian organs of the "Literary Bureau"! It may be asked what purpose can be served by manœuvres of this kind, seeing that the smuggling of Austro-Hungarian semi-official opinions into the foreign press would need to take place on a much larger scale than is practically possible if foreign public opinion and foreign governments are really to be influenced. The answer is that however futile single manifestations of Press Bureau activity may seem to be, they form part of a system which is extremely insidious and is sometimes extremely effective. While agents are attempting to influence the press abroad and "well-disposed" correspondents are seconding them from Vienna, efforts are simultaneously made to influence the Vienna Embassies or Legations of the governments upon which it is desired to produce an impression. The personal foibles of Ambassadors or Ministers are studied and played upon. If an Ambassador be vain, his vanity is assiduously flattered ; if he have compromised himself by imprudent conduct or language, he is made to feel that his recall will not be asked for provided he lend himself to the propagation of Austro-Hungarian official views. Diplomatists are human and fear nothing so much as having it whispered that they are not "agreeable persons" to the governments to which they are accredited. They wish also to be thought "well-informed" and, as the acquisition of reliable information and sure judgment entails in Vienna harder and more constant work than most diplomatists care to undertake, they are reluctant to close their doors to the emissaries sent to inoculate them with "confidential" information. These emissaries are of several kinds. The most efficient are the editors or members of the staff of semi-official journals. The information they supply is, as a rule, so delicately adjusted to the taste of the diplomatic victim that he is not infrequently misled into allowing it to colour his reports to his government. At critical moments, additional means of influencing foreign opinion are employed. Foreign journalists of note are encouraged to come to Vienna, are granted easy access to Austro-Hungarian Ministers and other personages of State and are able to declare without fear of contradiction that their information is "invariably drawn from the very best sources." When they leave Vienna arrangements are made to keep them periodically supplied with "information" of equal quality; and it is only when, as during the Balkan crisis of 1912–1913, events perversely flout their predictions and belie their "positive knowledge" that unwary readers begin to doubt their infallibility.

The "Literary Bureau" has, besides, at its service a number of what may be termed demi-semi-official organs and agencies in the shape of lithographed or printed *Correspondenzen*. A *Correspondenz* is a news-sheet printed as manuscript and subsidized from the secret funds. Into it the "Authorities" pour information for which they would not care to be made directly responsible. Most of the untruths designed to create an "atmosphere" favourable to Austro-Hungarian policy that are systematically disseminated in and from Vienna on Balkan, Albanian and Southern Slav topics pass through these semi-clandestine *Correspondenzen*. The *Politische Correspondenz*, the prototype of such news-sheets, stands, however, in a class by itself. It is frankly and admittedly semi-official. Its editor is directly subordinate to the Head of the Foreign Office Press Bureau, whose responsibility for its publications is acknowledged ; but its demi-semi-official contemporaries have no recognized status and masquerade as independent undertakings. The Press Bureau is always able to disavow them, though they are invariably edited in accordance with the views which it desires to propagate.

Since the publication of Busch's *Bismarck ; Some Secret Pages of His History*, the English public has had at its disposal a classical account of the Press Bureau of the German Foreign Office and of its tortuous methods. No indiscreet scribe has yet ventured to reveal from the inside the workings of the Vienna Press Bureau nor to explain the manner in which it co-operates with its sister institution in Berlin. Austro-Hungarian press officials have, however, confessed in unguarded moments that, just as there exists a secret military convention between Austria-Hungary and Germany, so there exists an arrangement by which the Austro-Hungarian semi-official organs are placed at the disposal of Germany in regard to international questions affecting interests mainly German, while the German semi-official press is placed at the disposal of Austria-Hungary when Austro-Hungarian interests are principally involved. When the interests of the two countries clash, confusion ensues. During the summer of 1905 a German Foreign Office organ alleged that in case of the outbreak of war between Germany, France and England over the Morocco question, Austria-Hungary would be bound to give Germany armed support. The assertion was immediately challenged in Vienna, not by the *Fremdenblatt* or any other prominent Foreign Office organ, but by the (now defunct) Conservative-Catholic *Vaterland.* So authoritative was the tone of the *Vaterland* article that interested enquirers asked the " Literary Bureau " why an utterance of such importance had been relegated to the comparative obscurity of the *Vaterland* instead of appearing in a recognized Foreign Office organ. The explanation given was that German control over the Austro-Hungarian press was, in virtue of the

reciprocity arrangement and for other reasons, so strong that
no Austrian journal of note would accept criticism of Germany
even though the criticism were furnished with the *imprimatur*
of the Austro-Hungarian Foreign Office. The *Vaterland*
alone enjoyed sufficient independence or was considered un-
important enough to escape the German yoke. Since that
time the Austro-Hungarian Foreign Office press has acquired
a greater measure of independence, possibly because the
Balkan crisis that began with the annexation of Bosnia-
Herzegovina in October 1908 has thrust Austro-Hungarian
interests into the foreground and has compelled the more
official of the German semi-official organs to respect an
arrangement of which the working was previously unilateral.

Yet the pernicious facts remain that the Austro-
Hungarian press is almost entirely under official control
when dealing with questions of foreign policy and that the
public rarely gets an inkling of the merits of a situation
that may involve the country in war. During the Morocco
crisis of 1905–1906, Austro-Hungarian ignorance of the
position of affairs in Europe was complete. Not until after
the Conference of Algeciras in April 1906, did any Austrian
journal lay before its readers an intelligible account of the
origin and course of the crisis. The German Press Bureau
conducted its campaign against France and England even
more in Austro-Hungarian than in German journals. Even
when, after the diplomatic defeat of Germany at Algeciras,
the *Neue Freie Presse* allowed M. Georges Clemenceau to
state in its columns the bare facts concerning the recent past
—facts that gave the lie to the inventions which the *Neue
Freie Presse* and its contemporaries had previously foisted
upon the public—it continued tranquilly its campaign of
conscious untruthfulness and left its readers bewildered.
Similarly, before and during the annexation crisis of 1908–
1909, Austrian journals, under the influence of Count
Aehrenthal's Press Bureau, rigorously excluded from their
columns all information contrary to the official thesis, and
waged war, not only against Russia and Servia, but against

the best interests of the Monarchy itself. Nemesis overtook
the Press Bureau and its organs during the recent Balkan
war. Events belied official and semi-official doctrine so
rapidly and unmistakably that the public actually awoke to
the situation and understood for a moment the deleterious
effects, moral and material, of Government control of the
press and of the constant inoculation of the public mind
with mendacious statement and misleading suggestion.

But, it may be urged, the press itself is largely to blame
for abetting such abuse of public opinion. Seeing that the
chief Austrian organs are financially independent, voluntary
collusion with the Government is surely more reprehensible
than mere corruption would be. It is difficult satisfactorily
to answer these objections. The larger organs of the
Austrian press are financially independent but on questions
of foreign policy they fear the Government. Confiscation
may await those that fall into the pernicious habit of holding
aloof from "official circles." The trend of public feeling is
against the systematic adoption by any journal of an "anti-
patriotic," that is to say anti-official, attitude, even though
the attitude be inspired by consideration for the higher
interests of the country. However much the people may
grumble and cavil at official policy, the feeling that after
all it is the business of the government to look after public
affairs and that "the authorities" know better than any
unofficial wiseacre what should or should not be done, is too
strong to permit the growth of a powerful body of independent
opinion. Indirect criticism is tolerated and at times even
welcomed, but it is taken for granted that it will exercise
no practical effect. The Viennese atmosphere of amiable,
sceptical, satirical indifference affects the whole tone of the
press and causes any writer who takes public interest to
heart in a manner not approved of by the authorities to
be considered eccentric or, at best, to be suspected of
having some private axe to grind under cloak of vociferous
solicitude for the public welfare.

Within these limitations the Austrian-German press is,

in many respects, technically excellent. It is, on the whole, better written and better printed than the majority of journals in Germany. Its arrangements for reporting political speeches in Parliament are, on occasion, extremely efficient. An important speech delivered in Magyar at Budapest as late as one p.m. will often be printed *in extenso* by the *Neue Freie Presse* or the *Neues Wiener Tagblatt* an hour later. It is taken down in German shorthand by bilingual Jewish reporters who read their notes through the telephone to stenographers at Vienna and these in their turn dictate them to type-writers or, when time presses, to the type-setters. Similarly, on weighty occasions, the proceedings in the House of Commons or the Palais Bourbon will be telegraphed very fully to the *Neue Freie Presse*, which, despite its many failings, is not so far americanized as to think its readers incapable of concentrating their attention for more than five minutes on one subject. But, alongside of these laudable features, the reports of foreign events in which Austria-Hungary has or is supposed to have a special kind of interest, are apt to be trimmed and cut, even by the Official Telegraph Agency, with singular disregard for accuracy. Fair play and good faith sometimes seem to be concepts foreign to the Austrian journalistic mind. *Suppressio veri* and *suggestio falsi* are by no means tabooed. No journal feels called upon, out of mere regard for truth or impartiality, to expose itself to a *diminutio capitis* ; and he who has occasion to correct deliberate misstatements and misrepresentations will be well advised to devise a formula not wounding to the *amour propre* of the journal in question. To compel an Austrian newspaper, by invoking Clause XIX. of the Press Law, to eat its own words is a draconian proceeding tantamount to a declaration of war. In such a case an editor is considered to be well within his rights if he append a malicious postscript to the compulsory rectification. Far wiser then—from the Viennese standpoint—to adopt a " formula " which the journal can print without loss of " face," and to trust the public to read between the lines.

Vienna and "Vienna"

The " Viennese standpoint " is, simply, to avoid unpleasant-
ness, to take life easily, sceptically, and to get out of it as
much thoughtless enjoyment as possible.   Abroad, Vienna
has a reputation for "gaiety," dating, perhaps, from the Congress of 1815.   Of this reputed gaiety, the critical stranger
sees little.   He sees a whole population trying to be gay,
but little spontaneous merriment.   Centuries of absolutist
government working upon a temperament compounded of
Celtic versatility, South German slackness and Slav sensuous-
ness, have—thanks to the constant efforts of the authorities
to turn attention away from public affairs and towards
amusement—ended by producing a population of *dilettanti*,
disposed to take nothing seriously save the pursuit of
pleasure.   The result is depressing to those not born to the
Viennese manner or capable of assimilating the Viennese
standpointlessness.   The Viennese themselves hold their
city incomparable—as indeed it is, after its fashion.   Their
pride in it and in themselves as its inhabitants is intense,
far deeper-rooted and livelier than the pride of the Parisian
in Paris.   For this pride there are many valid reasons.
No European capital has so Imperial an air, none finer
boulevards, none a more magnificent park at its gates or
more delightful surroundings.   First impressions of Vienna
are usually seductive.   The combination of stateliness and
homeliness, of colour and light, the comparative absence of
architectural monstrosities and the soft Italian influence
everywhere apparent, contribute, together with the grace
and beauty of the women, the polite friendliness of the
inhabitants and the broad, warm accent of their speech, to
charm the eye and ear of every travelled visitor.   Then, in
a brief space, the spell is often broken.   Disillusionment,
of the kind that overtakes a guest during too long a *tête-à-
tête* with a handsome hostess who is handsome but nothing
more, sets in and sometimes inclines strangers to harsh and
hasty judgment.   The defects of the city are felt to out-

weigh its attractions. The population appears soulless, its easy-going character amorphous, its politeness hollow, its honesty dubious and its vanity insufferable. The very architecture of Viennese buildings seems to stand in no relation to Viennese life save, perhaps, the Baroque which, with its apotheosis of unreality, somehow suits the character of a people that has latterly adopted with snobbish alacrity the unintelligible canons of "modern art." This disillusionment may last until the stranger discovers in some odd corner of the city a veritable Viennese and finds that beneath the appearance of gaiety there is much quiet, hard work, beneath the superficial politeness much real courtesy, alongside of childishness, great shrewdness and knowledge of mankind, and, amid scepticism and carelessness, an amazing richness of talent. The level of talent in Vienna is remarkably high though it is often a talent without object or intelligible purpose. The "stupidity" of the Viennese and of Austrians generally, by which strangers are so often struck, proceeds not from lack of wits but from absence of opportunity for the application of intelligence. The beginning of positive intelligence is discipline of attention. The Viennese have never been schooled to concentrate their minds upon matters more important than concerts, theatres, sports and amusements. Proof that their "stupidity" is due to lack of opportunity rather than of capacity is afforded whenever Austrians in general and Viennese in particular find employment abroad. The number of Austrians who have achieved intellectual and technical distinction in Germany, the United States, the Argentine Republic and other countries is astonishing. But at home they seem to be hypnotized by the general atmosphere of unreality. In their hearts the best of them often resent the impotence to which they are condemned by the political, social and moral conditions of their life ; yet they are loth to admit that Viennese life is not, in its way, ideal. "A Viennese," writes Bahr,[1] "is a man very unhappy about himself, who hates

[1] *Wien*, by Hermann Bahr, p. 9.

the Viennese but cannot live without them, who despises himself but is touched by his own condition, who constantly grumbles but wishes to be constantly praised, who feels miserable but finds comfort in wretchedness, who always complains, always threatens but puts up with everything except that any one should presume to help him—then he defends himself."

And again, in speaking of Viennese talent,[1] " Nowhere in the wide world is there so much talent as in Vienna, talent for everything, political and artistic. But it is talent of a special kind, attached to nothing, hanging in the air, a talent with nothing to express but itself, purposeless, void, a hollow nut. Here are young actors able to communicate feelings they do not feel ; here people, who are themselves empty, revel in the finest verses. Here is all political wisdom which no man knows how to use. No one has a will. Viennese talent is like an abandoned piano, containing all potentialities of sound, but silent. Men do not lack talent but talent lacks men. Every man hides his manliness. The fear, wrought into their fathers, is still too great. Hence the terror of the Viennese when a real man appears among them. They find him uncanny and would like to hide from him—unless they be in a theatre. On the stage they know it will be over in three hours. The Viennese are still able to bear reality as a representation though they are glad that the dangerous beast has been chained up with chains of art. A real man in real life, the Viennese have never tolerated ; neither Beethoven nor Hebbel nor Kürnberger nor Hugo Wolf nor Mahler. Real men are kept in the cage of an immense solitude. The Viennese never let them enter their beloved light and lusty life. Hence the great silence of Vienna. Nothing moves, nothing can happen. The boldest, the greatest acts have no effect ; they remain hidden. The thinker, the doer must hide himself—' isolated and power-less,' as Hebbel said—and take his thoughts and deeds home with him and stow them away in a secret drawer.

[1] *Wien*, pp. 77-78.

Outside, the attractive appearance of life in the dear, light, soft-living city goes on untroubled."

The problem of Vienna as, indeed, the problem of Austria and of the Monarchy is how to adjust appearances to reality and to bring more sincerity into life. Hitherto the "authorities" have striven to adjust reality to appearances. The argument that Vienna is not Austria and, still less, the Monarchy, holds good in the sense that life in the Austrian provinces and in parts of Hungary is more real and direct than in Vienna. Some writers, Bahr among them, maintain that Vienna no longer wields decisive influence and that the fate of the Monarchy and of Vienna will be settled by the Hapsburg peoples without much consideration for Viennese preferences. This view might be sound had the Hapsburg peoples a corporate life apart from Vienna or had they any common purpose save such as may be suggested to or imposed on them by Vienna. Though Vienna may be powerless to solve the problem of the Monarchy, it is powerful to impede solutions and to foment distrust and hatred among the Hapsburg peoples and even among peoples beyond the frontier. The Viennese atmosphere—which attains its fullest expression in the official, military and police spheres whose lack of moral sense and of ethical imagination has made the name "Vienna" a by-word throughout the Monarchy—affects, directly and indirectly, every aspect of political life in the Hapsburg Dominions. To trace the genesis of "Vienna" would be to write a psychological history of the Austrian Empire. It is mainly a product of education on Jesuit lines under a Dynasty which long believed its mission to be that of world-domination, the famous "A.E.I.O.U. policy"—*Austriae Est Imperare Orbi Universo.* In the spirit of domination, Dynasty and Jesuits found themselves agreed. Around them gathered a *clientèle* of German, Magyar, Czech, Polish, French, Italian, Irish, Scottish and Spanish families—largely reinforced during recent generations by baptized Jews—a *clientèle* united only in the determination to gain advancement and influence. As

Mickiewicz wrote seventy years ago, the Austrian Empire has never been German, Hungarian or Slav, but has been ruled by a caste of inter-related families battening on the Dynasty and its peoples. Bahr rightly says that one of the most pressing Austrian problems is how to break the power of this —now largely bureaucratic—caste of political middlemen and to adjust the structure of the State to the needs of the Hapsburg peoples. But it is an open question whether the power of the caste can be broken before it has broken the Monarchy. From Lemberg to Mostar and from Kolozsvár to Innsbruck, men of public spirit may be heard in different tongues but identical tone denouncing the arrogance, narrow-mindedness, faithlessness, and stupidity of "Vienna," and, to a lesser extent, of "Budapest," which now rivals "Vienna" in lack of moral consciousness. To visit the Hapsburg Monarchy in its length and breadth is to realize how great are its resources and how immense its possibilities, and to compre-hend that the bonds uniting its peoples are, or might be, stronger than the elements of division. But everywhere the blighting breath of the Capital can be felt and, on approaching Vienna, faith and idealism vanish. It is this moral void that makes most foreigners and many Austrians feel perennially strangers in the Austrian Capital. Its "Asiatic" character, to which Metternich and Kürnberger alike bore witness, repels those who would fain feel at home within its walls, and whom mere climatic or physical drawbacks would not deter. For forty years the Viennese have been studying how to draw a stream of foreign visitors to their city and for forty years have been astounded at their failure. They enumerate the attractions of Vienna, the multiplicity of its pleasures, the beauty of its monuments and the charm of its natural surroundings ; but they forget that for a capital to act as a magnet upon strangers it must have a soul of its own with which the stranger can secretly commune. Both Vienna and "Vienna" are soulless or, at least, their "souls" are so much in abeyance that neither thrills the thoughtful stranger with that inward satisfaction which moves the heart.

CHAPTER IV

FOREIGN POLICY

Soulevée par la question d'Orient, la question polonaise semble tranchée depuis 1815. Voilà un siècle que l'on travaille à résoudre la question d'Orient. Le jour où l'on croira l'avoir résolue, l'Europe verra se poser inévitablement la question d'Autriche. (Albert Sorel, *La Question d'Orient au XVIIIe Siècle*. Paris, 1902,.p. 280.)

THE recent wars in the Balkans have, to all appearances, driven the Hapsburg Monarchy back upon itself and dispelled the dream of a " March to Salonica "—so often disavowed but so long and stubbornly cherished by Austro-Hungarian statesmen and soldiers—as completely as the solution of the German and Italian questions in 1866 and 1870 destroyed the possibility of Hapsburg domination in Germany and Italy. The question whether the Balkan wars have solved "*la question d'Orient*," in the sense in which the late M. Albert Sorel referred to it, is not lightly to be answered ; but so much of it appears to have been solved as to suggest the likelihood that, unless Hapsburg diplomacy and statecraft speedily rise to the occasion, his prediction may presently come within measurable distance of fulfilment.

In many modern democracies matters relating to foreign policy are considered of secondary importance. Even where the vital significance of foreign affairs is recognized they are often treated as occult problems or as relics of a bygone age, encumbering a field that would otherwise be susceptible of cultivation by steam-plough and harrow. The United States long seemed to have adopted the maxim, " Happy the people that has no foreign policy " ; latterly they have awakened to the importance of foreign questions but have allowed their policy to be unduly influenced by Jewish financiers. France, whose position in Europe is always exposed to foreign aggression, has nevertheless repeatedly tolerated the management of her foreign affairs by men devoid of special training or knowledge ; and her diplomacy is often sadly banker-ridden. Italy has again and again placed her diplomatic interests at the mercy of politicians better fitted to shine in business or in the law courts than to handle affairs of State which a Cavour would have approached with trepidation. England has, at times, succeeded in combining pre-democratic tradition with parliamentary practice. In Austria-Hungary the pre-democratic method persists, in reality if not in appearance, and its drawbacks are seen to be even more serious than those of a purely democratic system. The management of foreign affairs in the Dual Monarchy is essentially a dynastic prerogative, usually exercised with the help of a diplomatically-trained minister who is in the first place, " Minister of the Imperial and Royal Household," and only secondarily, " Minister for Foreign Affairs." Andrássy alone possessed an influence over foreign policy equal, if not superior, to that of the Monarch. As former Premier of Hungary and co-author with Deák of the Dual System, he endeavoured so to shape Hapsburg foreign policy as to bring it into harmony with the Dual System, the efficient working of which demands the predominance of Germans over Slavs in Austria, and of Magyars over Slavs and other non-Magyars in Hungary. A foreign policy worked out on this basis was bound to be anti-Slav and anti-Russian in the Balkans if not in Europe. But the Dynasty, whose interests and ambitions always control foreign policy in the long run, could not close its eyes to the fact that the majority of its subjects are Slavs, and that by pursuing an anti-Slav policy it was courting disaffection at home and placing itself abroad in a position of subservience to Germany. The momentous question forced upon the Hapsburg Dynasty by the independence of the greater part of the Balkans is whether its home and foreign policy shall be brought into closer harmony with the numerical balance of power among its own peoples, or whether it will risk disaster by clinging to traditions that events have gone far to render obsolete.

Precedent suggests that, for the present, the dynasty will cling to tradition. The Hapsburg mind has rarely shown itself elastic. Misfortune has often had to correct conceptions of which the impracticability had long been evident to detached and even to inimical observers. Both Bismarck and Cavour understood that the Hapsburg policy of retaining sway in Germany and Italy while the energies of home peoples were being compressed by absolutism and desperate financial expedients were being employed to stave off bankruptcy, must end in defeat and collapse. Had Francis Joseph and his advisers learned from the Franco-Piedmontese Alliance of 1859 and the loss of Lombardy that Austrian rule in Italy was doomed, they might have purchased an alliance with Italy by the timely cession of Venetia, and have faced Prussia with such strength as to have retarded the unification of Germany under Prussian leadership. Pride, and the perpetual inability of Austrian statesmen to appreciate the force of the moral elements in a situation, made them strive to retain their power in Germany and Italy alike without attempting seriously to create at home conditions such as to assure to the dynasty the spontaneous support of its peoples. It has been the curse of the Hapsburg Monarchy that its internal problems have never been dealt with on their merits but have been treated tentatively from time to time as the interests of dynastic foreign policy may have seemed to require. After the rude lesson of 1859, it would have been possible to put the Monarchy on an internal basis of federalized unity and to have guaranteed the various Hapsburg races a fair chance of development without placing the dynasty in the position of unstable equilibrium it has held since the creation of the Dual System. It is true that such a transformation could not

have been effected without constructive statesmanship inspired by a broad sense of justice. The Bach " System " which
the disasters of 1859 overthrew, was not a good preparation
for lasting reform. The morrow of oppression is rarely the
best moment for expansive confidence. The Hapsburg
dynasty and the bureaucrats who surround it have yet to
learn that trust and gratitude grow but slowly on the ruins
of ill-treatment. Moreover, the Hapsburg conception of a
dynastic mission excludes the idea that Hapsburg peoples can
have cause for resentment. Peoples behave well and deserve
recompense when they second dynastic plans. They behave
ill and deserve correction when they oppose or thwart those
plans. The cessation of just punishment is a sign that
Imperial disfavour has ceased and that rewards may be
attainable by good conduct. Unless this standpoint be kept
in view, Hapsburg policy at home and abroad will ever be
unintelligible. The essays in constitutional reform made in
1860 and 1861 after the collapse of the Bach System were
not inspired by belief in the value of constitutional methods
per se, but by the empirical consideration that, since the
Bach System had worked badly as a basis for foreign policy,
something else must be tried. Whether the " something
else " were the Federalist Diploma of October 1860 or the
Centralist Patent of February 1861 was a matter of comparative indifference. Not until defeat at Sadowa had compelled the dynasty to reckon with a force—that of the
Magyars—obstinately refractory to its influence, did it consent
to the creation of a " something else " over which it could no
longer exercise full control. The Dual System, hurriedly
formed under the influence of disaster, made the Magyars co-
partners with the dynasty and left them a freedom of action
in dealing with the Southern Slavs and other non-Magyars
that was destined to compromise, perhaps irremediably, the
interests of the Monarchy as a semi-Slav state both at home
and in the Balkan Peninsula.

Prior to the establishment of the Dual System, the
Eastern Question began for the Monarchy on the banks

of the Save and beyond the South-Eastern Carpathians. Dualism shifted it farther west and made it begin for Austria at Budapest and for Hungary at Agram. The Austrian Imperialist and dynastic tendencies known as the *Drang nach Osten* found in Magyar resistance to an increase of the Slav elements in the Monarchy a formidable obstacle to expansion in the Balkans; and the Magyars, haunted by memories of Jellachitch,[1] strove so to keep the Croatians and Serbs in subjection that the Southern Slav world, without whose help or acquiescence an Austro-Hungarian " advance to Salonica " would have been a perilous adventure, gradually became distrustful of the dynasty and estranged from the Monarchy. Austria and the dynasty, for their part, could not work with the Southern Slavs without undermining Dualism. Thus the Dual System resolved itself into a system of political paralysis in which immobility became the only pledge of equilibrium.

The operation of the Dual System as a check upon Imperialist expansion was not understood at the outset. The Magyar authors of the System, Deák and Andrássy, especially the latter, conceived it as necessarily subordinate to the higher unity of the Monarchy in diplomatic and military matters. As long as Deák's influence prevailed in Hungary and Andrássy was able, as Austro-Hungarian Foreign Minister, to guide the foreign policy of the Monarchy, the veritable character of Dualism remained concealed. Magyar opposition to the acquisition of Bosnia-Herzegovina in 1878 first revealed the mind of the Magyar nation which would have preferred to see the Monarchy support Turkey against Russia and inflict a defeat upon the Slav cause. Andrássy was at heart an Austro-Hungarian Imperialist. Like his fellow-Magyars he disliked and distrusted the Pan-Slavist tendencies that inspired the policy of Russia, but he believed in the Balkan mission of the Monarchy. His faith

---

1 The famous Ban of Croatia who led the Croatians against the Magyars during the Revolution of 1848. His statue stands in the Jellachitch Square at Agram, holding aloft a drawn sabre pointing in the direction of Budapest.

in the political virtue of the Magyar people was too robust to allow him to entertain a particularist conception of its future or to imagine that the *globus hungaricus* must be a garden walled around and devoted solely to the intensive culture of Magyar chauvinism.   The acquisition of Bosnia-Herzegovina seemed to him less an end in itself than a stage in the advance towards the political if not the military conquest of the Balkans. Though he might not have been ready to endorse the sanguine and visionary promise of the Archduke Rudolph to the Archduchess Stéphanie at Constantinople in the early 'eighties, " Hier wirst Du Kaiserin sein ! " he would scarcely have discouraged an enthusiasm that was in complete harmony with the aspirations of Hapsburg rulers.   After having chained up the Russian bear by means of the Austro-German Alliance of 1879,[1] and having left open a door for an understanding with France by rejecting Bismarck's demand that the Alliance be directed equally against France and Russia, Andrássy retired from office with the feeling that, thanks to his efforts, the Dual System had proved its value as a basis for a vigorous foreign policy and that his secret convention (of July 13, 1878) with Russia had opened for the Monarchy a broad road into the Balkans.

Despite his shrewdness, Andrássy overlooked several important factors in the situation which he bequeathed in 1879 to Haymerle, his short-lived successor.   Andrássy had been a match for Bismarck.   Left to himself, Bismarck was able, without fear of control, to neutralize the efficacy of the Austro-German Alliance as a menace to Russia, by negotiating in 1884 a secret Russo-German Re-Insurance Treaty in order to prevent Russia from seeking an ally in France ; and the Emperor Francis Joseph, no longer restrained by the influence of the vigilant Magyar Statesman, was free to essay in Austria a Clerical and pro-Slav policy which Andrássy would scarcely have tolerated.   The Emperor was, moreover, dissatisfied that Andrássy should have contented himself with a mere European mandate to " occupy and administer " Bosnia-Herzegovina.

[1] Cf. p. 27.

He desired annexation outright, and did not regard the secret Austro-Russian Convention as a full equivalent. This Convention, signed on July 13, 1878, ran :—" Le gouvernement impérial de Russie s'engage de son côté à n'élever aucune objection, si, à la suite des inconvénients pouvant résulter du maintien de l'administration ottomane dans le Sandjak de Novi-Bazar, l'Autriche-Hongrie se voyait amenée à occuper définitivement ce térritoire comme le reste de la Bosnie et de l'Herzegovine." In return for this undertaking, Austria-Hungary promised to lend Russia diplomatic support in removing any obstacles that might arise to the execution of the provisions of the Treaty of Berlin. The origin of the secret Convention is still mysterious. Though Russia had consented to the acquisition of Bosnia-Herzegovina by Austria-Hungary during the meeting between the Tsar and the Emperor Francis Joseph at Reichstadt in 1876 and by supplementary agreements concluded at Budapest on January 15, 1877, and ratified, with an annexe, at Vienna (March 18, 1877),[1] the Russian plenipotentiaries, Gortchakoff and Shuvaloff, showed themselves at the Berlin Congress reluctant to sanction the occupation of the two provinces, and yielded only to German and English pressure. The original Russian idea seems to have been to purchase the neutrality of Austria-Hungary while Russia should establish her own hegemony in the Balkans by creating out of Turkish territory a big Slav State—Bulgaria. England had, on June 6, 1878, concluded with Austria-Hungary a convention providing that " le gouvernement de Sa Majesté Britannique s'engage à soutenir toute proposition concernant la Bosnie que le gouvernement Austro-Hongrois jugera à propos de faire au congrès." [2] Though the revision of the Treaty of San Stefano by the Berlin Congress had in part destroyed the Russian scheme, Russia finally gave way in regard to Bosnia-Herzegovina and the occupation of the Sanjak in return for a rectification

[1] *Wie wir zu Bosnien kamen: eine historische Studie*, von Dr. August Fournier, pp. 41, 43.

[2] *Graf Julius Andrássy: sein Leben und seine Zeit*, von Eduard Wertheimer, Band iii. p. 122.

of the Montenegrin frontier.   But this "compensation" hardly explains why Russia should have consented to the " definitive occupation " of the Sanjak " like the rest of Bosnia-Herzegovina " by the secret Convention of July 13 ; nor why Russia should ever afterwards have offered stubborn resistance to the transformation of this " definitive occupation " into an annexation.   The history of Austro-Russian relations on the subject of Bosnia-Herzegovina, both before and after the Congress of Berlin, is still obscure despite the contributions made to it by the Russian State Archivist, Gorjainoff, in his book *The Bosphorus and the Dardanelles* (1907), and authorized Austrian and Hungarian publications like Professor Fournier's *Wie wir zu Bosnien kamen* and Eduard von Wertheimer's *Andrássy.*   Since the abandonment of the Sanjak by Austria-Hungary at the moment of the annexation of Bosnia-Herzegovina in October 1908, the question has lost much of its practical interest, though it remains historically important as an episode which, like Austrian " ingratitude " towards Russia at the time of the Crimean War, continued to influence the relations between St Petersburg and Vienna long after the original cause of ill-feeling had disappeared.

The further question why Andrássy accepted an " occupation " instead of an annexation is more easily answered. Originally, annexation was contemplated.   Annexation alone corresponded fully to the ardent desire of the Emperor Francis Joseph to make up for the loss of Lombardy and Venetia by incorporating in his dominions two provinces of approximately equal extent.   The persistence of this desire was one of the main reasons why Baron von Aehrenthal, thirty years later, celebrated the Emperor's year of Diamond Jubilee by transforming the occupation into an annexation.   Andrássy was induced to abandon the idea of an immediate annexation partly by the prospect of Turkish resistance (which would have given Russia an opportunity to renew hostilities against Turkey) and partly by the strength of Austrian-German and Magyar opposition to the incorporation of the two provinces in the territory of the Monarchy. As at the moment of the annexation of 1908, neither Austria nor Hungary was prepared to sanction the acquisition of the new territory by the other ; and Hungary, jealous of her constitutional independence, deprecated the creation of an Imperial Reichs-land that might become an additional tie between her and Austria and eventually serve as the starting-point for a system of federalization which would diminish the relative importance of the Magyars in the Monarchy. Both the Austrian-Germans—then paramount in Austria—and the Magyars objected, moreover, to the increase of the Slav population of the Monarchy proper. Hence Andrássy was fain to accept the formula of "occupation and administra-tion," while surrounding it with guarantees that the title of the Monarchy to definite possession could not well be challenged save by force of arms. The Administration of the provinces was tacked on to the Austro-Hungarian Department for Joint Finance, and the head of the Depart-ment, or Joint Finance Minister, was made responsible not to the Austrian or Hungarian Parliament but to the Joint Parliamentary Delegations. This expedient was retained even after the annexation in 1908 and the granting of constitutional autonomy to Bosnia-Herzegovina eighteen months later. The inhabitants of Bosnia-Herzegovina are still without a properly regulated status in the Monarchy. They are not entitled to call themselves citizens of Austria or Hungary. They are *fra color che son sospesi*, and rank at best as second-class Hapsburgians. The end of the question of Bosnia-Herzegovina is not yet. It has become an integral part of the Southern Slav question and can hardly be settled save in the connexion with the larger issue whether Austria-Hungary will be able to solve the Southern Slav question in her own favour or whether it will, like the Italian and German questions of the nineteenth century, be decided against her. Upon this point the future of the Monarchy may turn.

The Servian authority Ristitch, in his *Diplomatic History*

of Servia, 1875–78 (vol. ii. pp. 251-252), relates, on the authority of Shuvaloff, that Bismarck originally suggested the Austro-Hungarian acquisition of Bosnia-Herzegovina. Though Andrássy's biographer, Eduard von Wertheimer, deprecates the assumption that Bismarck was the author of the idea and claims that Andrássy had long recognized the necessity of the occupation, it is extremely probable that the German Chancellor encouraged if he did not actually propose the expansion of the Monarchy in the Balkan Peninsula. Just as he subsequently encouraged France to occupy Tunis in order to divert French attention from the Franco-German frontier and to foment discord between France and Italy, so it was in his interest to turn Austro-Hungarian attention to the South-East both in order to deflect it from anti-German enterprises and to bring Austria-Hungary into potential conflict with Russia. If Russia and Austria-Hungary were watching each other with jealous suspicion, each would be more likely to cultivate a good relationship with Germany in the hope of securing German neutrality if not German support. A permanent opportunity for "honest brokerage" by Germany would thus be created. After the failure of the League of the Three Emperors, Andrássy and Bismarck were practically agreed upon the necessity of a formal alliance between Austria-Hungary and Germany — Bismarck in order to preclude the contingency of a Franco-Russian alliance against Germany into which a detached Austria-Hungary might be drawn, and Andrássy in order to obviate the danger of a single-handed struggle between the Monarchy and Russia in which Germany might play the part not only of a *tertius gaudens* but eventually of a claimant to a share in the spoils. Besides, the Austro-German Alliance was regarded by Andrássy and possibly also by Bismarck as a guarantee of the maintenance of the Dual System in Austria-Hungary, which both Andrássy and Bismarck regarded, for different reasons, as a safeguard against the triumph of anti-German and anti-Magyar tendencies in the Monarchy. Whether the Emperor Francis Joseph regarded the Alliance exactly in this light is an open question, which has been amply discussed in a previous chapter.[1] It is certain that the anti-German policy adopted by the Emperor in Austria during the Taaffe era (1879–93) would not have been possible or would at least have entailed diplomatic intervention by Germany had not Bismarck's mind been set at rest on the score of Austrian military loyalty by the existence of the Austro-German Treaty. Neither the Emperor Francis Joseph nor Count Kálnoky (who succeeded Haymerle at the Vienna Foreign Office in 1881) had any notion that Bismarck had departed far more explicitly than Austria-Hungary from the spirit of the treaty nor that, while Austro-Russian rivalry was at its height during the Bulgarian troubles of the 'eighties, Bismarck had already concluded with Russia (1884) the secret Re-Insurance Treaty that might have made the Austro-German Treaty inoperative if Austria-Hungary and Russia had come to blows.[2] Technically, Bismarck might defend

[1] " The Monarch and the Monarchy," pp. 26-28.

[2] The historic article in Bismarck's organ, the *Hamburger Nachrichten* of October 24, 1896, in which the former existence of a re-insurance treaty with Russia was divulged, ran: " . . . Very soon after the change of throne (in Russia, by the accession of Alexander III.) and the retirement of Gortchakoff, a good understanding was established between German and Russian policy and remained in this shape until 1890. Till then both Empires were completely agreed that, should one of them be attacked, the other would remain benevolently neutral, so that if, for instance, Germany were attacked by France, the benevolent neutrality of Russia was to be expected, and the benevolent neutrality of Germany if Russia were attacked without provocation. After the retirement of Prince Bismarck (March 1890) this understanding was not renewed, and if we (the *Hamburger Nachrichten* or, rather, Prince Bismarck) are rightly informed concerning events at Berlin, it was not Russia, ill-disposed by the retirement of Prince Bismarck, but Count Caprivi (Prince Bismarck's successor) who declined to continue the reciprocal insurance, although Russia was prepared to do so. Moreover, if the Polonizing era simultaneously inaugurated (in Prussia) is taken politically into account, there can be no room for doubt that the Russian Government must have asked itself what might be the aims of this Prussian Polonizing that stands in so flagrant contradiction with the traditions of Emperor William I."

The immediate cause of the publication of this sensational article was the visit of the Tsar and Tsaritza to France where, after the review at Châlons on October 9, 1896, the Tsar had assured President Faure that "a deep feeling of brotherhood in arms" existed between the French and the Russian armies. Angered by this proof that a Franco-Russian military alliance had been concluded and that his successors, Count Caprivi and Prince Hohenlohe, had failed to prevent it, Prince Bismarck employed his Hamburg organ to "throw a stone

his conduct by arguing that inasmuch as the Austro-German Treaty provided only against a Russian attack upon either of the two parties to the Alliance while the Russo-German Treaty of Re-Insurance provided against an unprovoked attack upon Russia by Austria-Hungary or any other country, there was no essential contradiction between the obligations which Germany had assumed, inasmuch as the Austro-German Treaty did not pledge Germany to support Austria-Hungary in an attack upon Russia. But morally it is impossible to resist the conclusion that Bismarck was running things very fine, and was, as Baron Marschall von Bieberstein argued, exposing the allied loyalty of Germany to the chance of a decision as to which party in a conflict had been the aggressor. The German

---

into the duckpond." Its effect was prodigious. For weeks the European press did little but discuss it. The German *Imperial Gazette* accused the ex-Chancellor of violating secrets of State and of exposing the allied loyalty of Germany to question. Prince Bismarck replied that his Treaty of Re-Insurance with Russia was perfectly compatible with the Austro-German Alliance, and claimed that, if Russia had no objection, the whole Triple Alliance *in corpore* would do well to contract with Russia a similar engagement. But the late Baron Marschall von Bieberstein, then German Foreign Secretary, hit the nail on the head in his speech to the Reichstag on November 16, 1896, by saying, "In our treaty of 1879 with Austria-Hungary we are pledged to assist the Monarchy with our whole armed strength if the Monarchy is attacked by Russia. This position is perfectly clear. But if the revelations (of the *Hamburger Nachrichten*) are accurate, the Re-Insurance Treaty with Russia might have brought us into the position of being asked—in case of an Austro-Russian conflict—for benevolent neutrality by the one party and for support with our whole armed strength by the other party ; and we should then have had to decide which of the two parties was the aggressor."

Scarcely less interesting than the revelation of the secret Re-Insurance Treaty was Bismarck's suggestion that the pro-Polish policy, tentatively adopted by the Emperor William II. at the beginning of his reign, contributed to cause Russia to doubt German intentions. Bismarck always made the oppression of the Poles an asset in his policy towards Russia, and succeeded unfortunately in hypnotizing Russia into a belief that the oppression of the Poles is likewise a pre-eminent Russian interest. The joint oppression of Poland thus became, and has remained, a bond of union between Germany and Russia. The present German Emperor departed for a moment from this sinister principle but subsequently reverted to it and sanctioned Prince Bülow's policy of expropriating the Prussian Poles. Germany thus placed in the hands of Russia a trump card which the Russian Government has hitherto failed to use. The position of Russia in Europe might be immensely strengthened and her political preponderance over Germany and Austria-Hungary assured at one stroke were she to grant her Polish subjects a measure of autonomy and to treat them as fully qualified Russian citizens.

Emperor and Count Caprivi, who in 1890 allowed the Re-Insurance Treaty to lapse because the situation it created was "too complicated," had both common sense and right-mindedness on their side. Some future indiscretion may perhaps show whether the German Emperor did not subsequently change his mind and revert in practice, if not by formal Treaty, to the re-insurance policy of Bismarck.

The revelation of the Re-Insurance Treaty by Bismarck led indirectly to a new era in Austro-Russian relations. Though unpleasantly impressed by the public announcement of the potential perfidy of Germany, the Austro-Hungarian Government instructed its official organs to dismiss the affair in a few words and treat it as a phase long past. The *Fremdenblatt* approved of the refusal of the German Government to supplement the Bismarckian revelations by divulging the details of the treaty. Nevertheless it was plain that the episode had inspired Austria-Hungary with retrospective resentment, and when, in the spring of the following year, the Emperor Francis Joseph returned at St. Petersburg the visit of accession paid to him at Vienna by Nicholas II. in August 1896, an Austro-Russian *rapprochement* took place in the form of an agreement in regard to the Balkans. On April 29, 1897, Counts Gołuchowski and Muravieff, the Austro-Hungarian and Russian Foreign Ministers, addressed from St. Petersburg to the Austro-Hungarian and Russian representatives in Servia, Bulgaria, Rumania, and Montenegro, identic notes declaring that the exchange of views between the Emperor and the Tsar had given the two sovereigns an opportunity of recognizing the correct attitude of those countries during the Greco-Turkish war, an attitude the more pleasing in that the Emperor and the Tsar were firmly determined to maintain the general peace, the principle of order and the *status quo*. In the following autumn Count Gołuchowski informed the Delegations that a basis for an Austro-Russian agreement had been found and that the "two powers principally interested in the Balkans" repudiated all idea of conquest and were determined to maintain the *status quo.* In reality the agreement between Austria-Hungary and Russia had not been attained quite so smoothly as these announcements appeared to indicate. During the conference at St. Petersburg between the two sovereigns and their advisers, Count Muravieff, at the instance of the Tsar, sketched briefly the Balkan policy of Russia, which was, in view of Russian activity in the Far East, at that moment eminently conservative. Count Gołuchowski replied on behalf of Austria-Hungary with a brilliant and exhaustive statement, in the course of which he advocated the annexation of Bosnia-Herzegovina by Austria-Hungary. He presented to Count Muravieff a memorandum containing the same suggestion which was, however, struck out by the Tsar when revising the memorandum as a basis for the agreement. Austria-Hungary was fain to accept the agreement on these terms and to postpone till a more convenient season the annexation of the occupied provinces.

THE FEBRUARY AND MÜRZSTEG PROGRAMMES

For some years the Austro-Russian understanding remained in the background of European politics. The war of 1898 between the United States and Spain (in regard to which Austria-Hungary took up a strongly anti-American standpoint and advocated collective European action against the United States), the Boer War, the Anglo-French dispute that ended in the Fashoda incident, and the growing estrangement between England and Germany, deflected public attention from the Balkans and turned it in the direction of " world-politics." But, towards the end of 1902, unmistakable signs that a serious insurrection in Macedonia was at hand and that Bulgaria and Turkey might be involved in hostilities, induced Russia to take up the question of Macedonian Reform. Count Lamsdorff, who had succeeded Count Muravieff as Russian Foreign Minister, made a rapid journey to Sofia and Belgrade in December 1902, and went thence to discuss the outlook with Count Gołuchowski at

Vienna. The two statesmen, representing the two "most interested" Powers, agreed upon a scheme of reforms for Macedonia and instructed the Russian and Austro-Hungarian Ambassadors at Constantinople to draft it. It was transmitted to Vienna and St. Petersburg early in February 1903 and presented to the Porte on February 21. Hence its designation as "the February Programme." It suggested, in the name of Austria-Hungary and Russia, the introduction of reforms in the vilayets of Salonica, Kossovo, and Monastir; proposed the appointment, for a term of three years, of a Turkish Inspector-General with the rank of Vizir and possessing authority over the Valis or provincial governors; insisted upon the engagement of foreign officers to reorganize the police and the gendarmerie; and urged the necessity for financial and fiscal reform. Under pressure from all the Powers, the Porte accepted this Programme and appointed Hussein Hilmi Pasha to be Inspector-General. His, mainly bureaucratic, activity availed nothing to prevent the terrible insurrection of the summer of 1903, so that, chiefly in response to English public opinion firmly voiced by Lord Lansdowne, Counts Gołuchowski and Lamsdorff decided in the early autumn of 1903 to amplify and render more stringent the provisions of the February Programme. At the end of September 1903 the Tsar, accompanied by Count Lamsdorff, visited the Emperor Francis Joseph at Schönbrunn and went thence with him to the Emperor's shooting-box at Mürzsteg in Styria. Here, while his Austro-Hungarian colleague was out with the guns, Count Lamsdorff drew up the famous Mürzsteg Programme which was to play so large a part in Balkan affairs during the next five years. An English proposal for a more drastic series of reforms and especially for greater efficacy of control than Austria-Hungary and Russia appeared to desire, reached the Vienna Foreign Office two hours after Counts Gołuchowski and Lamsdorff had started for Mürzsteg. Diplomatic rumour assigned their departure at an earlier hour than originally contemplated to a desire to avoid the English proposal. In any case Lord Lansdowne's suggestions found no place in the Programme communicated to the Austro-Hungarian and Russian Ambassadors at Constantinople in the form of identic instructions dated Mürzsteg, October 2, 1903. The chief points of this Programme were the appointment of Austro-Hungarian and Russian Civil Agents attached to the person of the Inspector-General, Hilmi Pasha, whom the Civil Agents were to accompany on all his journeys of inspection, with authority to report to the Austro-Hungarian and Russian Ambassadors at Constantinople and also directly to their Governments.   Since the task of the Civil Agents would be to watch over the introduction of the reforms and the pacification of the inhabitants, the Programme specified that their mandate would expire two years after their appointment. The Programme further proposed that a foreign General should enter the service of the Ottoman Government to re-organize the Gendarmerie with the help of assistants chosen among the officers of the Great Powers.   The third clause of the Programme provided that after the pacification of the country, the Ottoman Government should be requested to modify the territorial delimitation of the Turkish ad-ministrative districts, in view of a more regular grouping of the various Macedonian races.[1]   The fourth clause of the Programme demanded the reorganization of the Turkish administrative and judicial system in such a manner as to favour the admission of native Christians and to develop local autonomies.   In conclusion, the Programme proposed

---

[1] This clause of the Mürzsteg Programme gave the signal for a ferocious war of all against all in Macedonia, especially between Greeks and Bulgars.   Armed Greek bands sought to exterminate the Bulgar inhabitants of various mixed districts and *vice versa*, in order that, when the "more regular grouping" of the different races should take place, these districts should appear to be purely Greek or purely Bulgar.   After some years of atrocious butchery which the Turkish authorities encouraged and which the European Gendarmerie Officers were powerless to prevent, the Powers decided to abrogate Clause III. of the Programme and to warn the Balkan States and races that no account would be taken of districts thus "conquered" in an eventual change of Turkish administrative delimitation.   The abrogation of the clause was decided upon, subject to the approval of Russia, at an interview between Baron von Aehrenthal and Viscount (then Sir Charles) Hardinge at Ischl in August 1907 ; but the credit for

the formation of mixed Musulman and Christian Commissions under the surveillance of the Austro-Hungarian and Russian Consuls to investigate political crimes and to repair the havoc wrought by the insurrection ; and insisted that the Ottoman Government should again pledge itself to introduce the reforms specified by the February Programme.

Adopted by the Porte under pressure from the Powers, the Mürzsteg Programme gradually led to a substantial improvement of the situation in Macedonia. Austro-Hungarian and Russian Civil Agents were appointed. An Italian General was chosen as Instructor-in-Chief (but without command) of the reformed Gendarmerie. Macedonia was divided into five sectors, each of which was allotted to the officers of a Great Power.[1] Germany held aloof from the work of Gendarmerie reform, though she was represented by a Consul on the International Commission formed at Salonica for the control of Macedonian finance. This commission did excellent work and began to evolve order out of chaos. Lord Lansdowne, whose firmness in promoting the reforms deserves unstinted praise, had striven from the outset to internationalize the work both in order to increase its efficiency and to allay Turkish apprehensions that Rumelia would become a politico-administrative preserve of Austria-Hungary and Russia. The internationalization of the reform of the Gendarmerie and of the financial control was largely the result of his efforts, which were supported by Italy and, after the Anglo-French Agreement of April 1904, by France. The Austro-Hungarian Foreign Minister, Count Gołuchowski, was obliged reluctantly to admit that the mandate of the Austro-Hungarian and Russian Civil Agents

directing the attention of Europe to the sanguinary effects of the clause is due chiefly to Sir (then Mr.) Henry Paul Harvey, late Financial Adviser to the Egyptian Government and at that time British representative on the International Commission at Salonica for the Control of Macedonian Finance. Accompanied by Lady Grogan, who had undergone much hardship in relieving the sufferings of the Macedonian population, Mr. Harvey rode through the disputed districts, collected evidence and laid it before the British Foreign Office.

[1] The Kossovo sector was assigned to Austria-Hungary, that of Monastir to Italy, Salonica to Russia, Drama to Great Britain, and Seres to France.

had been limited by the Mürzsteg Programme to a period of two years and required the express consent of Europe for its renewal. The principle of all-round internationalization came to be increasingly accepted, and when, after the end of the Russo-Japanese War, Russia adopted a more liberal internal policy and turned her eyes again towards Europe and the Balkans, Russian opposition also ceased. This gradual transformation of the Austro-Russian Agreement of 1897 and of its products, the February and Mürzsteg Programmes, into a thoroughly international system of reform and control in Macedonia, was one of the most important features of the European situation during the years 1905–7. From the continued resistance of Austria-Hungary to the process of internationalization proceeded the breach of the Austro-Russian Agreement of 1897 and its consequences in the form of the Austro-Russian rivalry that persisted throughout the years 1908–12 and assumed so threatening a form during the crisis of last winter.

BARON VON AEHRENTHAL

When, in 1903, Russia and Austria-Hungary agreed upon the February and Mürzsteg Programmes, they were doubtless inspired to some extent by solicitude for the welfare of the Balkan Christians, but were also, and perhaps principally, anxious to preserve their political influence in the Balkans. The name " Mürzsteg " has often been used as a catchword to denote a policy of agreement between Austria-Hungary and Russia for the moral if not the actual partition of the Balkans. Nothing has transpired entirely to substantiate this view, at least as far as Russia is concerned, though in the case of Austria-Hungary there may have been the *arrière-pensée* that, by engaging jointly with Russia in the work of reform, the Monarchy would be pegging out for itself a future sphere of influence in such manner as to keep open the road to Salonica. Russia, then engaged in a diplomatic, and on the eve of an armed struggle with Japan, desired, by agreement with Austria-Hungary, to prevent the single-handed intervention of the Monarchy in the Balkans, while not appearing to neglect the cause of the Balkan Christians. The Macedonian Reforms were therefore designed by Russia to improve the lot of the Balkan Christians while guaranteeing them and Russia against the expansive tendencies of Austria-Hungary. Count Gołuchowski, the Austro-Hungarian Foreign Minister, was much criticized in Austrian Imperialist circles for not taking advantage of Russian embarrassments in the Far East and of the revolutionary movement that accompanied and followed the Russo-Japanese War, to intervene in the Balkans, annex Bosnia-Herzegovina, establish a firm hold over Servia and make the Hapsburg Monarchy politically mistress of the Morava and Vardar valleys. But Count Gołuchowski, though not a genius, was a statesman of upright mind and endowed with a large measure of common sense. The idea of playing false to Russia was repugnant to him. He felt, moreover, that to force on a Balkan crisis by single-handed intervention would be to incur risks which the Monarchy might not be able to face. From 1903 to 1906 both Austria and Hungary were involved in severe internal crises. In Austria, parliamentary government had practically ceased to exist and with it the constitutional possibility of raising money for extraordinary military purposes. In Hungary, Parliament was in revolt against the Crown and not disposed to sanction even a modest increase of the Army. The idea that the Monarchy might escape from its internal embarrassments by a policy of foreign adventure was indeed ventilated by some advisers of the Crown but neither the Emperor nor Count Gołuchowski gave it serious consideration. Besides, the German conflict with France and England over Morocco—the German Emperor's provocative visit to Tangier (March 31, 1905) took place within a month of the defeat of Russia at Mukden (February 24 to March 10, 1905)—caused Germany to deprecate any Austro-Hungarian action which, while endangering German interests in the Near East, might diminish the efficacy of the support which the Monarchy could give to Germany in case of European complications. In other words Germany was prepared to take advantage of Russia's weakness on her own account but would have looked askance at any Austro-Hungarian attempt to follow her example. In these circumstances Count Gołuchowski wisely adhered to the principle *quieta non movere* and co-operated steadily, though perhaps without enthusiasm, in the work of Macedonian Reform ; but he was careful to remind Germany, through his organs in the press, that the *casus foederis* could not arise for the Triple Alliance in connexion with transmarine questions, and that, should Germany become involved in a conflict with England and France over Morocco, Austria-Hungary would not be bound to lend her armed support. Simultaneously he began to work for the improvement of Austro-Hungarian relations with Italy—then ranged alongside of the Mediterranean Powers against German pretensions in the Morocco question —and ratified, during meetings with the Italian Foreign Minister at Abbazia (1905) and Venice (1906), the Austro-Italian Agreement in regard to Albania, which he had concluded verbally with the Marquis Visconti Venosta in 1897 and by an exchange of notes in 1900. Germany, whose reading of the Triple Alliance has usually been that close and direct relations between Vienna and Rome are undesirable, inasmuch as they diminish the power of Germany over her allies and tend to give unnecessary independence to Austria-Hungary and Italy, watched these tendencies with disfavour ; and despite the help loyally given by Count Gołuchowski to Germany at the Conference at Algeciras in the spring of 1906, the German Emperor dealt him a blow that went far to render his position untenable. By way of marking his displeasure at the Francophil attitude of Italy during the Conference of Algeciras, the Emperor William addressed to Count Gołuchowski a telegram praising his action during the Algeciras Conference as that of a " brilliant second on the duelling-ground." The telegram was published

—whether spontaneously or not is unknown. Contemporary diplomatic rumour pretended that the publication had been asked for by the German Ambassador in Vienna who was alleged to have expressed astonishment that the Austro-Hungarian Foreign Minister should not have made known to the world so "flattering" a testimonial. In any case, the suggestion that Austria-Hungary was a mere "second" to Germany wounded Austro-Hungarian pride; and when, in the following autumn, difficulties arose between the Hungarian Government and Count Gołuchowski, the latter took occasion to withdraw from office. In him the Emperor Francis Joseph lost a faithful servant and the Monarchy a statesman whose qualities his fellow countrymen have since learned to appreciate at their true value.

Baron von Aehrenthal, the Austro-Hungarian Ambassador at St. Petersburg, who succeeded Count Gołuchowski at the Vienna Foreign Office, was a man of a very different stamp. Gołuchowski had been jovial, loquacious, light-living but withal a diplomatist whose word was his bond, and in whom no ambassador had ever detected the shadow of deceit. Aehrenthal was a Bohemian-German with a strain of Jewish blood who had been brought up in the Clerical and bureaucratic school of Kálnoky. A man of few words, to each of which he gave a special meaning— a meaning not always identical with that understood or intended to be understood—secretive, ambitious and hard-working, he brought with him to the Ballplatz new methods and a new spirit. Ambassadors who had welcomed his appointment as that of a diplomatist with whom it would be easier to transact serious business than with the genial, society-loving Gołuchowski, complained within a few months that Aehrenthal "avait établi autour du Ballplatz une épaisse atmosphère de mauvaise foi." He came from St. Petersburg with a reputation for Russophilism—a reputation valuable to a diplomatist on the Neva, embarrassing to a statesman on the Danube. Before he had been a year in office he was accused of servility towards Germany

—an accusation not damaging to a Minister whose position could not have been consolidated without the good-will of Berlin. Whether he was ever sincerely Russophil may be doubted. A shrewd English observer who knew him well at St. Petersburg averred that, in his heart of hearts, Aehrenthal despised the Russians. His friends in Russia belonged to a small coterie of ultra-conservative Grand Dukes and politicians whose ideas on Russia and on the principles of government were in harmony with his own. He surveyed European politics from a Russian reactionary angle of vision, distrusting Liberal States and constitutional tendencies. Towards England his original attitude was one of distrustful contempt qualified by ignorance. Germany he respected for her attachment to *Realpolitik*, her indifference towards ethical considerations and her readiness to employ any means for the attainment of her ends. His programme was to resuscitate the old League of the Three Emperors for the defence of conservative and monarchical principles—but with its pivot at Vienna, not at Berlin. By this means he hoped to restore to the Hapsburg Monarchy a greater measure of diplomatic independence than it had enjoyed since the conclusion of the Austro-German Alliance and to make Germany and Russia by turns serve Hapsburg purposes. Within the limits of his conception of Hapsburg interests, Aehrenthal was an ardent patriot who brought to the service of his patriotism a cool head and a statesmanlike fibre of which the value was diminished only by inexperience and by a resentful and sometimes ungovernable temper. His readiness to trade upon the good faith of others was in no respect due to moral cowardice ; and his tenacity in the pursuit of his aims would have ensured him greater success than he achieved had it not been accompanied by mental inelasticity and by reluctance to tack as rapidly as changes of wind and current might require. Experience and adversity matured his judgment ; and by his death in 1911 the Monarchy, which had paid and is paying heavily for his education in practical statecraft, was deprived of his services at the moment when they would have been most valuable. The figure of Aehrenthal is not devoid of a certain tragic grandeur and the mark he left on the Monarchy is, for good or evil, indelible.

On succeeding Count Gołuchowski in October 1906, Aehrenthal's immediate intention was to revive the closer and more exclusive co-operation with Russia that had marked the beginning of the Austro-Russian understanding of 1897 and, up to 1906, the execution of the February and Mürzsteg Programmes. The British tendency towards the complete internationalization of the work of Macedonian Reform appeared to him reprehensible both in itself and because it implied a readiness on the part of Russia to fall into line with the Western Powers and to accept their Liberal standpoint. The greater part of the Mürzsteg Programme had already been executed. The Administrative and especially the Judicial Reforms contemplated by Clause IV. of the Programme alone awaited definition and application. Aehrenthal wished the Judicial Reform to be organized on an Austro-Russian as distinguished from the all-round international basis that had been adopted for the Financial Reform. M. Isvolsky, the new Russian Minister for Foreign Affairs, decided, however, towards Christmas 1906 to admit the internationalization of the Judicial Reform and thus confirmed Aehrenthal's suspicion that Russia was drawing closer to England. Within a few days of receiving the Russian intimation, Aehrenthal conceived and discussed with intimate friends the policy, which he executed a twelvemonth later, of abandoning the Austro-Russian Agreement of 1897 and of ceasing to support the work of Macedonian Reform in return for a concession from Turkey for the construction of an Austro-Hungarian railway through the Sanjak of Novi Bazar from the Bosnian frontier terminus at Uvatz to the Turkish railhead at Mitrovitza. Nevertheless he did not at once abandon all idea of co-operation with Russia on another basis, nor of preventing the Anglo-Russian *entente* which he apprehended as an obstacle to his scheme

of reviving the Three Emperors' League. In the spring of
1907, after a visit to Prince Bülow at Berlin, Aehrenthal
made to M. Isvolsky a proposal of which the details have
never been divulged, though its general character is known
to several European governments. It was to the effect that
the Austro-Russian understanding of 1897 should be enlarged
so as to include Germany on the one hand and France on
the other. The basis of this *entente à quatre* was to be a
scheme of "compensations" all round, including, probably,
the annexation of Bosnia-Herzegovina for Austria-Hungary,
the opening of the Dardanelles for Russia, the diplomatic
and financial support of France for Germany in the Baghdad
Railway question and a benevolent attitude on the part of
Germany towards French policy in Morocco. In what
form these proposals were made is not precisely known,
but it is known beyond possibility of denial that M. Isvolsky
declined Aehrenthal's suggestion for an *entente à quatre*
early in May 1907. The Russian Foreign Minister doubtless felt that the proposals were meant to be a master-stroke
of Austro-German diplomacy but that it was not quite clear
whether Russia and France would secure commensurate
advantages. The opening of the Dardanelles did not
depend upon Austria-Hungary alone, and the withdrawal
of Austro-Hungarian opposition would still have left Russia
face to face with England and other Powers. True, the
object of estranging Russia from England might have been
attained and, in the meantime, Austria-Hungary would
have secured Russian consent to the annexation of Bosnia-
Herzegovina. Similarly, a Franco-German "deal" in regard to the Baghdad Railway would have given Germany
an immediate and France a merely prospective advantage.
The main object of the proposals was naturally to break
up the Anglo-French *entente* and to thwart the growing
rapprochement between England and Russia or, in other
words, to prevent the formation of the Triple Entente
which Aehrenthal and Germany alike regarded as a
serious danger. M. Isvolsky was too Liberal in his views

and too convinced that Russian disasters had been, at
least indirectly, due to the German influences which had
encouraged Russia to turn her eyes away from Europe, to
welcome suggestions of which the ultimate effect would
have been to bring Russia once again under German
influence and to perpetuate the conflict between Russia
and England. England had given Russia sufficient proofs
of good faith during 1903, the year preceding the Russo-
Japanese War, to convince Russian statesmen that there was
no truth in the German thesis that England had promoted
the war in order to weaken Russia. While Germany had
persistently supported the Russian view that Japan was
bluffing and would "climb down" at the last moment if
Russia remained firm—private letters from Prince Bülow
maintained this view as late as January 1904—England
had used diplomatic and private influence to convince
Russia that Japan had her teeth set and to persuade the
Russian Government to avoid war by a friendly settlement.
The Russian Government, suspecting that England was
acting only as diplomatic "second" to her ally, Japan, paid
no heed to these warnings and advice, which were nevertheless renewed with insistence before hostilities became
inevitable. Not only did England not promote the war
in the Far East but she did her utmost to ward it off, if
only out of fear that she herself might be drawn into it.
Nevertheless, the thesis that Japan would give way at the
last moment triumphed at St. Petersburg over the British
thesis that Japan was in deadly earnest ; and when war
broke out at the beginning of February 1904, King Edward
and Lord Lansdowne were able with a clear conscience to
seek ways and means of localizing a conflict they had striven
to prevent.

These ways and means led within three months to the
Entente Cordiale between England and France. France had
replied to the Anglo-Japanese Alliance of 1902 by concluding
with Russia a Convention that practically extended the Dual
Alliance to the Far East. Since France, like England, had

vainly used her influence at St. Petersburg to prevent the Russo-Japanese War, it was clearly to the interest of both countries not to be drawn into hostilities in spite of themselves. They therefore " paired " and neutralized each other. This negative agreement might not have been practicable but for the success of King Edward's first visit to Paris in May 1903. From the moment of his accession, King Edward had worked to promote more cordial relations between England and France, not only out of a sincere liking for France but from recognition of the dangers to which England had been and might again be exposed by Lord Salisbury's policy of " splendid isolation." The South African War had revealed the shortsightedness or rather the over-longsightedness of that policy which kept the gaze of England fixed upon the uttermost parts of the earth and led her to overlook stumbling-blocks and pitfalls at her very threshold. At the darkest moment of the South African War a proposal had been made to revive against England the Franco-Russo-German Coalition that had been directed against Japan after the Treaty of Shimonoseki. France and Russia had declined the suggestion but the lesson was not lost upon King Edward, then Prince of Wales, who determined, on ascending the throne, that England should not again be exposed to such a danger. He therefore sought to improve relations with France and at the same time to render Russia a service by preventing the war in the Far East. In the latter respect he failed but his failure actually gave England an opportunity of arranging with France to " contract out " of the Russo-Japanese struggle and of concluding, three months later, a more positive convention in the form of the Anglo-French Agreement of April 8, 1904 concerning Egypt and Morocco.

The conclusion of the Russo-Japanese War by the Treaty of Portsmouth and the growing tendency of Russia towards constitutional reform naturally led to an improvement in Anglo-Russian relations. Confidence in British good faith, the first condition of such an improvement, had been steadily growing in influential Russian circles ; and some Russian diplomatists formerly Anglophobe, like the late M. Zinovieff, Russian Ambassador at Constantinople, had discarded their prejudices and become frankly Anglophil. These developments were highly displeasing to the German and Austro-Hungarian Governments. Germany, not unnaturally, placed an " objective " construction upon King Edward's " subjective " desire to remove points of friction between England and her Continental rivals, and accused England of aiming at the encirclement and isolation of Germany. Austria-Hungary, or rather Aehrenthal, descried in the Anglo-Russian *rapprochement* an obstacle to his scheme of reviving the Three Emperors' League and a tendency dangerous to Austro-Hungarian policy in the Balkans. Since the days of Andrássy the Vienna Foreign Office had based its dealings with England upon the principle that British antagonism to Russia strengthened the position of the Monarchy as the rival of Russia in the Near East ; and upon the consideration once defined by Andrássy in conversation with a British Ambassador at Vienna in the phrase that, in case of an Anglo-Russian conflict, " Austria-Hungary could apply a strong mustard plaster to the back of Russia."[1] Unlike Andrássy, Aehrenthal was Anglophobe or, at least, very contemptuous of British power in Europe. " What can England do to us ? " he asked repeatedly of visitors who warned him during the Annexation Crisis not to ignore British influence in the Near East. Nevertheless the possibility that Russia might come to an agreement with England seriously disturbed his calculations and led him in the spring of 1907 repeatedly to complain to Prince Urussoff, the Russian Ambassador at Vienna, of the Anglophil tendencies of the Russian Ambassador at Constantinople. M. Isvolsky's rejection of the Bülow-Aehrenthal proposal in May 1907, for an Austro-Russo-Franco-German *entente* caused Aehrenthal to suspect that Russia was on the eve of succumbing to British blandishments and, after the con-

[1] Wertheimer, *Graf Julius Andrássy*, Band ii. p. 17.

firmation of his suspicions by the publication of the Anglo-Russian Convention of August 31, 1907, he matured the plan which five months later brought about the first open breach between Vienna and St. Petersburg.

Rumours that Aehrenthal was contemplating the abandonment of the Mürzsteg basis were current in Vienna during the spring and summer of 1907. They arose chiefly from the pessimistic language employed by Aehrenthal himself in regard to the condition of Macedonia and the prospects of the Judicial Reform in conversation with diplomatic and other personages. It was further rumoured that the Archduke Francis Ferdinand, the Austro-Hungarian Heir-Presumptive, had, in conjunction with the Chief of General Staff, begun to study the question of a railway through the Sanjak of Novi Bazar. Aehrenthal feigned, however, to be interested in the completion of the work of Reform in Macedonia, and actually drafted the Judicial Reform jointly with M. Isvolsky during the latter's visit to Vienna in September–October 1907. M. Isvolsky considered that the joint authorship of the Reform placed its authors under an obligation to support it at Constantinople and to insist upon its application. Aehrenthal thought that the Reform might be made an object of barter with Turkey. Having agreed with Aehrenthal that the draft Reform should be submitted to a Conference of Ambassadors at Constantinople prior to its presentation to the Porte, M. Isvolsky left Vienna for St. Petersburg, and proceeded some weeks later to visit the Tsar at Livadia. Questioned by the Tsar as to his arrangements with Austria-Hungary, the Russian Foreign Minister reported that he and Aehrenthal were in entire agreement, and that they had together crossed every " t " and dotted every "i" of the last reform prescribed by the Mürzsteg Programme; whereupon the Tsar produced a secret despatch from Constantinople stating that Aehrenthal had offered the Porte to drop the Judicial Reform if Turkey would grant Austria-Hungary a concession for the construction of a railway through the Sanjak of Novi Bazar.

Indignant that doubt should thus be cast upon the good faith of his Austro-Hungarian colleague, M. Isvolsky replied that the despatch must be founded on a malicious rumour ; and the Tsar, accepting M. Isvolsky's argument, threw the despatch into the fire. Nevertheless, it was speedily proved to have been accurate and M. Isvolsky's confidence to have been misplaced. In the course of December 1907, the Dragoman of a European Embassy at Constantinople actually obtained a copy of the Austro-Hungarian proposal to the Porte ; and when the Conference of Ambassadors met to consider the Judicial Reform, the Austro-Hungarian Ambassador, Marquis Pallavicini, joined his German colleague, the late Baron Marschall von Bieberstein, in obstructing it. Towards the middle of January 1908, Count Berchtold, the Austro-Hungarian Ambassador at St. Petersburg, was instructed to inform M. Isvolsky that Baron von Aehrenthal would announce to the Delegations at the end of the month that Austria-Hungary had applied for and had been granted a concession to construct the Novi Bazar Railway. Despite M. Isvolsky's entreaties that the announcement should not be made public, Aehrenthal, who was anxious to score a parliamentary success, informed the Delegations on January 28, 1908, that the Railway would be constructed and that it would "constitute a new and important route from Central Europe to Egypt and India"!

The precise purpose of this pompous announcement has never been quite clear. In view of facts subsequently brought to light, it may be doubted whether Aehrenthal himself knew exactly what effect he meant to produce by bartering the Judicial Reform for the Novi Bazar Railway. Analysis of his work as Austro-Hungarian Foreign Minister leads irresistibly to the conclusion that his foresight and power of imagination were inferior to his tenacity and power of resistance. He possessed also a faculty for self-deception that often led him and his subordinates to believe a given situation to be other than it really was. It is conceivable that he may have thought a railway through the Sanjak to be a great acquisition for the Monarchy—the very Sanjak which he was to abandon nine months later, ostensibly as a pledge of his friendly disposition towards Turkey and as a sign to Europe that the Monarchy no longer dreamt of territorial expansion, but really as a concession to Italy and in obedience to the Austro-Hungarian General Staff, which insisted that, in case of war, the Sanjak would be a veritable death-trap for Austro-Hungarian troops and that the real line of advance towards Salonica lay along the Morava valley through the heart of Servia.   Aehrenthal appears not to have known, when negotiating with Turkey for the railway and when announcing triumphantly to the Delegations the impending construction of a new route from Central Europe to Egypt and India, that his line would be considerably longer than the existing line by way of Belgrade and Nish, and that the conversion of the Eastern extension of the Bosnian Railway from Sarajevo to Uvatz to a normal gauge, would be almost impossible from an engineering standpoint and prohibitively expensive from the standpoint of the financier.   These elementary facts he learned later.   Meanwhile the blow had been struck at Russia, and, as far as Austria–Hungary was concerned, the work of Macedonian Reform was at an end.

In the light of Aehrenthal's subsequent conduct and of his rancorous controversy with M. Isvolsky that filled the ensuing years, it seems probable that his principal motive was a desire to destroy the position of his Russian colleague, whom he regarded as responsible for the Anglo-Russian *rapprochement*.   Could Isvolsky be compelled to resign by public proof that he had been outwitted, Aehrenthal and Prince Bülow may have thought that it would be easier to break up the understanding between Russia and England.   But Aehrenthal, who knew only the old, reactionary Russia, and was, like many Austrian bureaucrats, totally unable to reckon with moral values in politics, miscalculated the effect of his manœuvre.   Instead of turning against M. Isvolsky for having allowed himself to be duped, Russian public opinion turned against Austria-Hungary and Aehrenthal for having played him false. M. Isvolsky, for his part, neutralized the Novi Bazar Railway scheme by putting forward a proposal for an anti-Austrian railway from the Danube to the Adriatic —a proposal which Aehrenthal accepted " in principle," with the mental reservation that much would happen before he accepted it in practice. In France and England indignation at Aehrenthal's trickery was almost as hot as in Russia. On February 25, 1908, Sir Edward Grey criticized, in moderate but telling language, the action of Austria-Hungary in seeking a private concession from Sultan Abdul Hamid at a moment when the Powers were engaged in coercing him into accepting the Judicial Reform. The British Foreign Secretary insisted that it would be the duty of the other Powers now to take the work of reform vigorously in hand and to compel the Porte to appoint a Governor-General for Macedonia. Aehrenthal complained to the British Ambassador in Vienna that Sir Edward Grey's speech was " an unfriendly act," and assumed an attitude of injured innocence. " Who could have foreseen," he asked, " that the Sultan would use the Austro-Hungarian application for the railway as a weapon to destroy the Concert of Europe?" But he found no reply to the Ambassador's pertinent rejoinder, " Who put a sword into the hand of a skilful fencer?"

Meanwhile the situation was fast developing. Under the influence of the Austro-Hungarian abandonment of the Mürzsteg Programme, England and Russia began to concert means to ensure the efficacy of the Macedonian Reforms. During the meeting between King Edward and the Tsar at Reval on June 9 and 10, 1908, Sir Charles Hardinge and M. Isvolsky, who accompanied their respective sovereigns, agreed upon a draft programme which is understood to have contemplated the appointment of a Governor-General for Macedonia. King Edward and the Tsar, for their part, are credibly reported to have tabooed politics entirely — a circumstance which did not prevent Aehrenthal and the

German-Jewish press of Austria-Hungary and Germany
from treating the Anglo-Russian interview as a conspiracy
against the *status quo* and as an attack, which Austria-Hungary
and Germany must resist, upon the sovereignty of the Sultan
and upon the administrative integrity of his dominions.   In
all the Jewish Freemasonic Lodges of Salonica and Macedonia, which served as meeting-places for the "Young
Turkish" conspirators against Abdul Hamid, the Austro-
German version of the Reval Meeting was disseminated and
the doctrine was preached that action must be accelerated
in view of the peril threatening the Ottoman Empire.
On July 24 the Turkish Revolution broke out, the final fillip
having been given by the betrayal of the Young Turkish
conspiracy to Abdul Hamid, who had despatched to Salonica
a trusty agent with a large sum of money to discover its
ramifications.   Compelled to choose between delay with the
probability of detection and "removal," and the chance of
success by immediate, albeit hazardous, action, the Young
Turkish leaders decided to act, and the late Major Niazi
Bey took to the mountains at Resna.   The story of the
Young Turkish Revolution, with its triumphs and dis-
appointments, need not here be told.   It is written in the
events that have convulsed the Near East during the last
five years.   Its course and its consequences radically transformed not only the Balkan Peninsula but also the position
of the Hapsburg Monarchy.

As has been shown, Austro-Hungarian statesmen had
long aimed at converting the "occupation and administration"
of Bosnia-Herzegovina into an annexation.   Andrássy's
original idea was to annex the provinces outright, and
Russia had doubtless consented to an annexation in the
agreements of 1876 and 1877, as well as by the secret
convention of July 13, 1878, although the last named
referred only to an *occupation définitive.*   The agreements
of 1876 and 1877 were made in view of the impending
Russo-Turkish War, and were intended to purchase Austro-
Hungarian neutrality while Russia established a big

Bulgaria and freed the Orthodox Christians of European Turkey. Thanks to the spirited help of Rumania, Russia compelled Turkey to sue for peace, and succeeded by the Treaty of San Stefano in marking out a Bulgaria that would have lain athwart the path of Austria-Hungary had the Monarchy ever attempted to advance towards Salonica. In these circumstances it would have mattered little to Russia that Austria-Hungary should have incorporated Bosnia-Herzegovina in the Monarchy. With the exception of the Montenegrins, the Serbo-Croatians or Southern Slavs seem long to have been left out of account by Russian statesmen. Servia, then ruled by King Milan Obrenovitch, was regarded almost as an Austrian satrapy. Russia had not acquired a clear consciousness of the potential importance of the Southern Slav question as a whole. Had the Treaty of San Stefano remained intact, it is probable that Russia would not have objected to the annexation of Bosnia-Herzegovina, and even of the Sanjak of Novi Bazar by Austria-Hungary. But Andrássy who, like Bismarck and Disraeli, was determined that the Pan-Slav cause should not triumph and that the Treaty of San Stefano should be revised, inflicted upon Russia at the Congress of Berlin so deep a humiliation that the Russian attitude towards the acquisition of Bosnia-Herzegovina by the Monarchy necessarily changed. Russia had borne the losses and the cost of the war against Turkey while Austria-Hungary, without raising a finger or incurring other expense than that of having supported some thousands of refugees from Bosnia-Herzegovina during the insurrection of 1875–76, was "compensated" with two Turkish provinces. British policy has rarely been worse inspired than when, under the Oriental guidance of Disraeli, it secured Cyprus as the price of peace with dishonour, helped Austria-Hungary and Germany to tear up the Treaty of San Stefano and incurred the moral responsibility for the carnage and havoc of the recent Balkan wars.

The unexpected resistance encountered by the Austro-Hungarian troops during the occupation of Bosnia-Herzegovina and the difficulty subsequently experienced in crushing Bosnian risings, put the idea of annexing the provinces beyond the range of practical politics for nearly twenty years. Servia, moreover, came increasingly under Austro-Hungarian diplomatic control, especially after the defeat of her army at Slivnitza in 1885 and the intervention of the Monarchy to check the march of the victorious Bulgarians. Since Servia seemed destined to fall, sooner or later, into Austro-Hungarian hands, there could be no reason to rouse sleeping dogs by pressing for the annexation of Bosnia-Herzegovina. It seemed a sounder policy for Austria-Hungary to prepare a situation such as to bring Bosnia-Herzegovina and Servia, at one stroke, within the confines of the Hapsburg realms. The abdication of King Milan in 1889, the growth of Russian influence in Servia under Queen Nathalie in the early 'nineties, the quarrels and reconciliations between Milan, Nathalie, and their son Alexander, the return of Nathalie to Servia in 1895 followed by that of Milan as commander-in-chief of the army in 1897, appear, however, to have convinced Austria-Hungary that it would be safer to annex Bosnia-Herzegovina as soon as possible. As has been stated, the idea of annexation was mooted by Count Gołuchowski during the Emperor Francis Joseph's visit to St. Petersburg in April 1897. Russia negatived the suggestion and the matter dropped. Some nine years later, in the summer of 1906, Count Gołuchowski again broached the subject in conversation with the Russian Ambassador in Vienna, Prince Urussoff, who once more deprecated the idea. In the meantime the outlook in Servia had been radically changed by the assassination of King Alexander and Queen Draga during the night of June 10–11, 1903, and Servian policy under King Peter Karageorgevitch had tended to become more Russophil. The obscure history of the plot to remove King Alexander and Queen Draga may never be fully elucidated. The plot may, as has been alleged, have been hatched under Russian auspices but its existence was certainly known to the Austro-Hungarian

Government which was fully informed of the meetings held by the conspirators in a well-known café of the Vienna Ringstrasse. Early in March 1903 the late M. de Kállay, Joint Austro - Hungarian Finance Minister and Chief Secretary for Bosnia-Herzegovina, informed the writer that King Alexander was in a perilous position and might not have many weeks to live ; and when, immediately after the arrival of the news of the assassination, the writer reminded M. de Kállay of this prediction, he replied, "Quite true ; and that will prove to you that what I tell you about the East is apt to be well-founded. Alexander was doomed and the intrigues of Nicholas of Montenegro have been nipped in the bud." The writer objected that Peter Kara-georgevitch was the son-in-law of King, then Prince, Nicholas of Montenegro. "Yes," answered M. de Kállay, "but his relations with his father-in-law are so bad that he is not dangerous. Besides, the Karageorgevitchs have always had two elements in their policy—not to quarrel with Austria-Hungary and not to quarrel with Turkey, their most power-ful neighbours." "Then," returned the writer, "the accession of Karageorgevitch does not mean trouble in the Balkans ? " "I did not say that," rejoined M. de Kállay. "Karageorge-vitch may be obliged to make himself popular by engaging in some national enterprise, though, as he is no longer young, I do not anticipate trouble in that direction ; it is Nicholas of Montenegro who, seeing the defeat of his schemes to put his second son, Mirko, on to the Servian throne, may try to push forward to Prizrend through the Albanian Catholic country so as to work round towards Servia from the South. It will be the business of Turkey to deal with him."

This conversation took place at the Joint Finance Ministry in the Johannesgasse at Vienna towards 10.30 A.M. on June 11, 1903, the morning following the night of the assassination. On June 12 the Austro-Hungarian Foreign Office organ, the *Fremdenblatt*, commented upon the assassination in a tone so cynical that the French Ambassador felt bound, before transmitting the comment

to his Government, to ask Count Gołuchowski whether the
Fremdenblatt article—with its declaration that the change of
régime was a matter of comparative indifference to Austria-
Hungary, who required only that Servia, whether ruled by
Obrenovitch or Karageorgevitch, should maintain good
relations with the Monarchy—really represented Austro-
Hungarian official views. Count Gołuchowski, who had
not yet seen the article in print, read it through in the
Ambassador's presence and confirmed the accuracy of its
standpoint. A violent attack in the *Zeit* upon such callousness on the part of the official organ of a Monarchical State
towards the assassination of Crowned Heads, moved the
Fremdenblatt rapidly to change its tone and to refer thereafter to the assassination in terms of horror. Nevertheless
the impression persisted in the Diplomatic Corps that the
Austro-Hungarian Government was by no means displeased
at the removal of the Obrenovitch dynasty; and it is an
interesting fact that when Peter Karageorgevitch passed
through Vienna on his way from Geneva to assume the
crown at Belgrade, the Austrian authorities refrained from
interfering with the crowd of Serbo-Croatians that assembled
to welcome him at the Western Railway Station, although,
among other manifestations, cheers were given for " Peter,
King of Croatia ! " Austro-Servian relations remained indeed
tolerably good until the end of 1905 when Austro-Hungarian
equanimity was upset by the conclusion of a Customs Union
between Servia and Bulgaria, and Count Gołuchowski, as a
punitive measure, declared a tariff war against Servia.

From this measure of coercion dates the regeneration of
Servia. The Austro-Hungarian Foreign Minister, Count
Gołuchowski, who appears to have neglected the first signs
of a *rapprochement* between Servia and Bulgaria, acted
hastily and angrily upon learning that the Customs Union
was virtually concluded and that it had been ratified by
acclamation in the Bulgarian Sobranye. With less circumspection than he was wont to display, he resolved to bring
Servia to her knees by excluding Servian cattle, swine, and

agricultural produce from the Austro-Hungarian market. The "Pig War" thus begun was destined to inflict greater damage upon the Monarchy than seemed conceivable at the moment. It drove Servia into a policy of economic expansion and obliged her to seek in Egypt, France, England and elsewhere the market she had lost in the Dual Monarchy. It deprived the inhabitants of the Monarchy of their regular supply of cattle and meat, and exposed them to the extortionate tactics of the Agrarian parties in Hungary and Austria which hastened to raise the prices of meat to an unprecedented level. It damaged even the Agrarians themselves by preventing the periodical renewal of their live stock from the Servian reservoir; but, most of all, it damaged the Monarchy by creating an atmosphere of animosity between Vienna and Belgrade, and by stimulating the Servian spirit of self-reliance. The Servian Government which, in normal circumstances, would probably have purchased in Austria the military material required for the reorganization of its army and would thus have become to some extent dependent upon Austria, turned instead towards France, and purchased field-artillery, ammunition and other supplies from Creusot. At the same time, Servian ill-will towards the Monarchy was increased by the attempts of the Hungarian Government to destroy the Coalition that had been formed by Serbs and Croats in the Croatian Diet, and to combat, by means of the Agram High Treason trial, the supposed pro-Servian tendencies among the Southern Slavs of the Monarchy. This, briefly, was the Austro-Servian situation in the summer of 1908 when the Young Turkish Revolution suddenly changed the terms of the Balkan problem, and convinced Baron von Aehrenthal that the annexation of Bosnia-Herzegovina could no longer be delayed.

THE ANNEXATION CRISIS

Prior to the Turkish Revolution (July 24), and after the Anglo-Russian meeting at Reval on June 9-10, 1908, Baron von Aehrenthal had received from the Russian Foreign Minister, M. Isvolsky, an important memorandum, or *Aide-mémoire*, dated June 19, on pending Balkan issues. Though the text of this document has never been published, it is understood to have suggested that these issues, including the annexation of Bosnia-Herzegovina and the opening of the Dardanelles, should be settled between Austria-Hungary and Russia by mutual consent on a European basis. The object of the *Aide-mémoire* was, in M. Isvolsky's view, to define more exactly certain features of the Austro-Russian agreement of 1897 which had been modified by Baron von Aehrenthal's action in obtaining from Turkey the concession for the Novi Bazar Railway. What reply Aehrenthal made to the *Aide-mémoire* is not known, nor has the relationship of the *Aide-mémoire* to antecedent Austro-Russian correspondence ever been clearly established. M. Isvolsky, whose ambition it was to revise the Treaty of Berlin in a sense favourable to Russia, doubtless surrounded his suggestions with saving clauses and considerations ; but the interesting fact remains that, after the Reval meeting and before the Turkish Revolution, he intimated to Baron von Aehrenthal the readiness of Russia eventually to consent to the annexation of the occupied provinces. In making this intimation M. Isvolsky was doubtless influenced by the manifold symptoms of an approaching Balkan Crisis and by the wish to prepare for it in friendly intelligence with Austria-Hungary. What course the Austro-Russian negotiations would have taken had not the Young Turkish Revolution broken out at the end of July is now a question merely academic. The Revolution certainly strengthened Aehrenthal's desire to carry through the annexation without delay and to use M. Isvolsky's *Aide-mémoire* as a lever to obtain Russian consent. When the archives of the Austro-Hungarian Foreign Office are opened to some future historian, the workings of Aehrenthal's mind may be clearly revealed ; but to contemporary observers acquainted with the main facts of Austro-Hungarian and Russian action, there still appears much that is mysterious in Aehrenthal's management of the matter.

In Austria, counsels were divided both as to the moment and the method of effecting the annexation. The Austrian historian, Dr. Friedjung, then an intimate friend and adviser of Baron von Aehrenthal, stated in the *Neue Freie Presse* of March 25, 1909—the famous article that led to the Friedjung trial of December 1909—that Herr Rappaport, the Austro-Hungarian Civil Agent in Macedonia, had been instructed to inform the Young Turkish Committee at Salonica of the Emperor Francis Joseph's intention to grant a constitution to the occupied provinces but had received the " highly offensive " reply that the right which the Austro-Hungarian Monarch proposed to exercise belonged exclusively to the Suzerain of the provinces—the Sultan. This impertinence on the part of the Young Turks, added Dr. Friedjung, assuredly hastened the necessary resolve of Austria-Hungary.

It is indeed probable that Baron von Aehrenthal committed the imprudence of consulting the Committee of Union and Progress in regard to the proposed annexation, after having, some months earlier, rejected an appeal made to him by Young Turkish emissaries for financial assistance. The view that the restoration of the Turkish Constitution had rendered inevitable the granting of some form of constitutional autonomy to Bosnia-Herzegovina was current in Vienna at the beginning of August 1908, and a foreign authority who was consulted on the subject tendered the advice that the spontaneous gift of a Constitution would greatly strengthen the position of the Monarchy in regard to the two Provinces. Whereas a decree of annexation would be likely to evoke protests from Turkey and from several European Powers, the granting of a Constitution, argued this authority, would meet with no serious objection and would be in itself a clear assertion of Austro-Hungarian sovereignty over the Provinces. To the objection that the Bosnian Musulmans might take advantage of constitutional autonomy to elect deputies to the Turkish Parliament, the authority in question replied that, in this case, the Bosnian Musulmans would themselves supply Austria-Hungary with a valid reason for annexing the Provinces outright since, in such circumstances, annexation would be a legitimate act of political self-defence against the abuse of liberties magnanimously granted. This sage advice went unheeded, although the considerations on which it was based are understood to have been put forward during the Austrian Cabinet Council which, on August 18, 1908—the Emperor Francis Joseph's birthday—discussed the proposed annexation and sanctioned it in principle. The view prevailed that the annexation must be effected as a simple act of Austro-Hungarian sovereignty. But before the annexation was proclaimed on October 6, 1908, Baron von Aehrenthal's diplomatic errors sowed the seeds of future embarrassment for the Monarchy.

On August 13, 1908, King Edward paid what was to prove his last visit to the Emperor Francis Joseph at Ischl. On his way thither he had visited the German Emperor at Friedrichshof Castle near Homburg. The question of an Anglo-German Agreement for the limitation of naval armaments was then in the foreground of public discussion and is understood to have been touched upon in the conversations between King Edward, the Emperor William, and their advisers. In any case the result was negative, and, on reaching Ischl, King Edward is believed to have opened his heart to his old friend, the Emperor Francis Joseph, and to have suggested that the Austro-Hungarian Monarch should use his good offices with the Emperor William in favour of a naval agreement which, in the opinion of King Edward, would contribute notably to diminish the tension of Anglo-German relations. Either spontaneously, or under the influence of Baron von Aehrenthal whose anti-English tendencies were then pronounced and who suspected King Edward of attempting to win over Austria-Hungary to the Triple Entente in order to complete the "encirclement" of Germany, the Emperor Francis Joseph refused to entertain the British suggestion, and King Edward left Ischl for his annual "cure" at Marienbad in a disappointed mood. Possibly on account of this contretemps, but more probably because the Emperor Francis Joseph and Baron von Aehrenthal feared British opposition to the annexation of Bosnia - Herzegovina at a moment when Turkey seemed to be entering upon an era of progress and reform, nothing was said to King Edward at Ischl in regard to the intended annexation. On August 14, 1908, at Marienbad King Edward dismissed as entirely improbable a suggestion that Austria-Hungary was preparing to annex Bosnia - Herzegovina, and remarked that otherwise the Emperor Francis Joseph would surely have alluded to the plan in conversation with him. King Edward was not alone in this optimism. The Russian Foreign Minister, M. Isvolsky, who was then staying at Karlsbad, expressed, as late as August 26, the conviction that Austria-Hungary would not engage in so serious an adventure as the annexation. "Otherwise," said M. Isvolsky, "she would raise a grave question that would demand European treatment." An Austro-Hungarian Ambassador accredited to a Great Power stated early in September, after repeated conversations with Baron von Aehrenthal, that the idea of annexing the two Provinces had been abandoned. Yet by the beginning of September M. Isvolsky had received information that the annexation was decided upon and that it would be accompanied by the proclamation of Bulgarian independence. At Karlsbad on September 4, he informed the late M. Milovanovitch, the Servian Foreign Minister, that both the annexation and the proclamation of independence were inevitable, and asked M. Milovanovitch to suggest a scheme of compensations for Servia. On September 10 M. Milovanovitch returned to Karlsbad and proposed to M. Isvolsky the scheme of compensations which the Russian statesman and Sir Edward Grey afterwards supported. Thus it is clear that before starting from Karlsbad on September 15 to meet Baron von Aehrenthal at Buchlau in Moravia—the residence

of Count Berchtold, then Austro-Hungarian Ambassador at
St. Petersburg—M. Isvolsky was prepared to negotiate with
Austria-Hungary on the basis of the annexation of Bosnia-
Herzegovina and the proclamation of Bulgarian independence. The details of the Buchlau Meeting have never been
divulged though many interesting indiscretions have been
committed in regard to them. It is doubtful whether the
full truth will ever be known, since the chief conversation
took place *en tête-à-tête* between the Austro-Hungarian and
Russian Foreign Ministers who communicated only the
general results of their negotiations to the diplomatists
who accompanied them ; but it is certain that on leaving
Buchlau, M. Isvolsky believed himself to have attained a
complete agreement with Aehrenthal on all points under
discussion. Whether Baron von Aehrenthal was of the
same opinion is a matter for conjecture. He went to
Buchlau with a suite of diplomatists and Foreign Office
officials whose functions were intended by him to be those
of witnesses in case of subsequent contestation. In after-
dinner talk he skilfully extracted from M. Isvolsky admissions in regard to the agreement privately attained, and
quite as skilfully avoided giving any clear undertaking as
to the manner and moment of the action contemplated.
Aehrenthal's apologists aver that he informed M. Isvolsky
that Bosnia-Herzegovina would be annexed "au moment
favorable" ; and a well-informed pro-Russian writer in the
Fortnightly Review stated, in the autumn of 1909, that
when M. Isvolsky insisted on receiving considerable previous
notice of the intended date of annexation, Baron von
Aehrenthal unhesitatingly replied, "Why, certainly ; that
is a matter of course." This statement has never been and
probably could not be challenged by Aehrenthal's apologists.
M. Isvolsky consequently left Buchlau in the belief that he
would have ample time to prepare for the execution of the
part of the agreement in which Russia was mainly interested
—probably the question of the opening of the Dardanelles
—and to arrange that the projected modifications of the

status quo in the Near East should take place smoothly with general European assent.

How M. Isvolsky could place such confidence in the good faith of a statesman like Aehrenthal who, not a year earlier, had tricked him deplorably in regard to the Novi Bazar Railway concession, is a psychological mystery. Possibly the brilliant prospect of being able to revise the Berlin Treaty in favour of Russia blinded him to the danger attending any secret negotiations with Aehrenthal whom M. Isvolsky knew to be, figuratively speaking, thirsting for his blood. As the ally of France and the friend of England he was, moreover, under a moral obligation immediately to inform the French and British Governments of what had taken place at Buchlau ; but, lulled by a sense of false security, he preferred to wait until he should, three weeks later, have an opportunity of conferring personally at Paris and in London with the French and British Foreign Ministers. The sequel is best stated in the words of Dr. Friedjung, the pro-Aehrenthalian historian, who wrote in the *Österreichische Rundschau* of October 1, 1908 (p. 7) : " Both statesmen were satisfied with the results attained (at Buchlau), and each of them took the measures he thought necessary, albeit in very different ways. Isvolsky travelled slowly and comfortably to his meeting with Tittoni, stayed a full week in Italy, saw King Victor Emmanuel in one of his castles, and, believing himself sure of the assent of the Triple Alliance, arrived tranquilly in Paris on October 3. In the meantime Aehrenthal worked with fiery zeal and astonished the world by the Emperor Francis Joseph's (annexation) manifesto of October 5 (issued on the evening of October 6 at Vienna and promulgated at Serajevo on October 7). He created a *fait accompli*, while Isvolsky still stuck fast in long-winded preparations."

In view of the agreement at Buchlau that M. Isvolsky should have considerable previous notice of the intended date of the annexation, Dr. Friedjung's allegations, which bear a highly official character, amount to a charge of deliberate bad faith against his then friend, Baron von

Aehrenthal. It has been stated without denial that the only notice given to M. Isvolsky was in the form of a private letter from Aehrenthal that reached him on October 3, 1908, when he arrived in Paris from his visit to King Victor Emmanuel at Racconigi. Saturday, October 3, was indeed an important day in the history of the Annexation Crisis. On October 1 and 2 the Austro-Hungarian Ambassadors to France, Italy, England and Germany had been despatched from Budapest, where the Court was then residing, with letters from the Emperor Francis Joseph to inform the Heads of the States to whom they were accredited that the Emperor had decided to extend his sovereignty to Bosnia-Herzegovina on October 6. Two, at least, and probably all of these Ambassadors had been informed by Baron von Aehrenthal that the proclamation of Bulgarian independence would precede the Annexation by one day. But in order that this arrangement might not become known, they were instructed not to deliver the Emperor Francis Joseph's letters before Monday, October 5. Count Khevenhüller-Metsch, the Austro-Hungarian Ambassador to the French Republic, found, however, on Saturday, October 3, when requesting an audience of President Fallières for Monday, October 5, that the President would be at Rambouillet on that day. Count Khevenhüller therefore resolved to present the Emperor's letter on Saturday afternoon, October 3. In the course of the audience President Fallières remarked, " La lettre de Sa Majesté annonce l'annexion de la Bosnie-Herzégovine. Et l'indépendance de la Bulgarie ? " Whereto the Austro-Hungarian Ambassador truthfully but incautiously replied, " C'est tout arrangé, Monsieur le Président. La Bulgarie nous devancera d'un jour." This important admission was communicated by the French Government to Sir Francis Bertie, British Ambassador at Paris, who immediately informed the British Foreign Office. On the afternoon of the same day, October 3, Sir W. E. Goschen, the British Ambassador to the Austro-Hungarian Court, then at Budapest, enquired officially in pursuance of precise instructions, whether Baron von Aehrenthal had any knowledge of an impending proclamation of Bulgarian independence. Baron von Aehrenthal, who had on the previous evening announced to the Italian Ambassador the impending annexation of Bosnia-Herzegovina with the result that the Ambassador had suddenly and mysteriously started for Rome, seemed to expect that the British Ambassador would enquire about the annexation. Surprised by his question concerning Bulgarian independence, Baron von Aehrenthal answered that he had no knowledge of an impending proclamation of Bulgarian independence, that he did not consider it to be imminent, and added that there was no mention of it in Austro-Hungarian reports from Sofia. The British Ambassador telegraphed this official denial to London where it arrived almost simultaneously with his colleague's telegram from Paris reporting Count Khevenhüller's statement to the President of the Republic. The proclamation of Bulgarian independence on Monday, October 5, and the public announcement of the annexation at Vienna on Tuesday, October 6, showed that Count Khevenhüller had spoken the truth. It is satisfactory to record the hitherto unpublished fact that before taking up his new post at Berlin (to which he had been appointed by King Edward on the previous August 13, during the King's journey from Linz to Ischl), the British Ambassador, Sir W. E. Goschen, took an opportunity to tax Baron von Aehrenthal with untruthfulness in the presence of several diplomatic witnesses.

Why Baron von Aehrenthal should have lied officially to the British Ambassador is not clear. In ignorance of the indiscretion committed by Count Khevenhüller in Paris, he may have feared that premature divulgation of the Austro-Bulgarian scheme would evoke a British protest against what was likely to be regarded in England as a conspiracy against the regeneration of the Ottoman Empire. The exact degree in which Aehrenthal worked in secret intelligence with King, then Prince, Ferdinand of Bulgaria cannot be definitely ascertained. Prince Ferdinand with Princess Eleonora had paid a significant visit to the Austro-Hungarian Court at Budapest on the previous September 23, a week after the Buchlau meeting, and had been received with royal honours. It is certain that intercourse between the Emperor Francis Joseph and Prince Ferdinand was not, on that occasion, entirely harmonious, and that a sharp difference of opinion arose between them in connexion with the Order of the Golden Fleece, which Prince Ferdinand coveted but which the Emperor Francis Joseph considered him not to deserve on account of his strained relations with the Vatican.[1] (The distinction was subsequently bestowed in somewhat cavalier fashion upon King Ferdinand who received it as one of a batch of less distinguished candidates.) Baron von Aehrenthal, who had vainly advised the Bulgarian Ruler not to ask for the Golden Fleece, subsequently declared that he had also implored him not to precipitate the proclamation of Bulgarian independence—but Baron von Aehrenthal's testimony can scarcely be regarded as conclusive. More weight attaches to an assurance transmitted by the Emperor Francis Joseph to King Edward—in answer to King Edward's deprecatory reply to the Emperor's letter announcing the Annexation—that the question of Bulgarian independence had not been mentioned between him and Prince Ferdinand at Budapest. But, after the Budapest visit, Prince Ferdinand went to Vienna where he conferred repeatedly with Baron von Aehrenthal and presided over a Bulgarian Cabinet Council secretly held in the Coburg Palace towards the end of September. Nevertheless, the decision to proclaim the independence of Bulgaria was not finally communicated to the Bulgarian ministers until the night or early morning of October 4–5, when another Cabinet meeting was held on board Prince Ferdinand's yacht at Rustchuk. At mid-day on the 5th, independence was proclaimed at Tirnovo. One reason for King Ferdinand's haste is alleged to have been his fear of European opposition, and it is conceivable that, when once informed that the annexation of Bosnia-Herzegovina and

---

[1] The Vatican has never forgiven the Bulgarian Ruler for consenting to the conversion of his son, Prince Boris, to the Orthodox Faith.

the proclamation of Bulgarian independence had been agreed upon in principle by the Austro-Hungarian and Russian Foreign Ministers, Prince Ferdinand decided to force the pace and to be the first to bolt through the paper walls of the *Status Quo*. Though the haste of Prince Ferdinand may perhaps be held to afford a plausible explanation of Baron von Aehrenthal's failure to keep faith with M. Isvolsky, it cannot justify his untruthfulness to the British Ambassador, nor can his subsequent asseverations be taken as proof that, until October 4, he really had no knowledge that Bulgarian independence would be so rapidly proclaimed. The information and the instructions he gave to Count Khevenhüller and other Austro-Hungarian ambassadors as early as October 1 conclusively prove the contrary.

The Annexation was received with an outburst of joy in Austria-Hungary, with almost hostile reserve by Germany, whom Baron von Aehrenthal had scarcely consulted, and with indignation in Russia, England, France and Italy. Austrians felt that the Monarchy had once again asserted its political individuality and its power of independent decision. Baron von Aehrenthal became popular overnight and was christened "the Austrian Bismarck." In Russia, anti-Austrian feeling ran high. It was felt that M. Isvolsky had again been duped. During his visits to Paris and London M. Isvolsky strove indeed to repair the damage done by his single-handed agreement with Aehrenthal, and urged that a European Conference must meet to deal with the new situation and to revise the Treaty of Berlin. England and France accepted the idea of a Conference, though England is understood to have deprecated the raising of questions like that of the Dardanelles at a moment when the new *régime* in Turkey was struggling to establish itself. Aehrenthal, with the support of German diplomacy which had been obliged by self-interest to fall into line with him, resisted the idea of a Conference unless its programme should be strictly defined beforehand and the discussion of the annexation of Bosnia-Herzegovina limited to a mere registration of the

accomplished fact.   Austro-Russian relations grew more and
more strained.   Mobilization began on both sides of the
frontier.   Austria-Hungary filled Bosnia-Herzegovina with
troops and concentrated a large force in Croatia-Slavonia
and Southern Hungary.   In the North, arrangements for
the intervention of German troops were contemplated, so
that any aggressive movement on the part of Russia might
bring the German army also into action.   In Servia excite-
ment reached a delirious pitch, and the occupation of
Belgrade by Austria-Hungary was daily expected.   Had the
Servian army been at the moment of the Annexation as
ready for war as it was towards the end of the crisis, the
Servian Government would undoubtedly have thrown it into
Bosnia-Herzegovina in the hope of raising an insurrection,
which, to judge by the precedents of 1878 and 1882, would
have created a formidable embarrassment for the Monarchy.
Simultaneously the Young Turkish Committee proclaimed a
boycott of Austro-Hungarian merchandise and practically
suspended Austro-Hungarian trade with Turkey until the
spring of 1909.   Under the pressure of this situation,
Aehrenthal reluctantly adopted a policy he had previously
scorned and came to terms with Turkey.   His original thesis
had been that Turkey had lost nothing, save a fictitious suze-
rainty, by the Annexation and had been amply compensated
for this loss by the withdrawal of Austro-Hungarian garrisons
from the Sanjak of Novi Bazar.   The hostility of England
and Russia, the boycott of Austro-Hungarian vessels and
merchandise in Turkish ports, the danger of a Turco-Servian
alliance against the Monarchy, the uncertain attitude of
Italy, which, despite a secret agreement between Aehrenthal
and the Italian Foreign Minister, Signor Tittoni, prevented
the despatch of a single warship from the Adriatic to protect Austro-Hungarian commerce in the Levant, convinced
Aehrenthal, sorely against his will, that he must ease his
position and legalize the title of the Monarchy to Bosnia-
Herzegovina by securing Turkish assent to the Annexation.
After much negotiation Aehrenthal waived his original

demand that the Turkish boycott should cease before
Austria-Hungary could contemplate any diplomatic agreement with the Ottoman Empire and, on February 26, 1909,
an Austro - Turkish Convention was concluded on the
following points : (1) Austria-Hungary expressly renounced
all the rights acquired in regard to the Sanjak of Novi Bazar
by and in pursuance of the Berlin Treaty ; (2) The Austro-
Turkish Convention of April 21, 1879, concerning the
Sanjak and the occupation of Bosnia-Herzegovina was
abrogated ; Turkey recognized that all differences of view
between Austria-Hungary and the Ottoman Government had
ceased ; (3) Natives of Bosnia-Herzegovina resident in or
emigrating to Turkey were to retain their Ottoman
nationality ; (4) The liberty and exercise of the Musulman
religion in Bosnia-Herzegovina were guaranteed and it was
established that the name of the Sultan, as Khalif, should
continue to be mentioned in the public prayers of Bosnian-
Herzegovinian Musulmans ; (5) Austria-Hungary agreed to
pay the Ottoman Government an indemnity of £T2,500,000,
nominally as an equivalent for the Vakuf[1] properties possessed
by Turkey in Bosnia-Herzegovina ; (6) Austria-Hungary
promised to conclude a treaty of commerce with Turkey,
consented to an increase of the Turkish customs from 11 to
15 per cent *ad valorem*, to the creation of Turkish State
monopolies in petroleum, cigarette paper, matches, alcohol,
and playing cards ; (7) Austria-Hungary agreed to suppress
her post offices in Turkey as soon as the post offices of
other Powers should be suppressed ; and (8) to support at
a European Conference or otherwise the demand of Turkey
that the Capitulations be replaced by International Law.

This Convention was not the only concession which
Baron von Aehrenthal found himself obliged to make before
the end of the Annexation Crisis. Under pressure from
Russia and Italy, he consented, early in April 1909, to
modify Article XXIX. of the Treaty of Berlin in such manner
as to suppress clauses 5, 7, 8, 9, 10, and 11 of the Article,

[1] Pious Foundations.

which limited the sovereignty of Montenegro over her own littoral and gave Austria - Hungary the right to police Montenegrin waters. Austria-Hungary and Italy originally demanded that clause 6 of Article XXIX. should be replaced by a clause obliging Montenegro to maintain the commercial character of the Port of Antivari and declaring that no military works could be erected there ; but, on representations from Russia and France, who urged that a statement from Montenegro in regard to the commercial character of Antivari would be sufficient, Aehrenthal consented to the abrogation of clause 6 also, and thus opened Antivari and Montenegrin waters to the warships of all nations. The opening of Antivari as a free port (October 23, 1909) was celebrated on New Year's Day 1910 by the arrival of a French naval squadron, which had been sent in virtue of an agreement between France, Russia, and Italy to greet Prince Nicholas on having attained the fiftieth year of his reign. In the following August an Italian squadron with the King and Queen of Italy also visited Montenegrin waters to attend the Diamond Jubilee celebrations and to be present at the proclamation of Montenegro as a Kingdom.

These concessions on the part of Austria-Hungary to Turkey and Montenegro were more than counterbalanced by the obduracy with which Baron von Aehrenthal refused any kind of concession to Servia. True, Servia had no legitimate grievance. The annexation of Bosnia-Herzegovina seemed, indeed, to have dispelled the Servian dream of obtaining possession of the Provinces, but the dream could not be claimed as a " moral asset " of Servia save in a spirit of hostility towards the Monarchy. Besides, Aehrenthal suspected Servia of fomenting a pan-Serb agitation in Croatia-Slavonia, Bosnia-Herzegovina and Dalmatia. The Hungarian Government had been engaged since 1907 in an attempt to reduce Croatia-Slavonia to the condition of vassalage in which those provinces had been kept from 1868 till 1906, and from which they had only escaped in consequence of a coalition between the chief Croat and Serb

parties of Dalmatia and Croatia-Slavonia in 1905. This
Coalition had formed a fighting alliance with the Hungarian
Coalition of opposition parties which had resisted the
Crown from the end of 1904 until April 1906. If the
Dynasty and the Austro-Hungarian Government had viewed
with displeasure the co-operation of Croats and Serbs,
that neutralized the ancient Hapsburg policy of playing
off the one Southern Slav element against the other,
they had been thoroughly alarmed by the alliance of the
Serbo-Croatian and the Hungarian Coalitions. The condition
of the alliance was that when the Hungarian Coalition should
take office at Budapest, the Serbo-Croatian Coalition should
be allowed freedom in the administration of Croatia-Slavonia.
The Hungarian Coalition came to terms with the Crown in
April 1906 and, notwithstanding pressure from Vienna,
fulfilled its bargain with the Serbo-Croatians by establishing
a *régime* of comparative liberty in Croatia-Slavonia. For
the first time since the conclusion of the Hungaro-Croatian
Settlement in 1868, these two provinces were allowed to
breathe freely ; but the execution of various details of the
alliance between the two Coalitions met with so much
opposition in Vienna that Dr. Wekerle, the Hungarian
Coalition Premier, found himself unable to obtain the
Emperor's sanction to the appointment of two patriotic
Croatian officials at Agram whose nomination the Serbo-
Croatian Coalition considered urgent. The Serbo-Croatians
consequently resolved to apply pressure. It had been
announced that the Emperor would attend the combined
naval and military manœuvres near Ragusa that were to take
place in the autumn of 1906. The Serbo-Croatian leader,
M. Supilo, informed the Hungarian Premier that unless
the two officials were appointed immediately, the Emperor
would be received in dead silence by the Serbo-Croatians
of Dalmatia. The threat was not idle. In August 1906
the Lord-Lieutenancy of Dalmatia at Zara discovered that
the Slav population was firmly resolved to make a demonstration of silence against the Emperor should he attend the

manœuvres before the requisite appointments had been made in Croatia. An official was despatched in hot haste to warn the Emperor's aide-de-camp, Count Paar; and a few days later the announcement appeared that, as the Emperor was a bad sailor, the Heir-Presumptive, Archduke Francis Ferdinand, would attend the manœuvres in his stead. By a strange coincidence the appointments of the Croatian officials at Agram were actually sanctioned on the day of the Archduke's arrival at Ragusa, but, as the news was not known to the population, he was received in silence. On visiting the municipality in the evening he was painfully impressed by the absolute stillness of the immense crowd that filled the square and blocked the streets, a stillness all the more significant in comparison with an ovation that had been given to Prince Danilo of Montenegro by the same population in the afternoon. Similar frigidity marked the attitude of the population of Trebinje in the Herzegovina, which the Archduke visited officially on the following day. Efforts had been made by the Bosnian officials to induce the Serbs of Bosnia-Herzegovina to petition the Archduke in favour of the annexation of the provinces, but the reply had been given that the Serbs would not send even a deputation to greet the Archduke should there be any question of annexation. In these circumstances it is comprehensible that the Heir-Presumptive should have left Dalmatia with an impression the reverse of favourable, and that he and the Austro-Hungarian Government should have resolved to combat the growing sense of solidarity among the Southern Slavs of the Monarchy and between them and those beyond the frontier. As usual, "Vienna" made the mistake of not believing this sense of solidarity to be in any way spontaneous, and of attributing it exclusively to the work of Servian or pan-Serb agitators. Therefore, when an individual named Nastitch—who had received a subsidy from the Prince of Montenegro after turning evidence against his accomplices in a mysterious conspiracy, apparently promoted by Austro-Hungarian *agents provocateurs*, against the life of the Prince—offered the Hungarian Government, in 1907, " revelations " concerning the pan-Serb propaganda, which he alleged to be carried on from Belgrade in Croatia-Slavonia, advantage was taken of his " information " to open an era of persecution against the Southern Slavs of the Monarchy. On the strength of Nastitch's allegations, a High Treason prosecution was begun at Agram against more than fifty innocent Serbs. The trial of these victims, which became a European scandal, embittered the feelings of the Southern Slavs of the Monarchy and created an atmosphere favourable to the propagation of the Southern Slav unitary ideal. It is unquestionable that the Servian Government profited by this situation and that, in some cases, its emissaries and its secret funds found their way into Bosnia-Herzegovina ; but the Austro-Hungarian authorities grossly exaggerated the extent of Servian political and pecuniary influence and underestimated the natural tendency of members of one and the same race to draw together at moments of stress or persecution. In these circumstances, the Austro-Hungarian authorities became the willing dupes, if not the accomplices, of other unscrupulous informers who supplied them with " proofs " that there existed a widespread plot among the Serbs and Croatians of the Monarchy in conjunction with the Serbs of Bosnia-Herzegovina and with the Servians [1] of the Kingdom, to establish a "Greater Servia" at the expense of Austria-Hungary. Baron von Aehrenthal believed or affected to believe in the plot, instructed Austro-Hungarian Ambassadors to draw the attention of foreign governments to it and to inform them that it had driven Austria - Hungary to annex Bosnia - Herzegovina. The " proofs " of the existence of the plot consisted of documents fabricated partly under the supervision of a member

---

[1] The term " Servian " indicates the members of the Serb or Serbo-Croatian or Southern Slav race who are subjects of the Servian Crown. The term " Serb " is applied to the members of the same race who live outside the frontiers of Servia and are of the Orthodox Faith. Thus the Montenegrins are Serbs but not Servians. The term "Croat" or "Croatian" indicates the Catholic members of the Serbo-Croatian race who inhabit Croatia-Slavonia, Dalmatia, and Bosnia-Herzegovina.

of the Austro-Hungarian Legation at Belgrade and partly with the help of the police at Agram and Semlin. It is difficult to resist the suspicion that these " proofs," of which several scores were accumulated by the Austro-Hungarian Foreign Office and by the General Staff, were intended to constitute an overwhelming case against Servia in the event of an Austro-Servian war. Early in 1909 when war, or, as the Austrian expression ran, a " punitive expedition" against Servia was believed to be imminent, a selection of these " proofs" was placed at the disposal of Dr. Friedjung, who based upon them a series of articles intended to be a war-blast. In these articles, of which the first was published on March 25, 1909, Dr. Friedjung accused M. Supilo, the Serbo-Croatian leader, and several other prominent Serbs and Croatians of the Monarchy, of corrupt and treasonable intercourse with the Servian Government. The publication led to the famous Friedjung trial of December 1909,[1] in which the " proofs " were demonstrated to be clumsy forgeries ; and to the disclosure made by Professor Masaryk in the Delegations of 1910 that the forgeries had been largely the work of a man named Vasitch who had been employed for the purpose of forging them by Captain von Sviento-chowski of the Austro-Hungarian Legation at Belgrade. During the Friedjung trial, Count[2] Aehrenthal informed a foreign visitor that he had never believed in the authenticity of the " proofs " of the conspiracy ; and he hastened, as soon as their veritable character was revealed, to disavow them in his official organ, the *Fremdenblatt.* He appeared insensible to the discredit which the exposure of his methods had cast upon the Monarchy. His principles that all is fair in diplomacy and that " accomplished facts are the most conclusive proofs," doubtless explain his conduct ; and but for the withdrawal of Russian support from Servia after the intervention of the German Ambassador at St. Petersburg on

[1] Cf. pp. 100-105.
[2] Baron von Aehrenthal was raised to the rank of Count on the Emperor Francis Joseph's birthday, August 18, 1909.

March 24, 1909—the day before the publication of the
Friedjung article—Aehrenthal's methods might have been
placed beyond possibility of detection by an Austro-
Hungarian invasion of Servia and by the execution, under
martial law, of the Serbo-Croatians whom the forgeries
charged with high treason. But, according to a homely
Italian proverb, " Il diavolo fa le pentole ma non i coperchi." [1]
It is a singular but perhaps not quite fortuitous circumstance
that Germany, who secured the capitulation of M. Isvolsky to
Austria-Hungary, should thereby have rendered her ally and
Aehrenthal himself a signal disservice.

The attitude of Germany towards Austria-Hungary
during the Annexation Crisis throws vivid light upon the
character of German diplomacy. Aehrenthal had never been
quite popular at Berlin. He was suspected, not without
reason, of seeking to obtain for Austria-Hungary a large
measure of diplomatic independence, and of conceiving
Austro-German relations as being based on the principle of
give and take, not, as some German statesmen had imagined,
on the principle of " take " alone. He had neglected to
inform Germany of his plans for the annexation of Bosnia-
Herzegovina until the last moment, and had thus placed
German diplomacy in an awkward position at Constantinople
where Germany was made to appear the accomplice of a
State that had struck a heavy blow at Turkish prestige.
Prince Bülow, the German Chancellor, resented Aehrenthal's
independent action and hesitated for some weeks as to the
course to be pursued. It is on record that his attitude was
finally determined by the arguments and expostulations of
the late Herr von Holstein—long the *Éminence grise* of
the German Foreign Office—who emerged from retirement
to entreat the Chancellor not to leave Austria-Hungary in
the lurch. Otherwise, argued Holstein, the Austro-German
Alliance would be ruined. Aehrenthal had shrewdly counted
upon this consideration and had reckoned that, in her own
interest, Germany would be obliged to support him. Yet

[1] " The lids of the Devil's saucepans do not fit."

he, who was cunning above all things and proud of his cunning, left out of account the cunning of Prussian diplomacy.   Germany supported him throughout the crisis but at the decisive moment when the question of peace or war was on the point of decision and when Aehrenthal believed himself, in view of the military unreadiness of Russia, to be about to compel M. Isvolsky to recognize the Annexation and to abandon Servia, Germany instructed her Ambassador at St. Petersburg to inform M. Isvolsky that in case of war with Austria-Hungary, Russia would also have to face the armed strength of Germany.   The exact terms and circumstances of this intervention have never been revealed.   Malicious tongues have suggested that Russia, having decided not to risk a European war, invited Germany, directly or indirectly, to present a mock ultimatum in order that Russia might yield to Germany rather than to Austria-Hungary, her principal antagonist.   However this may be, it is a fact that forty-eight hours before the German intervention, the Russian military authorities had resolved not to make war.   M. Isvolsky always displayed reticence in regard to the exact circumstances of the incident, which he described to those entitled to enquire as "une mise-en-demeure péremptoire."   But whether tragi-comedy or quasi-tragedy, the Russian submission was made, and Count Pourtalès, the German Ambassador to the Russian Court, was able to telegraph to Berlin, on March 24, 1909, M. Isvolsky's declaration "that Russia would formally declare her unreserved adhesion to the abolition of Article XXV. (concerning Bosnia-Herzegovina) of the Treaty of Berlin in case Austria-Hungary should apply for Russian recognition of the Austro-Turkish Convention." [1]   The news reached Aehrenthal late on March 24.   An attempt was at once made to stop the publication of Dr. Friedjung's "War-trumpet" article in the *Neue Freie Presse* on the following morning, but the story runs that the printing presses were

---

[1] *Austro-Hungarian Red-Book*, 1909, "Diplomatische Aktenstücke betreffend Bosnien und die Herzegovina, Oktober 1908 bis Juni 1909," p. 113.

already in motion and the first edition of the journal printed. The Friedjung trial with its exposure of Aehrenthal's methods thus became inevitable. On March 25 Baron von Aehrenthal instructed the German Ambassador in Berlin to express his "grateful satisfaction" to Prince Bülow for the action of Count Pourtalès—his only recorded expression of thanks for the "service" rendered. Aehrenthal felt that by snatching from his brow at the last moment the crown of laurel he believed himself about to receive, Germany had "got level" with him for his independent conduct at the beginning of the crisis. So deep was his resentment of German action that, even after the Emperor William had, in a famous speech at the Vienna Rathaus on September 20, 1910, claimed Austro-Hungarian gratitude for the help Germany had given "with Nibelungen faithfulness" "in shining armour" to her ally in the hour of need, Aehrenthal's only acknowledgment was contained in the colourless phrase, "Recent events have shown that our alliances have a real value." This phrase, which formed the principal feature of Aehrenthal's statement to the Delegations on October 13, 1910, irritated the Austrian-German parties and served to nourish the attacks and intrigues constantly directed against Aehrenthal up to the eve of his death by the German Ambassador in Vienna and by the press and politicians under German diplomatic influence.

Aehrenthal retained office until his death in February 1912. During his later years at the Ballplatz his policy underwent a notable change. Partly on account of failing health and partly because experience had corrected his previously inadequate knowledge of the European situation, he remained on the defensive and became by degrees an element of stability in Europe. The Annexation Crisis having been closed by the decision of Servia to bow to the inevitable and to declare that "her rights had not been affected by the *fait accompli* created in Bosnia-Herzegovina and that she would consequently conform herself to the decision of the Powers in regard to Article

XXV. of the Treaty of Berlin," Aehrenthal was free to
pursue a policy less hazardous and more in accordance with
the veritable interests of the Monarchy.   The submission of
Servia, without other compensation than the vague promise
of a commercial treaty, was largely due to the conciliatory
influence of England at Belgrade.   Though Sir Edward
Grey was under no obligation to support Servia and had only
promised the Servian Foreign Minister, M. Milovanovitch, to
advocate Servian claims " as long as they should be seconded
by Russia," the British Foreign Secretary was better than
his word and lent his good offices to Servia even after
Russia had given way.   He obtained a modification of the
humiliating formula to which Austria-Hungary demanded
Servian adhesion and saved the Servian Government from
the bitter feeling that it had been abandoned by all the
Great Powers.   After the crisis, Austro-Hungarian relations
with England gradually grew less strained, thanks in part to
Aehrenthal's tardy recognition that England counts for
something in European politics, but chiefly owing to the old
friendship between King Edward and the Emperor Francis
Joseph.   The improvement would have been more rapid had
not Aehrenthal prevented a post-Annexation meeting between
King Edward and the Emperor at Ischl in August 1909.
Nevertheless, during the King's last stay at Marienbad in that
year, an exchange of courtesies took place between him and
the Emperor ; and an amicable controversy between leading
organs of the Austrian and British press resulted in a
definition of the British standpoint in regard to Austria-
Hungary which subsequently found King Edward's entire
approval.   That definition ran : " The idea that it has been
the object of Great Britain to detach other countries from
their alliances, or to surround Germany·with a ring of semi-
hostile States, is one of those perversions of the truth which
have been too readily propagated in Germany and accepted
in Austria-Hungary.   British policy has been inspired by
an honest and wholly non-offensive desire to remove points
of friction between England and other countries.   This

desire animates it still and lies behind the wish that relations
with Austria-Hungary may regain their former cordiality.
But clearness is an essential condition of the fulfilment of
this wish ; and for the avoidance of misunderstanding it is
eminently desirable to know whether, in their relations with
Austria-Hungary, British statesmen will have to reckon
with a Power conscious of its own individuality or with a
Power that, at every critical juncture will feel bound, over
and above its obligations as an ally, to identify itself with
another Power towards which British intentions are not less
amicable, but in dealing with which Great Britain has a
different class of interests to safeguard." [1]

While Anglo-Austrian relations thus tended to regain
some degree of cordiality, Austro-Russian relations were
further envenomed by an acrimonious controversy between
Count Aehrenthal and M. Isvolsky. Accompanied by a
press campaign on both sides and spiced with threats of
the publication of secret documents, the controversy gradually acquired such a degree of animosity that potent
influences had to be brought to bear to silence the Austro-
Hungarian Minister. Too passionate and resentful to be a
good controversialist, Aehrenthal was gradually driven into
a position from which he could only hope to escape by the
sacrifice of secrets of State. In a telegram to the editor
of the *Novoe Vremya* on November 8, 1909, Aehrenthal
actually suggested that both parties should publish all their
documents—and drew from Berlin strong disapproval of
a suggestion that would have been justifiable only on the
eve of war. The controversy then lapsed but its effects
remained and continued to encumber Austro-Hungarian
action down to and throughout the recent Balkan crisis.
Aehrenthal's management of the Annexation and his subsequent conduct placed indeed a heavy mortgage upon the
diplomatic freedom of the Monarchy—a mortgage not yet
entirely paid off.

In other respects, and particularly in his dealings with

[1] *The Times*, August 30, 1909, leading article, p. 7.

France and Italy, Aehrenthal was more fortunate. Even during the Annexation Crisis he contrived to retain with France relations more cordial than those with England and Russia. In this respect he reverted to the tradition of Andrássy, who had declined to direct the Austro-German Alliance of 1879 equally against France and Russia. During several phases of the Morocco conflict between France and Germany, Aehrenthal frankly dissociated himself from the German standpoint, especially in regard to the incident of the Casablanca deserters. A desire not to be entirely at the mercy of Germany in a European crisis was, in part, the motive for this conduct, but his main purpose was to gain for Austria-Hungary free access to the French money market. In this he failed. France, considering that Austro-Hungarian political dependence upon Germany is too marked to allow the Monarchy real freedom of decision, and that the relations between Austro-Hungarian and German Banks are so close as to place money lent to the Monarchy practically at the disposal of Germany, declined repeatedly to sanction the floating of Austrian or Hungarian loans on the Paris market. Aehrenthal resented this refusal as at once unjust and impolitic. He argued that France could not expect him to be independent of Germany unless she provided him with the necessary means, and argued that her attitude would compel him to identify himself more closely than ever with Germany. But the French Government shrewdly appreciated the circumstance that Germany would have demanded the immediate dismissal of Aehrenthal had he made a serious attempt to gain independence, and that his action in placing a temporary veto upon the expropriation of the Prussian Poles and upon the German scheme for levying navigation dues on the Elbe, had already aroused such suspicion and resentment at Berlin as to make his position precarious. Aehrenthal was, indeed, in many respects a tragic figure. He aimed sincerely at restoring the prestige and marking the diplomatic individuality of the Monarchy in Europe, but he came to his task inadequately equipped, burdened with an erroneous conception of international dynamics and handicapped by training and temperament. Like many Austro-Hungarian diplomatists, he knew little of the internal affairs of the Monarchy and sought to go his way regardless of them. He thus allowed the Austrian and the Hungarian Governments to undermine what ought to have been the twin bases of a successful Southern Slav and of a more successful Italian policy. He died worn out by a struggle against the enmities he had aroused, and bequeathed to the Monarchy little more than the memory of the hours of conscious pride it had enjoyed during the Annexation Crisis. Viewed retrospectively, the brightest side of Aehrenthal's work seems to have been his later treatment of Italy and his perception of the truth that a confidential relationship with Italy is the only practical guarantee of such diplomatic independence as the Monarchy may hope, in present conditions, to achieve. This truth, to which Kálnoky had been blind and which Gołuchowski only learned during his last two years of office, Aehrenthal comprehended within eighteen months of his appointment to the Ballplatz. As long as he believed in the possibility of reviving the League of the Three Emperors, he regarded Italy, like England, as an almost negligible quantity; and, at the outset, he looked upon Italy, in so far as he took her into consideration, as a troublesome member of the European family. In April 1907 his attitude was indicated by an unofficial message which he caused to be conveyed to the Italian Foreign Minister, Signor Tittoni, whom he thanked for friendly declarations made in the Italian Chamber, but added that he (Aehrenthal) would appreciate Italian friendliness still more if the character of Italian diplomacy at Belgrade were in conformity with the public statements of the Foreign Minister. This characteristically Aehrenthalian message was delivered to Signor Tittoni on the evening of April 18, 1907, after his return from the interview between King Edward and King Victor Emmanuel at Gaeta. Signor Tittoni, in reply, expressed surprise that his Austro-Hungarian colleague should be so misinformed in regard to the action of Italian diplomacy at Belgrade ; allowed his visitor to convince himself of Aehrenthal's mistake by showing him the instructions given to and a recent report received from the Belgrade Legation ; and requested him to inform Baron von Aehrenthal of their contents and to give him the following significant message. " Tell Aehrenthal from me," said Signor Tittoni, " that if he really wishes to promote good relations between Austria-Hungary and Italy, he had better pay me here in Rome the visit he has constantly expressed his intention of making.   Sooner or later the question of King Humbert's unreturned visit to Vienna will have to be settled, and it would be a good beginning if the Austro-Hungarian Foreign Minister would visit me at Rome. Tell Baron von Aehrenthal further that my relations with the Vatican are good enough to enable me to assure him that he will meet with no difficulties from that quarter."

This message was duly delivered ; but Aehrenthal—who had in the meantime visited Prince Bülow at Berlin and had, probably at the instance of Germany, made his proposal to Russia for an *entente à quatre* [1] designed to exclude England and Italy from a share in the settlement of Near Eastern questions—received it in silence and avoided any discussion of Austro-Italian relations beyond complaining that the visit paid by King Victor Emmanuel and Signor Tittoni to Athens on April 8, 1907, had encouraged the activity of Greek bands in Macedonia and had caused the Greeks to believe that Italy was on their side, notwithstanding the straightforward language which Aehrenthal admitted King Victor Emmanuel and Signor Tittoni to have used in conversation with the King of Greece and his Ministers.   Through another channel the Italian Foreign Minister soon received information that Aehrenthal would not visit him at Rome.   When in July 1907 Aehrenthal paid his visits to Signor Tittoni at Desio and to King Victor Emmanuel at Racconigi, he already knew that neither his dream of reviving the Three Emperors' League nor the scheme for an Austro-Russo-

[1] Cf. p. 230.

Franco-German *entente* would be feasible, and he therefore addressed himself to the cultivation of Italian goodwill with greater sincerity than he had previously displayed.

Save at rare intervals, the character of Austro-Italian relations since the formation of the Triple Alliance in 1882 had been "allied and inimical" rather than "allied and friendly." Prior to the alliance, Italy had wavered between France and the Central Empires, seeking to gain the advantages of friendship all round without incurring marked hostility in any quarter. Italian neutrality during the Franco-German War had, however, left upon French minds an impression of ingratitude which the high-hearted expedition of Garibaldi and its prowess at Dijon had failed to efface. French Catholic feeling had, moreover, been exasperated by the Italian invasion of the Pontifical State and the capture of Rome. Up to the "Seize Mai" 1877 Italy feared a French attempt to restore the Temporal Power of the Pope; and, in France, purely Clerical undertakings like the *Légion d'Antibes* and the *Zouaves Pontificaux* found indirect support in the conviction of many French politicians that Napoleon III. had sinned grievously against French interests in laying the foundations of Italian Unity at Magenta and Solferino, and in helping to create for France a formidable rival in the Mediterranean. Italy consequently sought a safeguard against French ill-will by courting the favour of Austria-Hungary, Germany, and particularly of Bismarck. Accompanied by his Ministers (Minghetti and Visconti Venosta) King Victor Emmanuel visited both Vienna and Berlin in September 1873. Bismarck, then in the thick of the *Kulturkampf*, complained that Italy had by her Law of Guarantees and her acquisition of Papal territory rendered the Holy See inviolable. He proposed that Italy should allow a German detachment to land at Civitavecchia (where, to the annoyance of Italy, the French Cruiser *Orénoque* had been lying at the disposal of the Pope since 1870) and march through to Rome in order to settle the *Kulturkampf* by force of arms. The Italian Ministers wisely rejected the proposal, and had subsequently the satisfaction of seeing the *Orénoque* recalled by Marshal MacMahon, who had succeeded Thiers as President of the French Republic. Italo-Austrian and Italo-German relations were, however, again improved by the return visit of the Emperor Francis Joseph to Victor Emmanuel in April 1875, and by that of the Emperor William I. to Milan in the following October. On the former occasion the Emperor Francis Joseph, who was accompanied by Andrássy, displayed rare magnanimity by drinking to the prosperity of United Italy in the very city which, only nine years previously, had been the last stronghold of Austrian power in Italy. The evolution towards an understanding, if not an alliance, between Italy and the Central European Powers was disturbed on March 18, 1876, by the fall of the Italian Right, which had believed the support of the two conservative Central Powers to be indispensable to the Young Italian Kingdom. The advent of the Left, or Radical Party, deprived Italy of the guidance of her most experienced statesmen, and placed her fortunes in the hands of men whose monarchical sentiments were not then thought to be above suspicion, and whose leanings towards Republican France deprived them of German and Austro-Hungarian confidence. Italy became practically isolated, and drifted without diplomatic leadership towards the Near Eastern crisis of 1877–78 and the Congress of Berlin. The return of the Italian Foreign Minister, Count Corti, from Berlin with "clean"—a euphemism for "empty"—hands, caused general disappointment in the Peninsula, while Crispi's irate but prophetic ejaculation in the Chamber, "Much good may they do her, these ill-gotten provinces," revealed the strength of Italian feeling against the Austro-Hungarian occupation of Bosnia-Herzegovina. But Italy continued to waver until Bismarck's master-stroke—the French occupation of Tunis—drove the Italian Government in 1881 once more to approach the Central Empires. Tentative negotiations for an alliance began. Bismarck feigned reluctance to admit Italy to the

Austro-German Alliance and met Italian suggestions with a
reminder that the way to Berlin lay through Vienna.   But
the Austro-Hungarian Foreign Minister, Kálnoky, had been
irritated by the Italian Irredentist manifestations, and was,
as a Clerical, disinclined to guarantee to Italy the possession
of the former States of the Church.   The Italian Foreign
Minister, Mancini, was for his part reluctant to guarantee
Austrian possession of Trent and Trieste.   Italy found herself in a position of extreme delicacy.   The advantages and
disadvantages of an alliance with Austria-Hungary and
Germany counterbalanced each other.   An understanding
with France and a continuance of the Irredentist movement
could not fail to arouse Austro-German hostility ; but
alliance with the Central European Powers would inevitably
draw upon Italy the hostility of France.   In the one case
as in the other Italy could count upon the moral support of
England but could not make of British friendship the basis
of a Continental policy.   Resentment against France on
account of Tunis would scarcely have sufficed to turn the
scale had not the question of the Temporal Power enabled
Bismarck to grasp the tongue of the balance and pull it
towards Berlin.

Since 1878 a new Pope, Gioacchino Pecci, better known
as Leo XIII., had occupied the chair of St. Peter.   Thanks
to the firmness and circumspection of Crispi, the Conclave
had passed off without other incident than an Italian warning
to the Sacred College that, if it left Rome to elect the
successor of Pius IX., the Vatican would be occupied by
Italian troops and be lost to the Church.   The Conclave
consequently preferred to remain in the Vatican.   But in
the summer of 1881 disorders had occurred during the
transfer of the remains of Pius IX. from St. Peter's to San
Lorenzo.   The Vatican had arranged the procession so as
to irritate Italian feeling and the Depretis-Mancini Cabinet
weakly played into the adversary's hands by neglecting
precautions for the maintenance of public order.   Tumults
consequently arose, and the world soon rang with a Papal

protest against "the miserable position of the Holy See." Bismarck, weary of the *Kulturkampf* and already on the highroad to Canossa, was anxious to conciliate German Catholic feeling. He therefore began a campaign in favour of the independence of the Papacy. Supported by Austria, he mooted the idea that Italy might be called upon to revise the Law of Guarantees in accordance with Catholic exigencies and that an International Conference might be convened to regulate the position of the Pope. His emissaries even suggested to the Pope that the Head of the Church would find at Fulda in Germany a free and tranquil refuge from the storms and the humiliations of Rome. Italy, with her army and navy in disorder, her relations with France precarious and her home affairs in a state of chaos, could scarcely have resisted Austro-German pressure, had it been seriously applied. Recognizing instinctively that the Italian character of the Papacy and of the Roman Catholic hierarchy is one of the greatest Italian national assets, the Government turned more decidedly towards Austria-Hungary and Germany and hastily arranged the visit of King Humbert and Queen Margherita to Vienna in October 1881 without stipulating any conditions for a return of the visit at Rome. Bismarck, as usual, treated Italy with arrogance, omitted from the Imperial message to the Reichstag in November 1881 all reference to King Humbert's visit to Vienna, and continued his campaign in favour of the Papacy. Nevertheless, negotiations for the alliance continued between Vienna and Rome. Kálnoky rejected the Italian wish that Austria-Hungary and Germany should pledge themselves to support Italian interests in the Mediterranean but finally consented to the stipulation of a reciprocal territorial guarantee and to a declaration that the allies would act in mutually friendly intelligence. A military convention provided that, in case of war, Austria-Hungary should guard the Adriatic on land and sea, while Italy should operate against the south-eastern frontier of France and place a second army at the direct disposal of her allies.

Save among German and Austrian Clericals the campaign in favour of the Pope's Temporal Power died down, having served its purpose as a whip to lash Italy into embracing the Central Powers.

Few episodes of modern European history illustrate more aptly than the entrance of Italy into the Austro-German Alliance the danger of entrusting the management of foreign affairs to the hands of untrained parliamentarians. Save in the case of men like Andrássy and Crispi, who acquired in exile a sense of international perspective, men devoid of traditions and influenced by ideas applicable, at best, to home politics, are liable to be outdistanced at every turn of the race. In the case of Italian parliamentarians the danger is peculiarly acute. Their quickwittedness and versatility lead them to underestimate the difficulties of diplomatic work. Count Alessandro Guiccioli, the brilliant biographer of Quintino Sella, truly observes that Italian public men find it especially hard to resist the temptation of appearing wily. This observation applies with force to men like the Italian Premier, Depretis, who, craftiest among the crafty in home affairs, believe foreign questions to be susceptible of treatment by similar methods conceived on a similar scale. Depretis thought that Italian adhesion to the Austro-German Alliance would, thanks to the secrecy of the pact, gain for Italy the advantage of an Austro-German guarantee of Italian territorial integrity without involving the disadvantage of French hostility. Thus, he imagined, foreign affairs would take care of themselves, while he reserved his attention for the short-range intrigue of parliamentary politics. But the secret soon leaked out, and Bismarck who had no reason to promote, by discretion, the intimacy of Franco-Italian relations, took no pains to hide it. Italy was therefore visited with French resentment, while Bismarck, having obtained from the Austrian and Russian Emperors at Skiernewice a promise of their benevolent neutrality in case Germany should be " compelled " to make war upon France, and having signed, without the knowledge of Austria-

Hungary, his Re-Insurance Treaty with Russia, proceeded to treat Italy with contempt. Matters mended only when Count di Robilant, who had held important diplomatic posts abroad and had looked askance at the formation of the Triple Alliance, was called from the Vienna Embassy in the autumn of 1885 to succeed Mancini at the Italian Foreign Office. Robilant stood his ground with Bismarck, dealt firmly with Kálnoky during the Bulgarian crisis of 1885–86, awakened in Italy some sense of the importance of Balkan questions, and arranged, with the help of Germany, an Anglo-Italian Naval Convention that safeguarded Italian interests in the Mediterranean. Crispi, who succeeded Robilant in 1887, forced the note of intimacy with Germany and improved Austro-Italian relations by stern repression of Irredentist tendencies. For this accentuation of devotion to the Triple Alliance, Italy paid dearly by the rupture of her commercial relations with France, and, during the second Crispi Administration (1893–96), by having to contend un-aided against the support lent to the Emperor Menelek by France and Russia during the Abyssinian campaigns. The disaster of Adowa (March 1896) that overthrew the second Crispi Cabinet was, to all intents and purposes, an outcome of the Franco-Russian policy of revenge upon Italy for having helped to form and for remaining a member of the Triple Alliance. Better days dawned for Italy when the veteran statesman, Visconti Venosta, resumed, in the summer of 1896, the control of Italian Foreign Affairs which he had previously held in 1864 and throughout the period 1869–1876. During a visit paid by the Austro-Hungarian Foreign Minister, Count Gołuchowski, to King Humbert at Monza in November 1897, a verbal arrangement was concluded that, in the event of the collapse of European Turkey, Austria-Hungary and Italy would abstain from territorial acquisitions in Albania and would co-operate in promoting Albanian autonomy. This arrangement was transformed into a written understanding during Visconti Venosta's last term of office in 1899–1900. In conjunction with a stipulation which is stated to exist in the Italo-Austrian portion of the Triple Alliance, to the effect that Italy is entitled to compensation for any extension of Austro-Hungarian territory in the Balkans beyond the limits of Bosnia-Herzegovina, the Visconti Venosta-Gołuchowski Agreement in regard to Albania has since formed and still forms the basis of Austro-Italian policy in the Eastern Adriatic. The agreement was confirmed during visits paid by Signor Tittoni to Count Gołuchowski at Abbazia in 1905, and by Gołuchowski to Tittoni at Venice in the spring of 1906. These visits corresponded to a tardy perception that, by their rivalry and mutual suspicion, Italy and Austria-Hungary were damaging their Adriatic interests to the advantage of Germany, whose *Drang nach Triest* has always been, and remains a much more positive and practical factor of European politics than the Austro-Hungarian *Drang nach Osten*, or the dream of a " March to Salonica." [1] The Austro-Hungarian statesman, like his Italian colleague, seemed at last to understand that the German method of retaining leadership in the Triple Alliance has usually been to prevent direct intercourse between Vienna and Rome, and, by fomenting suspicion of Italy in Austria-Hungary and suspicion of Austria-Hungary in Italy, to oblige the two allies to have constant recourse to the " good offices " of Germany. For long periods in the history of the Triple Alliance, the Italian " wire " to Vienna has, like the Austro-Hungarian " wire " to Rome, run through Berlin, and Berlin has rarely failed to levy a charge for the transmission of

---

[1] As long ago as 1860 the Prussian Foreign Minister, Schleinitz, addressed to Cavour through Count Brassier de St. Simon, the Prussian Minister at Turin, a note of protest against a decree published by one of Cavour's lieutenants in the *Corriere delle Marche* ordaining that vessels hailing from " the Italian city of Trieste " were to receive in Italian Adriatic ports the same treatment as Italian vessels. It is significant that the protest should have come, not from the Austrian, but from the Prussian Foreign Minister, who bade Cavour remember that Trieste was a " German city " (*ville allemande*), and urged that the decree of his lieutenant must therefore be disavowed. The text of the Prussian note was first divulged in Lamarmora's famous pamphlet, *Un po' più di luce sui fatti del 1866*, and afterwards reproduced in Chiala's *Lettere di Camillo Cavour*.

messages. Whenever a direct "wire" has been established between Rome and Vienna, the displeasure of Berlin has been curiously manifest and "untoward incidents" have usually "occurred" to mar the intimacy of the Adriatic allies.

Therefore, when Gołuchowski's successor, Aehrenthal, visited Tittoni at Desio in July 1907 and received his return visit on the Semmering in the following September, it was evident that Aehrenthal's original conception of Italy as a negligible quantity had given way to a more statesmanlike view. The two men rapidly became intimate. There is proof that after the Aehrenthal-Isvolsky meeting at Buchlau on September 15–16, 1908, Tittoni was informed of their agreement in regard to the Annexation, and that he discussed it with M. Isvolsky at Desio on September 29–30. What "compensation" Italy received for assenting in advance to the annexation can only be surmised, but it is probable that it consisted in Austro-Hungarian consent to the eventual acquisition of Tripoli by Italy, and also in an agreement that, at the moment of Annexation, Austria-Hungary should evacuate the Sanjak of Novi Bazar. Soon after the Annexation, Tittoni delivered at Carate a public speech of which the complacent tone—strongly at variance with the indignation of Italian public opinion—revealed the existence of some previous understanding between him and Aehrenthal. But at that moment Aehrenthal's reputation for reliability stood low, and during the debate on the Annexation in the Italian Chamber (December 1–4, 1908) the majority of speakers were agreed in regarding as worthless promises the "compensation" Tittoni had obtained. Anti-Austrian feeling ran riot, Irredentist sentiment again blazed forth and reports of a Garibaldian expedition to support Servia against Austria-Hungary in case of war were circulated by sundry Italian, German, and Austrian journals. It is a curious fact that Italians from Dalmatia, who were eager to join the "expedition," and who applied in person to General Ricciotti Garibaldi for enrolment, discovered that not only had he made no preparations for an expedition, but that the "Garibaldians" actually enrolled had been enlisted by agents notoriously connected with the German Consulate in a city of Northern Italy. Aehrenthal proved, however, as good as his word, and showed by his attitude of friendly neutrality towards Italy during the occupation of Tripoli in 1911, that the retention of Italian friendship appeared to him a necessity of the first order. Although he protested, as he was entitled under the Visconti Venosta-Gołuchowski Agreement to protest, against Italian naval operations off the Albanian coast in the autumn of 1911, he steadily resisted the influence of the Austrian Clerico-Military party, combined with that of the Jewish-Liberal press and of plutocratic interests, which worked in favour of an armed attack upon Italy. With his whole remaining strength he opposed the intrigues of General Baron Conrad von Hötzendorf, the Chief of General Staff, and of personages still more influential, and by compelling the Emperor to choose between him and Conrad von Hötzendorf, brought about the latter's resignation. Though Aehrenthal did not live to see the formation of the Balkan League and the expulsion of the Turks from the greater part of the Balkan Peninsula, he left to his successor, Count Berchtold, a valuable legacy in the form of an improved relationship with Italy that rendered possible the early renewal of the Triple Alliance in 1912, and the constant co-operation between Vienna and Rome during the recent Balkan crisis.

No episode of the Balkan crisis was more significant than the quasi-agreement improvised by Austria-Hungary and Italy for parallel if not joint action in Albania after the fall of Skutari. In its anxiety not to allow Montenegro to retain possession of Skutari—the centre of Austrian influence in Northern Albania—Austro-Hungarian diplomacy was on the point of agreeing to an Italian occupation of the important Albanian harbour of Vallona, the key of the Adriatic ; and the most militant Austrian politicians were prepared, for one mad week, to sanction the establish-

ment of Italy in a position from which it had always been
the object of Austro-Hungarian strategists to exclude her.
The Italian and Austro-Hungarian spheres of influence in
Southern and Northern Albania respectively were tentatively marked out, the valley of the Shkumbi river being taken
as the dividing line between them. But the moderating
influence of the Triple Entente and the skill with which
England obtained the command both of the international
fleet blockading the Montenegrin coast and of the international forces that occupied Skutari after the Montenegrin
evacuation, saved Austria-Hungary and Italy alike from the
complications which their precipitate action would have
entailed. It is a widespread and, possibly, a well-founded
belief that the partition of Albania between Austria-Hungary
and Italy would rapidly lead to war between the parti-
tioners ; and it is probable that those Austrian strategists
who were prepared to tolerate the Italian acquisition of
Vallona were influenced by a mental reservation that the
Monarchy would speedily find means to neutralize the Italian
advantage, if not to compel Italy to relinquish her grip
upon the Eastern Adriatic shore. On the other hand, Italy,
who early in the Balkan crisis had resented and practically
vetoed the Austro-Hungarian suggestion that Montenegro
should cede to Austria the mountain of Lovtchen which
commands the Bocche di Cattaro and diminishes the strategic
value of that magnificent harbour, was eager to occupy
Vallona, less because it might be converted into one of
the finest naval bases in the Adriatic than because its
possession would enable Italy at any moment to close the
strait of Otranto and to compel Austria-Hungary to give
battle there instead of awaiting an Italian attack near
the Austrian naval base of Pola, or in proximity to the
strategic curtain formed by the Dalmatian islands. It is
characteristic of the Austro–Italian Alliance that the parties
to it should be constantly contemplating and preparing for
war against each other. Prince Bülow once declared that the
only alternatives for Austria-Hungary and Italy are alliance

or war ; and he may have added, *sotto voce*, that in so far as
his efforts might avail, the Alliance should never be so cordial
as to preclude the possibility of a rupture, nor Austro-
Italian relations so bad as to preclude the maintenance of the
Alliance. Austria-Hungary, for her part, has rarely had a
clear notion of her interests in regard to Italy, nor followed
a consistent policy towards her Southern ally. At Court,
though not in the mind of the Emperor ; in the Foreign
Office, though not always in the mind of the Foreign
Minister ; in aristocratic society ; in the Army and Navy
and especially in the Church, there have always been, since
the unity of Italy was accomplished, influences and intrigues
working for " the chastisement of Italy," and propagating
the belief that only by fresh victories on the Lombard or
Venetian plains or by another battle of Lissa, can the
Monarchy restore its prestige in Europe and gain a free
hand in the Western Balkans. While the manifestations of
solidarity between the Germans of Austria and the Germans
of the German Empire have been winked at, the pro-Italian
sentiments of the Austrian Italians have been treated as
treasonable and the responses from Italy denounced as
" Irredentism." The Austrian corps of officers was, until
quite recently, trained to regard and to teach the rank and
file to regard Italy as *the* enemy ; and, but a few years back,
those who, in conversation with Austro-Hungarian military
men, ventured to question the necessity of an Austro-
Italian war or argued that such a war could only redound
to the advantage of Germany, were treated as amiable or
intriguing visionaries. Even at moments when Foreign
Ministers like Gołuchowski, Aehrenthal, or Berchtold were
striving for an agreement with the Italian Government on
points of foreign policy, the Lord Lieutenant of Trieste in
agreement with the Austrian Minister of the Interior pitilessly
expelled Italian subjects—no matter how long their residence
nor how inoffensive their character—from Trieste, Istria, and
Dalmatia, sometimes at the rate of ninety a month, and
refused nationalization papers to Italian applicants even if

they were natives of Trieste.[1]   Nevertheless, since the military
and economic potentiality of the Italian Kingdom have been
demonstrated by the gallantry of the Italian troops in Tripoli
and the comparative ease with which the Italian Exchequer
bore the burden of the war with Turkey (despite the hostility
of cosmopolitan financiers), there has been a change in the
attitude of Austria-Hungary towards Italy, and the former
tone of comminatory condescension has given place to a note
of semi-jealous admiration.   In December 1902 Gołuchowski
rejected with polite irony a suggestion from the Italian
Foreign Minister, Prinetti, that Italy had a right to be consulted by Austria-Hungary and Russia in regard to the
question of Macedonian Reform ; early in 1907 Baron von
Aehrenthal believed himself able to leave Italy out of account
when preparing to deal with Near Eastern issues ; but, in the
spring of 1913, Count Berchtold was fain to seek Italian
assent to the projected operations against Montenegro, and
was disposed to purchase it by admitting the Italian claim to
the lion's share of Albania !   On the part of Italy the fears of
an Austrian attack, that led to the fortification of the Italian
side of the Italo-Austrian frontier between the years 1902
and 1910, were gradually replaced by the singular notions
that the Southern Slav question represents almost as great
a danger for Italy as for Austria-Hungary, and that Italy is
interested in helping to keep Servia away from the Adriatic.
The crudity of these notions did not prevent them from
bringing the official attitude of Italy into harmony with
that of the Monarchy during the delimitation of Albania.
Most nations and many governments are ignorant of foreign
affairs, and the Austro-Hungarian Monarchy deserves perhaps
to head the list of States whose policy has been guided by
fundamental ignorance of some of the foreign questions most

---

[1] The recent expulsion of Italian officials from the employ of the Municipality
of Trieste is a logical continuation of this policy, but one which might perhaps
have been avoided had not Italy placed herself in a position of comparative
isolation by allowing her relations with France to become strained.   The
temptation to treat an isolated Italy with contempt is too strong for Austrian
bureaucrats to resist.

nearly affecting them. But in Italy also ignorance of the forces and conditions that appear destined to mould the future of the Eastern Adriatic is phenomenal. Contemporary Italian views of Adriatic questions, save of the Albanian question in its naval aspects, are still influenced mainly by sympathy with the estimable Italians of Dalmatia and Istria, who judge the whole problem of the Slav Adriatic littoral from the standpoint of their own struggle against the over-whelming numerical strength of the Southern Slavs in Istria and Dalmatia. The Italians of Dalmatia and Istria have one true interest—to save what can yet be saved of their culture and of the traditions of the Venetian Republic by frank agreement with their Slav fellow-subjects. Otherwise, their "national struggle" will but facilitate the endeavours of the equally short-sighted Austrian administration to Germanize the Adriatic. The Kingdom of Italy and the Austro-Hungarian Monarchy are indeed jointly interested in the Southern Slav question. Their safest policy would be to promote the union of the Southern Slavs in friendly intelligence with the House of Hapsburg, if not under its auspices. Only thus can the Hapsburg Monarchy and Italy alike escape the danger that threatens them both from the German *Drang nach Triest* and build athwart the German line of economic and political advance a solid Southern Slav barrier. Otherwise Italy may awaken too late to the fact that the Adriatic—of which the Eastern littoral from the Quarnero to Antivari is Serbo-Croatian—is in process of becoming not an Italian nor a Slav, but a German Sea. German shipping companies, scarcely disguised under Italian names, already challenge the supremacy of the Austrian Lloyd at Trieste ; German banks, bearing Viennese and Italian names, are gradually absorbing the commerce and controlling the interests of the port ; local German parties "support" the Triestine Italians in the "national struggle" against the invading Slav, while the Austrian authorities, for fear of "Irredentism," bar the importation of Italian capital from the neighbouring kingdom. North German enterprise is eating the heart out of Italian and Austrian Trieste and is preparing to substantiate the claim of Schleinitz that Trieste is a *ville Allemande.*

. . . . . .

The notions that the Southern Slav problem threatens the existence of Austria-Hungary, and that foreign states like Italy are vitally interested in opposing the Southern Slavs in order to assist in maintaining the Hapsburg Monarchy, deserve, however, to be considered from another than a merely Adriatic standpoint. The question whether it be not too late for Austria-Hungary to solve the Southern Slav problem in her own favour is hard to answer negatively in view of the victories of Servia and of the bad faith and wrongheadedness of Hapsburg statesmen during recent years. But in judging the affairs of the Hapsburg Monarchy, it is easy to underestimate its hidden powers of resistance, its secret vitality and the half-unconscious dynastic cohesion of its peoples. For these forces and qualities full allowance must always be made, even though the signs of their existence be overshadowed by symptoms of decrepitude and disintegration. After the Balkan victories over Turkey in the autumn of 1912, the impression was widespread in many parts of Austria and in some parts of Hungary that the Monarchy had received its death-blow. The prediction of a sanguine Southern Slav who wrote on the eve of the war, " If this war succeeds, the Monarchy will cease to be a Great Power," seemed to have been realized. An odour as of death was in every nostril. The mingled incompetence and insincerity that characterized such management of Austro-Hungarian affairs as was visible to the public eye, led an experienced and unprejudiced diplomatic observer to exclaim, " Jamais je n'ai vu des gens si acharnés à travailler contre leurs propres intérêts," and the saw, *Quos Deus vult perdere*, was a commonplace of conversation. But the Monarchy, though stricken, continued to live and have its being. To the question whether it could continue to exist, it seemed to reply, *Solvitur vivendo !* Gradually the consciousness dawned, even in minds not quick to perceive the essential lines of a situation, that if the existence of the Monarchy is threatened, the menace comes less from without than from within, and proceeds mainly from the ill-starred legacy of Sadowa—the Dual System. The perception dawned first among the partisans of Dualism, the "Liberal" Germans of Austria, and the Magyars and Judaeo-Magyars of Hungary, who instinctively drew nearer each other and sought to sink their differences in order to support the System that was fashioned to perpetuate their hegemony. Their defence is likely to be stout, especially in view of the successful re-occupation of Thrace by the Young Turks, and they may yet succeed in wrecking the Monarchy before it can reorganize itself upon a basis such as to give it and its dynasty a reasonable prospect of withstanding at once the German, the Russian, and the Southern Slav dangers.

Of these dangers the most apparent is the Southern Slav, the most immediately formidable the Russian (or perhaps the Russo-Rumanian), and the most insidious the German.

The Southern Slav problem has two main aspects, of which the one is represented by the undeniable tendency of all branches of the Serbo-Croatian race towards political union, and the other by the formidable obstacle which the Dual System places in the way of any rational Austro-Hungarian Southern Slav policy. Prior to the Balkan War the watchword of the most influential Austro-Hungarian Southern Slavs was "All together; within the Monarchy if possible, but in any case all together." After the war a feeling that it is hopeless to aim at union within the Monarchy spread and deepened, less perhaps on account of the consideration that the Greater Servia created by the war seems unlikely ever to come under the Hapsburg Crown than because of the disappointment and resentment engendered by the continued ill-treatment of Croatia-Slavonia, Bosnia-Herzegovina, and Dalmatia during and after the war. Hungary, to whom Croatia-Slavonia and half the influence over Bosnia-Herzegovina constitutionally belong, will never, it is assumed, voluntarily consent to treat the Southern Slavs in such manner as to allow them to become a counterpoise to the Magyar State in the Monarchy ; and no developments such as to prevail against the will of the Magyar State appear yet to be within sight. Hungary naturally clings to the possession of Croatia-Slavonia, through which lies her only route to the sea, and of Fiume, her only port, which she received from Maria Theresa as a *corpus separatum* of the Hungarian Crown in 1779 and has developed immensely since its restoration to her in 1870.   Fiume is the only window through which the Magyars can look out upon the world, and it is comprehensible that they should strive, by fair means and foul, to prevent the Southern Slav race from obstructing the view. Dalmatia is also claimed by the Magyars as historically and constitutionally theirs.   Every Hungarian coin bears the inscription, " Ferencz József I.K.A.Cs- Ès- M.H.S.D.O.AP.Kir." (Francis Joseph by the Grace of God, Austrian Emperor, and of Hungary, Croatia, Slavonia, Dalmatia, Apostolic King).   The Magyar solution of the Southern Slav question would be the re-incorporation with Hungary of Dalmatia and also of Bosnia-Herzegovina—which the Magyars identify with the Kingdom of Rama, whose banner figures at the coronation of Hungarian Kings.   But this solution presupposes the abandonment by Austria of all control over the Adriatic littoral beyond Trieste and the coast of Istria. During the first years of the Dual System, when the affairs of Hungary were guided by men of superior political talent, there appeared some reason to believe that the Magyars, acting as *primi inter pares*, would group round them the Southern Slav peoples and acquire, with their support, the leadership in the Monarchy.   This solution now seems to be past hoping for.   From the standpoint of the internal cohesion of the Monarchy, the Magyar State has acted as a repellent force, powerless for good, powerful for evil ; and, pending proof to the contrary, students of Hapsburg affairs are constrained to regard the Magyars rather as a liability than as an asset of the Crown. The instinct of self-preservation might perhaps work a miracle at the twelfth hour had not the present generation of Magyars been so steeped in chauvinism as to have lost all sense of their real position in Europe ; and, unless some heaven-sent leader arises in their midst, or unless " Vienna " blunders so egregiously as to warn them in time, the future may reserve for them trials as severe as any they have experienced during their chequered history. As for Austria, she cannot even address herself to the task of dealing reasonably with the Serbo-Croatian problem so long as the Dual System in its present form and the present Magyar State block the way. The Southern Slav danger may, indeed, be fended off for a time by preventing the economic development of the Serbo-Croatian race as Hungary has hitherto prevented the development of Croatia-Slavonia ; Austria (mainly at the instance of Hungary) the development of Dalmatia ; and Austria-Hungary combined that of Bosnia-Herzegovina. But the Serbo-Croatians are gradually learning the lesson which some of the Northern Slavs of the Monarchy, notably the Czechs and to some extent the Hungarian Slovaks, have learned from the Jews—the necessity of husbanding their own resources, creating their own banks, and developing their economic potentiality in such manner as to resist, first the local Jewish usurers and secondly international Jewish finance, which the Southern Slavs regard not without reason as the pioneer of Germanism. Patient effort, aided by the development of the Southern Slavs beyond the border, should enable the Serbo-Croatians of the Monarchy eventually to overcome or to undermine the obstructive policy of Vienna and Budapest, unless, indeed, Vienna and Budapest awaken to the folly of seeking to retain in economic subjection populations and territories whose development cannot in the long run be prevented without exposing the whole Monarchy to grievous peril. The fundamental internal problem that confronts the Hapsburg

Monarchy is how to modify or extend the Dual System without civil war and its attendant risks. Opinions differ widely as to the resistance which the Magyars could offer to an attempt to unify the Monarchy by force; but catastrophic contingencies of this kind are best ignored until all possibilities and hypotheses of pacific arrangement have been exhausted. One such hypothesis is that, in view of the impossibility of allotting Bosnia-Herzegovina either to Austria or to Hungary, and in view of the necessity of giving to the disjointed and artificially divided Serbo-Croatian provinces of the Monarchy some form of organization corresponding to their desires and needs, the joint rule now prevailing in the annexed provinces should be modified and extended so as to include Croatia, Slavonia, and Dalmatia. To this hypothesis there are doubtless weighty objections. Magyar Constitutional lawyers would abhor any admission of Austrian influence to Lands of the Crown of St. Stephen like Croatia-Slavonia; and Austrian feeling would run counter to any extension of Hungarian influence to the Dalmatian littoral. The Serbo-Croatians themselves might resent the reduction of Dalmatia and Croatia-Slavonia to the position of a joint Reichsland even were such reduction to be accompanied by complete local autonomy and economic advantages. But from the point of view of the Monarchy and of the Dynasty, this hypothesis might offer the advantage of creating a fresh link between Hungary and Austria and of avoiding the dislocation inseparable from any attempt to replace the Dual System by a Triple or a Federalist organization of the Monarchy. Were an Austro-Hungarian Serbo-Croatia to be constituted with a central Diet and a veritably autonomous Government, and were it entitled to send representatives direct to the Austro-Hungarian Delegations which would remain competent to deal with diplomatic and military matters, a tentative solution of the Austro-Hungarian side of the Southern Slav question might perhaps have been found. Most Austrians and some Hungarians would prefer to any such expedient a

policy that would make *tabula rasa* of existing arrangements and satisfy either the "Young Austrian" ideal of
federalized unity for the whole Monarchy, or the Magyar
ideal of Hungarian independence with complete Magyar
control over Croatia-Slavonia, Dalmatia, and Bosnia-Herzegovina. But the history of the Constitutional experiments
during the early 'sixties of last century scarcely encourages
belief in the practical value of a new arrangement drafted
on a "clean slate" by Constitutional theorists. The adaptation of what exists might produce more tolerable results and
be better adapted to the Austro-Hungarian genius for
"muddling along." Should, however, Vienna and Budapest
remain obdurate and continue to sacrifice the economic
development of the Serbo-Croatians to the maintenance of
the Dual System in its present form, the sense of economic
suffocation will inevitably be added to the sense of political
oppression that acts to-day as the strongest stimulant to
the feeling of Southern Slav solidarity. If and when the
Balkan countries, and especially Servia, develop their
economic resources and advance in prosperity, the position
of the Serbo-Croatian provinces of the Monarchy will
become intolerably anomalous unless Austro-Hungarian
statesmen face in time the problem confronting them. To-
day, in all its aspects, the Southern Slav question involves
danger for the Monarchy. If the danger be ignored or
trifled with there may presently be no means of averting it
save by a dynastic *coup d'État* or by an upheaval among
the elements that still believe in the future of the Hapsburg
polity.

Did the Southern Slav question stand alone, its solution
might be less difficult and call less urgently for treatment.
But in point of fact, it is only one link in the chain of notes
of interrogation that encircles the Hapsburg dominions.
In the south-east of Hungary the old question of Transylvanian autonomy and the newer question of Rumanian
Irredentism remain unsolved and may be thrust into special
prominence should, as a result of the Balkan crisis, the rela-

tions between the Monarchy and the Kingdom of Rumania grow less cordial. Here, as in the Southern Slav question, the short-sighted chauvinism of the Magyars has again been to blame. In the vain attempt to Magyarize a prolific and gifted race not inferior to themselves in intellectual capacity, though long downtrodden, the Magyars have undermined the loyalty of the Rumanes not only to the Magyar State but to the Hapsburg Dynasty, and have laid the axe at the root of the Austro-Hungarian system of resistance to Russia in South-Eastern Europe. Since 1878, when Russia estranged Rumania by annexing the part of Bessarabia assigned to Moldavia by the Treaty of Paris, Rumania has been compelled to rely on Austro-Hungarian support. Rarely have a state and a statesman been guilty of a more egregious blunder than were Russia and Gortchakoff in despoiling Rumania of territory after Prince Carol with his gallant troops had saved the honour of Russian arms at Plevna and had virtually turned in favour of Russia the adverse tide of the Russo-Turkish War. The result was to paralyse for decades the effective influence of Russia in the Balkans. Rumania for her part was doubly damaged—by the loss of her portion of Bessarabia and by the political impossibility — in her position of dependence upon the Monarchy—of applying diplomatic or military pressure to Austria-Hungary in order to secure better treatment for the Rumanes of Transylvania and freedom from the chicanery constantly employed by the Magyar frontier and railway authorities to impede the importation of Rumanian cattle and agricultural produce into the Monarchy. The exact nature of the political and military agreements concluded between Rumania and the Monarchy after the formation of the Triple Alliance has never been divulged, but the arrangements are supposed to include a reciprocal territorial guarantee and a military convention arranging for the simultaneous mobilization of the Austro-Hungarian and the Rumanian armies in case of Russian attack. How long such agreements would survive skilful diplomatic assault by Russia is an open question. A Russian Bismarck, or rather a Russian Cavour, would scarcely hesitate to efface the ungrateful blunder of 1878 and to promote a good understanding with Rumania by considerate treatment of those Rumanes who might still be left under Russian rule. Hitherto the only non-Rumanian Rumanes who have been considerately treated by their rulers are those of the Bukovina, where the Austrian authorities have shown an intelligent toleration that is eloquent of what the Hapsburg Monarchy might become were it governed from end to end in a spirit of impartial goodwill.

THE UKRAINE QUESTION

But in the Bukovina are to be found, alongside of Rumanes, the beginnings of a problem which may yet involve Austria-Hungary and Russia in a struggle even if it does not precipitate a European conflagration. The Ruthenes, or Little Russians, who inhabit the western districts of the Bukovina, practically the whole of Eastern Galicia, as far as Przemysl, and several Russian "Governments" like Podolia, Volhynia and Kieff, form a racially compact mass of some 30,000,000 souls, extending from the Dnieper to the Carpathians, and overflowing into North-Eastern Hungary.[1] Russia regards the Little Russians as an integral part of the Great Russian family and treats their language as a Russian dialect. Austria encourages the Ruthenes to regard themselves as a separate Slav race and their language as a well-characterized Slav idiom as distinct from Russian as from Polish. The linguistic question in its scientific aspects is one for philologists ; but in its political aspects it may presently acquire grave importance. Russia offers no facilities for education in the Little Russian language or dialect. Austria has created a number of Ruthene professorships at the University at Lemberg and treats Ruthene as one of the recognized official languages of the Empire. The Austrian side of every Austro-Hungarian bank-note

[1] Cf. pp. 128-30.

bears an inscription in Ruthene as well as in Polish and the language is taught in the primary schools of Eastern Galicia with the sole restriction that the learning of Polish is also obligatory. The only Russian means of counteracting Austrian efforts to encourage Austrian Ruthenes, or Little Russians, in the belief that they are a separate people, is a Russophil and Orthodox propaganda among the Austrian Ruthenes aided by the surreptitious introduction of Russian roubles into Eastern Galicia, so that the peasants may draw from the Russian inscription on the coins and from the portrait of the Tsar, the conclusion that the Great White Tsar is their rightful ruler. This conclusion is drawn more readily by those Austrian Ruthenes who belong to the Russian Orthodox Church than by those who are members of the Greek United Church, which is Roman Catholic in doctrine but Orthodox in rite. Of late years the Greek United Church, whose head in Galicia is Mgr. Count Szeptycki, a prelate of commanding character and attainments, has striven to extend its influence among the Little Russians beyond the Austrian frontier by urging upon them the consideration that membership of the Greek United Church enables them to be at once Catholic and Orthodox. The Russian Synod has, for its part, worked not without success, to promote in Eastern Galicia the conversion of Ruthene peasants from the Greek United to the Orthodox faith ; and the efforts of the Austrian-Polish authorities to combat this propaganda and their disinclination to recognize the conversions that have actually taken place, have given rise to the reports of religious persecution in Galicia that have found their way into the Western European press.

But alongside of this largely political strife of creeds runs a purely political movement which " Vienna " has for some years past been at pains to further. Its ostensible aim is the creation of an autonomous if not an independent Little Russian or Ruthene province to be called the Ukraine (the Borderland), and to consist of Eastern Galicia, part of the Bukovina and of the Little Russian districts of South-

Eastern Russia. The controversy whether the Little Russians should be called Little Russians or Ruthenes would then be settled by calling them Ukrainers or Borderers. The strongest party among the Austrian Ruthenes has already adopted this name and has sought to secure its adoption by the Little Russians of Russia. Exactly how much progress has been made in this direction is not known. Russians say, "Practically none"; Austrian Ukrainers say, "Immense"; but there is no doubt as to the objects which the Ukrainers are pursuing with the help of "Vienna" and with the encouragement of the Greek United Church. These objects are the establishment of a purely Ruthene or Ukraine University at Lemberg, the capital of Galicia; the ejection of the Polish landlords and authorities from Eastern Galicia; and the establishment of an independent Ruthene Diet at Lemberg as the legislative organ of a self-governing Ruthene, or Ukraine, Hapsburg province, that would be destined to be the nucleus of the Greater Ukraine of "Viennese" dreams —a Ukraine to be formed under Hapsburg auspices when, with German help, Russia shall have been duly defeated and dismembered.

This idyllic programme is unfortunately complicated by the Polish question, not only in its narrower Galician bearings but in its full significance as a principal factor in the relations between Austria-Hungary, Russia, and Germany. Until "Vienna" began to encourage the Ukraine movement and to connive at the efforts of the Ruthene leaders to shake off Polish supremacy in Eastern Galicia, the Austrian Poles were among the most loyal and reliable subjects of the Hapsburg Crown. The older generation of Austrian Poles is loyal still, especially in Western Galicia and Cracow where the pinch of the Ruthene or Ukraine movement is not yet felt; but among the younger generation of Austrian Poles there are noticeable tendencies towards Russophilism, or rather towards a conception of the Polish cause that would develop into Russophilism were Russia sufficiently far-sighted to mitigate the disabilities under which the Poles of Russia

labour.   The Austrian Poles resent the efforts of "Vienna"
to drive them in double harness with the Ruthenes along an
anti-Russian road.   They know that the road may end
on the brink of a precipice, and find no solace in the
reflection that, while the Hapsburg Car of State might be
saved at the last moment by cutting the traces, the Poles,
and possibly also the Ruthenes, would risk being dashed to
destruction.   The Austrian Poles, moreover, find difficulty
in co-operating heartily with the Ruthenes, to whom their
relationship has for centuries been one of master to servant,
or rather of landlord to peasant.   The Ruthenes are a
peasant people.   Their natural leaders, the aristocracy, were
attracted in past centuries to the Polish or to the Russian
Court, and were polonized or russified.   Many prominent
Polish nobles are thus of Ruthene origin.   Hitherto only
one prominent member of these families, Mgr. Count
Szeptycki, has resumed Ruthene or Little Russian or
"Ukraine" nationality, but should the Ukraine movement
progress, his example may find imitators.   In the meantime
the Ukraine movement is led mainly by the sons of the
Greek United clergy and by others of low social rank who
stand near enough to the people to command its confidence.
Apart from its general political aims, the movement bears
largely a Radical and almost anarchical character which has
more than once found expression in political assassination.
The Conservative Polish aristocracy is naturally out of
sympathy with a movement that threatens at once its
material welfare and its political convictions ; and, despite
attempts on the part of the Polish Conservatives of Cracow
to promote an agreement with the Ruthenes for a division
of influence in the Diet of Lemberg and in Galicia generally,
the prospects of peace between the two races are faint.   The
Roman Catholic Archbishops of Galicia intervened in the
spring of 1913 to prevent a Polish-Ruthene electoral settlement on the ground that it would have increased the influence
of anti-religious and Radical elements, and especially of the
Jews.   The Jewish problem is indeed an important factor in

the whole complex of questions and tendencies that are
agitating Galicia and Russian and Austrian Poland, no less
than in the Near Eastern problem with which those questions are intimately connected ; and as the realization of the
Ukraine ideal and the consequent dismemberment of Russia
would affect the greater part of the Russian Jewish zone
and might free the Russian Jews from the disabilities and
restrictions imposed upon them, Jews sympathize as a rule
with the Ukraine cause and also with the Polish cause, in so
far as it is directed against Russia. The position in which
Russia may be placed by the Austro-Polish and Ukraine
movements calls for the careful attention of Russian statesmen and should lead them to consider whether the system
of administrative oppression maintained in Russian Poland is
not a grave impediment to the freedom of Russian diplomatic,
if not of Russian military action. The Russian Poles are
attached to Russia by strong ties of economic interest. The
wide Russian market is open to their manufacturers while
the Russian tariff protects them against German competition. But no considerations of interest can assure loyalty
as long as the Poles are governed by Russian bureaucrats
who receive double pay for administering a "rebellious
province," and may consequently be trusted not to admit
that the province has ceased to be insubordinate. Indeed,
the Russian *Tchinovniks* and the Okhrana, or Political Police,
are under strong suspicion of having promoted sundry
"Polish" revolutionary manifestations with the object of
convincing the Tsar's Government, and the Tsar himself, of
the necessity of maintaining what is practically a state of siege
in Poland. In these endeavours the Russian bureaucracy is
strongly supported by German influence, which works, directly
and indirectly, to prevent any reconciliation between Russia
and the Poles, and seeks to maintain the idea that the division
and oppression of the "turbulent and undisciplined" Polish
race is a primary interest of Conservative and order-loving
empires like Germany and Russia !

The question of Poland which grew out of the Eastern
Question in the latter part of the eighteenth century may
again be brought into the foreground of European politics
by the semi-solution of the Near Eastern Question during
the recent Balkan wars ; and, as the late M. Albert Sorel
acutely foresaw, it may, in conjunction with the Southern Slav
question, raise, sooner or later, the " Question of Austria."
The eyes of the Hapsburg Monarchy, long turned covet-
ously towards the Balkan Peninsula, may, unless Austro-
Hungarian diplomacy can completely undo by intrigue the
effects of the Balkan wars, presently be constrained to look
in another direction.   Should the Monarchy seek a new
orientation, its efforts may tend in the direction indicated
by the Austro-Polish and Ukraine movements—movements
which cannot, however, attain their objects without active
co-operation between Austria-Hungary and Germany.   The
antagonism between Austria-Hungary and Russia that grew
up in consequence of Baron von Aehrenthal's abandonment
of the Mürzsteg basis and of his annexation policy, enabled
Germany again to assume the direction of Austro-Hungarian
foreign affairs and to " mediate " profitably between Vienna
and St. Petersburg.   In Austria-Hungary apprehensions are
sometimes expressed, and are more often felt than expressed,
lest Russia and Germany one day agree to partition the
Hapsburg dominions.   If not baseless, these apprehensions
are certainly exaggerated.   Germany seems unlikely to consent to any essential dismemberment of Austria-Hungary as
long as the German Empire is able, by a policy of economic
and political penetration, to use the Monarchy as its instrument.   A main object of this penetration is to give Germany
command of the route to Trieste and, through the Adriatic,
to the Mediterranean.   The Hapsburg Monarchy will probably be exposed to no mortal peril as long as it refrains
from serious insubordination to Germany ; and should a
European conflagration ever arise out of the numerous unsolved international issues in Europe or the Near East,
the Monarchy might hope, in the event of victory, to

obtain with German help a considerable slice of Russian
territory. In the event of defeat its existence, like that
of the German Empire in its present form, might be en-
dangered. But catastrophic hypotheses are best left out
of account in these days of intertwined interests and of
armies so colossal that defeat could hardly fail to be
attended by revolutions fatal to thrones and to the existing
social order ; and calm consideration of the complicated
factors involved leads rather to the conclusion that the
Hapsburg Monarchy has but one sure way of escape from its
difficulties into a more prosperous and tranquil future—the
way of evolution, gradual or rapid as circumstances may
permit, towards a form of internal organization better adapted
than the Dual System to the permanent needs of its peoples.
A far-sighted Polish statesman of Little Russian stock and
wide German and classical culture was wont to define the
ideal form of the Monarchy as a " Slav house with a German
façade " ; but, like most framers of formulas, he paid too
little heed to the standpoint of the Dynasty and ignored the
question whether the House of Hapsburg will be able so to
adapt itself to altered circumstances as to renounce its ancient
traditions and to content itself with the prestige that comes
of ruling justly over peoples free to manage their own affairs
and spontaneously loyal to the Monarch as their Supreme
Moderator. The power of the Hapsburg Dynasty is still the
strongest element in the Monarchy—stronger, in the last
resort, than the influence of the Austrian Germans, the
Austrian Slavs, the Magyars, the Church, or the Jews. Its
power is still, to all intents and purposes, absolute ; but it is
exposed to the danger that threatens all absolutisms, be they
military, political, religious or financial—the danger of regarding their own existence as an end in itself, and of allowing
their conduct to be guided solely by considerations of short-
range expediency. Such considerations are poor substitutes
for the principle proudly inscribed on the outer gateway of the
Vienna Burg,"Justitia Regnorum Fundamentum." In a polity
divided as to race, public opinion and power of resistance

into a dozen entities, the triumph of a non-ethical standpoint of government is singularly facilitated. Yet, in an era when race affinities are strong and economic interests increasingly potent, a dynasty and its ministers need to be guided by maxims more lofty than those that spring from the apparent balance of immediate advantage. If the Hapsburg Dynasty is to retain the power it has hitherto wielded and, while remaining indispensable to its own peoples, to become a centre of attraction and a symbol of good government to peoples outside its dominions, it must rise superior to the lower expediency represented by the line of least resistance and comprehend the perennial efficacy of the higher expediency represented by the principle of Justice.

INDEX

Abbot, G. E., quoted, 163.
Abdul Hamid, Sultan, 237, 238.
Absolutism, revival of, in Austria, 34-9.
Adler, Dr. Victor, Austrian Socialist leader, 134-5, 156.
Adowa, 1896, 274.
Aehrenthal, Baron von, Joint Minister for Foreign Affairs, 53, 190, 199, 237, 294, Abandonment of Judicial Reform in Macedonia in return for concession for construction of railway through Sanjak of Novi Bazar, 229-30, 234-7, and Abrogation of Clause 3 of Mürzsteg Programme of Macedonian reform, 222 *note*, and Annexation of Bosnia-Herzegovina, 214, 243-63, Austro-Turkish Convention, 1909, 255, Character and work, 227 - 9, 267, Controversy with M. Isvolsky, 1909, 265, proposed *Entente à quatre*, 230 - 1, 233, Foreign policy, 228, 233, 263-7, 276, 277, 279-80, and Friedjung trial, 1909, 100, 101, 103, 104-5, and Macedonian Reform, 229-30, Meeting with M. Isvolsky at Buchlau, Sept. 1908, 247-50, Modification of Treaty of Berlin, 1909, 255-6, and alleged Serbo-Croatian plot, 260.
Agram High Treason trial, 1907–8, 190, 243, 259.
Albania, agreement between Austria and Italy concerning, 226, 274, 277-8.
Albert, Archduke, 72.
Alexander II., Tsar of Russia, meeting with Emperor Francis Joseph at Reichstadt, 1876, 213.
Alexander, King of Servia, assassination, 1903, 240-2.
Algeciras Conference, 1906, 226-7.
Andrássy, Count, the Elder, 9.
Andrássy, Count, 20, 21, 22, 29, 33, 52,

Andrássy, Count—*continued*
68, 266, 270, 272, Appointment as Minister of the Imperial Household and for Foreign Affairs, 23, and Austro-German Alliance, 216, and Dual System, 211, Foreign policy, 23-8, 208, 211-12, 233, and Occupation of Bosnia-Herzegovina, 214-16, and Revision of San Stefano Treaty, 238-9.
Antivari, opening of, as free port, 1909, 256.
Arbeiter Zeitung, the, organ of Social Democratic party, 135, 190, 191.
Aristocracy, influence, position of, etc., 131-4.
Army, 60-73, Administration, 63-4, Languages, 64-6, Magyar attacks on unitary character of, 68-70, Military families, 62, Officers, 61-2, Organizations, 63, Red tape and mandarinism, 70, Title of " Imperial *and* Royal," 32.
Army Order of Sept. 16, 1903, 66-7.
Army, Hungarian, Magyar demand for substitution of Magyar for German language, 32-3.
Austrian Constitution of 1848, 14.
Austrian Constitutional Statute of 1867, 17-20, 33.
Austrian Federal Constitution of 1860, 15.
Austrian-Germans: Opposition to annexation of Bosnia-Herzegovina, 214-15, Relations with Emperor, 1867–1906, 10.
Austro-Hungarian Bank, gold policy, 139-40.

Bach, Alexander, and Concordat with Rome, 1855, 114, 115, " System " of, 14-15, 24, 56, 99, 210.
Badeni, Count, Austrian Premier, Dis-

THE END